In Defense of Christian Patriotism

ALSO BY DANIEL DARLING

Agents of Grace: How to Bridge Divides and Love as Jesus Loved

A Way with Words: Using Our Online Conversations for Good

The Characters of Christmas: The Unlikely People Caught Up in the Story of Jesus

In Defense of Christian Patriotism

DANIEL DARLING

BROADSIDE BOOKS

HarperCollins books may be purchased for educational, business, or sales promotional use. For information, please email the Special Markets Department at SPsales@harpercollins.com.

harpercollins.com

FIRST EDITION

Library of Congress Cataloging-in-Publication Data
Names: Darling, Daniel, 1978– author.
Title: In defense of Christian patriotism / Daniel Darling.
Description: New York, NY: Broadside [2025] | Includes bibliographical references and index.
Identifiers: LCCN 2025008690 (print) | LCCN 2025008691 (ebook) | ISBN 9780063413948 (hardcover) | ISBN 9780063413931 (ebook)
Subjects: LCSH: Christianity and politics—United States. | Patriotism—Religious aspects—Christianity. | United States—Religion. | United States—Politics and government.
Classification: LCC BR526.D365 2025 (print) | LCC BR526 (ebook) | DDC 277.308/3—dc23/eng/20250515
LC record available at https://lccn.loc.gov/2025008690
LC ebook record available at https://lccn.loc.gov/2025008691

ISBN 978-0-06-341394-8

25 26 27 28 29 LBC 5 4 3 2 1

TO MY LATE MOTHER, WHO TAUGHT ME HOW TO LOVE THIS COUNTRY.

CONTENTS

Introduction: **REJECT EMBARRASSMENT; CHOOSE GRATITUDE** xi

Part I: Patriotism Is a Duty

Chapter 1: **SINCE WHEN IS FAITH IN POLITICS SCARY?** 3

Chapter 2: **YOU CAN'T OBEY GOD AND HATE YOUR COUNTRY** 27

Chapter 3: **WHY CHRISTIANS SHOULD BE *MORE* INVOLVED IN POLITICS** 61

Chapter 4: **AREN'T NATIONAL MYTHS JUST MADE UP?** 97

Chapter 5: **THE CASE FOR AMERICAN EXCEPTIONALISM** 121

Part II: It Is Not Good for Man to Be Alone

Chapter 6: **CHRISTIANITY WON'T ABIDE LONE RANGERS** 141

Chapter 7: **THE WAR ON THE FAMILY** 167

Chapter 8: **CHRISTIANS CAN'T ABANDON SCHOOLS** 185

Chapter 9: **RESTORING "E PLURIBUS UNUM"** 205

Chapter 10: **SAVING AMERICA FROM YOUR BACKYARD** 219

Acknowledgments 229

Notes 231

Index 259

Reject Embarrassment; Choose Gratitude

AMERICA IS LIVING THROUGH A CRISIS. BUT IT'S PROBABLY A CRISIS YOU haven't noticed. It's a crisis of ingratitude.

I marvel at this every Fourth of July. Even conservative-leaning Christians who dare post something positive about the United States on her birthday feel the need to affix several caveats about her worst sins. It's even chic, among some progressive Christians, to post *only* about the injustices she has committed, as if there is nothing redeemable about the country that has given them the freedom and prosperity to have such a public voice. It should worry us that recent surveys show that younger Americans recoil at the idea of patriotism.[1]

Healthy self-criticism is good for any nation, but can a nation survive that refuses to believe the best parts of her own story? My thesis, then, is a bit counterintuitive to that of many prevailing narratives. A healthy patriotism is not only an *acceptable* posture for a Christian. I believe it is a *necessary* posture for a Christian.

In Scripture, God commands a number of loves. We are to love God, love our family, love our neighbors. But what about love of country? It can be easy for a modern Christian to dismiss this love as superfluous to Christian duty. However, a fundamental assumption of the Christian life is that we are to be grateful to God for the things that he gives us. The specifics of our birthplace fall under that category: our family, our home, our community. We are to honor *our* father in a way that's distinct from all the other fathers of the world, not because he is superior to them but because he is ours. We're to love our home as the place where God has planted us, not because it's the best of all possible homes but because it's a space we've been given to steward.

God must be the center of this. If we love those things without loving God more, it's easy to make them idols, since, after all, each is in some manner merely a reflection of him. "Lord, thou hast been our dwelling-place in all generations," the psalmist said (Psalm 90:1, ASV), and Paul wrote that God is "the Father, from whom every family in heaven and on earth is named" (Ephesians 3:14–15). We therefore can't properly love our family, our home, or our country without loving God first.

But the anti-patriots tend to see any expression of country love as idolatry. They say that patriotism may have been well and good forty years ago, but isn't this new form of "Christian patriotism" uniquely toxic and proud? And what about the Christian nationalists who are seeking to create a new theocracy?

It'd be easier to give credence to this view if hysteria about public Christianity hadn't been with us for decades. The pollster George Gallup declared 1976 to be "the year of the evangelical." A little-known Southern governor named Jimmy Carter had burst onto the scene, not only winning the Democratic nomination for president of the United States but defeating Gerald Ford to become America's thirty-ninth chief executive. Carter proudly talked of his "born-again" faith. That Baptist Sunday school teacher was a refreshing respite for a nation gripped by the shocking scandals of Watergate.

However, a wary *New York Times* headline declared, "Carter's Evangelism Putting Religion into Politics for First Time Since '60," describing Carter as "a deeply committed evangelical Christian."[2] Part of the mistrust was due to Carter shattering a time-honored custom: US presidents often talked about faith in general but never about their own personal faith.[3] His born-again language came out of a generation reared on Billy Graham's sermons and who placed a strong emphasis on personal conversion.

Of course, as it turned out, *The New York Times* didn't have much to worry about regarding Carter's actual policies. His born-again story is inspiring, but his faith ended up conveniently conforming to mostly left-wing policies. But even though Carter was a progressive Democrat, this seemed to mark the beginning of an intense focus in American media on the patriotism and political activity of conservative, churchgoing Christians, many of whom voted for Carter in 1976 and then switched their electoral allegiance to Ronald Reagan four years later. Though Christians have engaged civically from the beginning of the republic, believers as a voting block have been the subject of fascination since Carter's rise.[4] Every year, especially an election year, features numerous books, essays, and documentaries flooding the marketplace with the overwhelming implication that the involvement of Christians, particularly conservatives, in our national life is not only unhelpful, but dangerous.

The rise of Donald Trump and the shameful events of January 6, 2021, supercharged that sentiment in major media and even among many evangelicals, resulting in a tidal wave of apocalyptic warnings. In recent years we've seen books such as *The End of White Christian America*, *The Ballot and the Bible: How Scripture Has Been Used and Abused in American Politics and Where Do We Go from Here*, *Christians Against Christianity: How Right-Wing Evangelicals Are Destroying Our Nation and Our Faith*, *American Idolatry: How Christian Nationalism Betrays the Gospel and Threatens the Church*, *The False White Gospel: Rejecting Christian Nationalism, Reclaiming True Faith, and Refounding Democracy*, and *Kingdom of Rage: The Rise of Christian Extremism and the Path Back to Peace*, as well as the widely publicized documentary by Rob Reiner, *God & Country*.

This is often accompanied by op-eds in outlets such as *The New York Times* and *The Atlantic*, often by Christian leaders lambasting their own people for the crime of voting a certain way or identifying with a particular party. The picture painted by these works is one where hordes of conservative Christians are hovering at the gates, eager to transform the republic into Gilead. The problem would go away, these writers insist, if Christians would simply stop putting their trust in politics.

But a closer look suggests that for most of the critics, it's not political Christians that are the real problem but conservative policies. For instance, there are few irate think pieces aimed at progressive Christians, whose political activity is almost always described in positive terms. Consider, for instance, that a considerable number of self-described evangelicals don't vote,[5] according to the latest polling, and that progressive congregations are far more political than conservative ones.[6] If the problem is that Christians are "being political," shouldn't progressive Christians be the most dangerous group? Wouldn't Jimmy Carter be the father of Christian nationalism?

One progressive Christian singer sang in 2008, "God is not a flag / Not even American / And God does not depend on a government." He later apostatized, but in 2020, one of his songs would be the background track for a Joe Biden ad.

Of course, conservative Christians do often need a corrective word about the way we live in public. We have no shortage of cranks and grifters in our ranks as you'd expect of a group of sinners in a fallen world. The criticism and rebuke that comes our way often provide a welcome dose of perspective and warning. Yet so many of the hyperbolic jeremiads are far too sweeping in their denunciations and leave many of the faithful feeling guilty about engaging at all in the political life of the country they love.

Like most evangelicals, I was appalled by the shameful events of January 6, 2021. But I think we have to be careful about the use of that singular event motivated by a fairly extreme and antisocial group as a cudgel to condemn political involvement and to redefine patriotism as something sinister. The dominant media narrative wrongly and purposefully conflates ordinary, conservative, churchgoing Christians with a fringe group of thugs, some of whom crassly weaponized Christian symbols in service of misplaced passions. What's more, too little patriotism, not too much, was the problem that day.

I'm writing this book for Christians who love America but are afraid to express it for fear of being accused of idolatry. I'm writing this book for Christians who want to shape the life of their nation but are constantly being told to leave their faith in church on Sunday. I'm writing this book for confused followers of Jesus wondering what it looks like for Christians to faithfully steward their God-given citizenship.

I'm speaking to moms who look at a country that's made the world far more confusing for their children. To young Christian medical students who are forced to carry out their residencies in environments where they're asked to compromise their faith and the truth to do their job. To nonwhite Christians who are told they're white supremacists because they oppose the half-decade-old policies overthrowing the biblical vision for men and women. To people who feel like they're being gaslit by leaders who claim that every attempt to gain political power for conservative causes is motivated by power, while every left-wing attempt to do so is just "loving your neighbor."

As I speak to ordinary believers here in Texas and around the country, I meet good people who want to love America but are constantly being told that this passion is in direct conflict with their love for God. They aren't in love with the Republican Party but find it the only available institution that seems at least to listen to the issues about which they care. Yet they are told that to identify in this way is somehow wrong, maybe even dangerous.

Why does this matter? The United States is at a critical juncture in its history. We are approaching, as of this writing, the 250th anniversary of the signing of the Declaration of Independence. Rather than celebrate the fact that this miraculous experiment in human government has lasted this long, we are beset by ritual self-loathing and doomsday predictions of failure.

This attitude is myopic and ungrateful. It's a neurotic gloominess that seems a product more of decadence, recency bias, and provincialism than of honest analysis of this country. But more fundamentally, patriotism is about loving the place where God has planted you. We are a nation with an exceptionally rich pantheon of heroes, gifts, and virtues. And of course, a nation that has made profound mistakes. God has given us this country and, with it, the duty to love it. That's what patriotism is.

America isn't perfect. But who says a place must be perfect before it's worthy of love and gratitude? In other areas of our lives, we understand that love often consists of improving the object of love and that love itself is the motive for this repair.

Cancel the self-loathing. You never start a project of self-improvement with self-hatred; ask any therapist. Instead, let's roll up our sleeves and get to the work of renewing this country and passing the blessings of liberty on to the next generation. American Christians have to resist the misguided notion that to be faithfully Christian is to retreat from the public square. The nation desperately needs a stimulus of Christian courage, character, and compassion.

This book won't be a simplistic jingoistic tract, but I'll ask the questions I'm often asked in churches, schools, and gatherings. The first part of this book tackles some fundamental questions about the oddity of our historical moment: Where did the modern hostility to patriotism come from? Why does God want us to love our country? How can we do so when our country is so imperfect? Perhaps the biggest question under all of these questions: What does patriotism look like for today's Christians when it's gone wrong so often in the course of history?

I'll also defend things that in the past Christians found normal, such as national heroes, flags, and countries, and explain why, in the modern West, Marxism and secularism have taught people to be allergic to these ideas. I'd like to believe that Christians anywhere could read this book and be edified, but when I speak of patriotism, of course, I'll largely speak from the familiar reference point of America, my home.

Having answered these foundational questions, I'll spend the second part of the book highlighting ways beyond politics in which faithful patriots can best renew America through her most important mediating institutions: church, family, school, and local communities.

Throughout our history, people of faith have had a vital role to play in preserving this fragile American experiment for our children and grandchildren. We can do this while still understanding that even the greatest nations—including the United States—will one day give way to that far better country, that city whose builder and maker is God (Hebrews 11:10).

Thankfully, we are not the first generation of believers to wrestle with these questions. Since the dawn of the church age, Christians have understood their responsibility both to the kingdom of God and to the nation-states in which they've been placed by God. In one of the oldest Christian documents on record, the second-century Epistle of Mathetes to Diognotus, we read that "what the soul is in the body, Christians are in the world. The soul is dispersed through all the members of the body, and Christians are scattered through the cities of the world. . . . God has assigned them this illustrious position, which it were unlawful for them to forsake."[7]

These words, a not-so-distant echo of Jesus' own words in Matthew 5 and John 17, were written about and to Christians who faced far more hostility than Christians face in the secularized West. We can draw inspiration from that great cloud of witnesses in Heaven who saw Christianity as more than just a private exercise. With little agency and power, those early generations of believers loved their neighbors by engaging with their communities and their nation. They lived an otherworldly lifestyle of discipline, love, and self-sacrifice. They were marked not only by a distinctive ethic but by a distinctive advocacy for the most vulnerable.

Even more should we, in a representative republic such as the United States of America, live our days using whatever agency and influence we have to serve as "the soul of the body" for the flourishing of our neighbors. We can do this not with cynicism or anger but with genuine joy, believing fully the words Jesus said to his disciples before he went to the cross: "Be of good cheer. I have overcome the world" (John 16:33, ASV).

The cynical person lives life miserably, determined to criticize everything. The sentimental person lives a life of folly because they won't criticize anything. Christians are called to be neither cynical nor sentimental but grateful, not because the world is perfect but because we know that it will be. We love others because God first loved us. And we love our country for the same reason. Reject embarrassment. Embrace gratitude.

Part I

PATRIOTISM IS A DUTY

CHAPTER 1

Since When Is Faith in Politics Scary?

Because We have no Government armed with Power capable of contending with human Passions unbridled by . . . morality and religion. Avarice, Ambition, Revenge or Galantry, would break the strongest Cords of our Constitution as a Whale goes through a Net. Our Constitution was made only for a moral and religious People. It is wholly inadequate to the government of any other.[1]

—*John Adams*

Without God, there is no virtue, because there's no prompting of the conscience. Without God, we're mired in the material, that flat world that tells us only what the senses perceive. Without God, there is a coarsening of the society. And without God, democracy will not and cannot long endure. If we ever forget that we're one nation under God, then we will be a nation gone under.[2]

—*Ronald Reagan*

ON OCTOBER 25, 2023, LOUISIANA CONGRESSMAN MIKE JOHNSON STOOD before his colleagues and the world in the well of the US House of Representatives. It was his first speech since his unlikely ascension from being a mostly unknown congressman to Speaker of the House. In his remarks, he said, "I believe the Scripture, the Bible, is very clear that God is the one who raises up those in authority. He raised up each of you, all of us. And I believe God has ordained and allowed each one of us to be brought here for this specific moment and this time."[3]

As speeches go, it was unremarkable, similar to statements about the providence of God made by political leaders throughout

American history. Still, the political media reacted with horror. Late-night hosts teed up lame jokes usually reserved for Mike Pence. And progressives warned that a new dark era of Christian nationalism had dawned in America. That hyperbole happened, ironically, in reaction to Johnson, a Southern Baptist, who had spent his career fighting for religious liberty for those of all faiths and those with no faith at all.

Politico, never subtle, declared Johnson to be a "right-wing, white evangelical Christian nationalist" who had made a turn "away from democracy."[4] The religion scholars Andrew Whitehead and Samuel L. Perry, writing in *Time*, warned that Johnson "exemplifies this aspect of Christian nationalism disregarding the values of democracy to instead embrace any means through which political power remains in the 'right' hands."[5] Robert P. Jones, the founder of the Public Religion Research Institute polling firm and author of books such as *The Hidden Roots of White Supremacy: And the Path to a Shared American Future*, *White Too Long: The Legacy of White Supremacy in American Christianity*, and *The End of Christian America*, was less subtle in a quote published by *The New York Times*, labeling Johnson "the embodiment of white Christian nationalism in a tailored suit."[6]

If this freakout over public expressions of faith by a politician sounds familiar, that's because it is. I'm old enough to remember when George W. Bush first ran for president and had the audacity to say, when asked by a reporter who his favorite philosopher was, "Jesus Christ, because he changed my life." The headlines, then and throughout his presidency, were punctuated by hyperbolic warnings of a coming Christian theocracy.[7] Many commentators even compared George W. Bush to the Taliban.[8] You might be old enough to remember that same contempt for Ronald Reagan's subdued expressions of evangelical faith.

This modern tradition of freaking out over faith seems to be strangely one-sided. When Bill Clinton stood in a church pulpit to accuse Republicans of violating the Ten Commandments, he was praised by the press.[9] When former Vermont Governor Howard Dean, while running for president, said that Jesus was a "model" for his political life, there was no accompanying hand-wringing about medieval theocracy.[10] And *Politico*, the same outlet that trembled with fear that Speaker Mike Johnson had used Christian language to describe his calling, had once highlighted President Barack Obama for invoking the name of Christ more than his predecessor had.[11] Yes, that same George W. Bush who was also Taliban-like because he read his Bible every day. Make it make sense.

These are just a few examples. We could talk about the bizarre questioning of President Donald Trump's nominee for director of the Office of Management and Budget by Vermont Senator Bernie Sanders, the strange questions at the nomination hearing of Catholic Supreme Court Justice Amy Coney Barrett, or the ritual mockery of former Vice President Mike Pence's piety.

As absurd as all this sounds, the constant hand-wringing by the press, progressives, and a handful of religious scholars has had an impact on the way many Christians think about the role of faith in the life of our country. When President Trump unexpectedly stopped by a Washington, DC–area megachurch in the middle of a worship service after a round of golf, he was invited onstage, where pastor David Platt prayed over him. Even though the pastor's prayer was very thoughtful and could have been prayed over any public official, Platt was roundly criticized,[12] even by some Christian leaders.[13] The journalist Emma Green rightly questioned the freakout: "What's remarkable about this prayer is not that it happened, but that it shows how thoroughly the Trump era has opened the way for cynicism and outrage over even mundane, predictable Christian behavior."[14]

Green is right. Yet what's even more remarkable is that the mixing of politics and the pulpit is so common in progressive-leaning churches and barely registers a blip. Once, Senate Majority Leader Chuck Schumer stood onstage in a congregation and compared the appointment of Justice Ketanji Brown Jackson to the resurrection of Jesus.[15] Another time, Democratic Senators Elizabeth Warren and Cory Booker pounded church pulpits while declaring that fighting Republicans was a righteous act.[16] And the pastor of the Progressive Baptist Church once eagerly hosted the lesbian mayor of Chicago in his pulpit during a mayoral race and it generated very little public hand-wringing about the future of democracy.[17]

As a pastor, I'm not a fan of politicians in the pulpit. When I was a senior pastor, I never allowed them to speak on a Sunday and I never endorsed them. This is a policy I advise other pastors to take. I'm aware that politicians on both sides of the aisle often misquote or misapply Scripture for political advantage. But politicians invoking God, quoting Scripture, and appealing to Providence is an American tradition that is, overall, a good one. I agree with the longtime religion columnist Kenneth L. Woodward, who wrote:

> History is replete with efforts by Protestants to connect the American experiment in ordered liberty to some higher purpose, plan, or Planner. For the Puritans of Plymouth Rock that higher purpose was to establish God's new Promised Land. Later it was to establish a righteous—read Protestant—empire by (in Lincoln's tempered phrase) an "almost chosen people." In the Cold War era, when the spread of Communism was the nation's main concern, both liberals and conservatives advanced their political agendas by appealing to yet other forms of Christian nationalism. And so, in the biblical idiom of freedom and justice, did Martin Luther King Jr.[18]

The imbalanced reaction whenever religion and politics mix on the right is often less about genuine fears over the separation of church and state and more about animus toward conservative Christians. Just consider one author, Bradley Onishi, who described conservative Christians as "a clear and present danger to the United States of America . . . homegrown radicals who prioritize White Christian supremacy over multi-racial democracy."[19] Onishi is not alone, joined by the authors of such provocative books as *Confronting Christofascism: Healing the Evangelical Wound*, *Christians Against Christianity: How Right Wing Evangelicals Are Destroying Our Nation and Our Faith*, and *The Power Worshippers: Inside the Dangerous Rise of Religious Nationalism*. This is just a sampling of a burgeoning genre that sees Christianity's influence on government as a threat. The historian and political scientist Mark David Hall described these efforts as "impassioned polemics rather than serious studies."[20]

Debunking the Secular Story

Many people understand the story of America's founding as a triumph of secularism over religion. As the story goes, while in the bad old times in the bad old world, thousands had died in wars over religion waged by kings who claimed God's authority for any wicked whim, America represented the triumph of reason over superstition. Finally, we could create a civilization from the ground up, where meaning would come from the voting public, from the "People," not from God.

The only problem with this narrative is that it isn't at all how the United States' Founders perceived their experiment.

A more serious study of history would acknowledge the role Christianity has played in the life of the United States. This is part and parcel of the perennial debate over whether or not the United States is a "Christian nation." I don't particularly like that phrase, because I am not sure that a nation can be Christian in the sense that in the new covenant, it is people, not nations, that are saved by grace through faith. I agree with historians such as John Wilsey, John Fea, Mark David Hall, Thomas Kidd, and others who argue that the American project draws from both Enlightenment ideals and Protestantism.[21]

Yet though we may or may not use the exact term, it is indisputable that America was profoundly shaped by Christianity. Wilsey, a historian and theologian, offers this:

> What students of history can affirm is that religion has always enjoyed a special place in American society, not just since the founding but since the planting of the colonies. . . . Christianity has had an enormous impact on the development of the American identity, but secular ideas have been particularly formative as well.[22]

That special place Wilsey mentions is important to understand. The American Founders, some of whom were orthodox Christians and others were not, were not shy about the importance of Christianity to the American experiment.

John Adams, in a letter to the Massachusetts militia, underscored that this project of liberty would work only with "a moral and religious People. It is wholly inadequate to the government of any other."[23] George Washington, in his farewell address in 1796, stated:

> Of all the dispositions and habits which lead to political prosperity, religion and morality are indispensable supports. . . . And let us with caution indulge the supposition that morality can be maintained without religion. Whatever may be conceded to the influence of refined education on minds of peculiar structure, reason

> and experience both forbid us to expect that national morality can prevail in exclusion of religious principle.[24]

Benjamin Franklin, a Unitarian who, like John Adams and Thomas Jefferson, did not believe in the resurrection of Jesus Christ, nevertheless passionately believed in the necessity of a robust Christianity for the flourishing of his fledgling nation:

> All of us who were engaged in the struggle must have observed frequent instances of a Superintending providence in our favor. To that kind providence we owe this happy opportunity of consulting in peace on the means of establishing our future national felicity. And have we now forgotten that powerful friend? Or do we imagine that we no longer need His assistance.[25]

The Founders, regardless of their theology, could not help being influenced by Christianity because it was the environment in which they had grown up. That is why their words were peppered with references to Scripture and appeals to God's Providence. Though they resisted the idea of a state church, they were insistent that their new experiment in ordered liberty could not survive without the strong presence of religion.

It wasn't merely the Founders who believed that. You can take a casual tour through our history and find similar sentiments in appeals to America's Christian character by succeeding generations of American leaders.

Consider John Quincy Adams, who became the vice president of the American Bible Society, declaring in his first speech to Congress that America "owed a gratitude to the Omnipotent Disposer of all God for the continuance of the signal blessings of his providence."[26] In the early nineteenth century, as the Second Great Awakening swept through the country, biblical language was common. The historian John Fea wrote of that era that "the real debates . . . were not over whether God was on the side of the United States—that was a well-accepted belief. Rather the conflict centered on what kind of Christian nation the United States would be."[27]

At the center of the conversation was the debate over slavery, as both North and South appealed to Scripture to make their case.[28] Arguably our greatest president, Abraham Lincoln, raised by abolitionist Baptists in Kentucky and Illinois, drew heavily on Scripture in his campaigns and even more from the White House as he led a nation in the midst of a civil war. Consider his humble appeal to Providence in his second inaugural address:

> The Almighty has his own purposes. "Woe unto the world because of offenses! for it must needs be that offenses come; but woe to that man by whom the offense cometh." If we shall suppose that American slavery is one of those offenses which, in the providence of God, must needs come, but which, having continued through his appointed time, he now wills to remove, and that he gives to both North and South this terrible war, as the woe due to those by whom the offense came, shall we discern therein any departure from those divine attributes which the believers in a living God always ascribe to him? Fondly do we hope—fervently do we pray—that this mighty scourge of war may speedily pass away. Yet, if God wills that it continue until all the wealth piled by the bondsman's two hundred and fifty years of unrequited toil shall be sunk, and until every drop of blood drawn with the lash shall be paid by another drawn with the sword, as was said three thousand years ago, so still it must be said, "The judgments of the Lord are true and righteous altogether."[29]

Scholars differ on the exact nature of Lincoln's faith, whether he held to the eclectic religious syncretism he had maintained on his journey to the White House or if he returned to his parents' faith in his final years. What we do know about Lincoln is that he was profoundly shaped by Christianity, lived by a healthy fear of Providence, and was shaped by the idea of natural law, which God "planted in our bosoms."[30] In his most famous speech, the Gettysburg Address, his use of "four score and seven" is a direct allusion to the King James Version's numbering system.

Lincoln's words are not unique. After the Civil War era and into the twentieth century, American leaders spoke without reservation about America's Christian character in ways that today would make secularists blush and cause a minor media firestorm. The elections of 1896 and 1900, for example, featured two candidates who were known for their strong evangelical faith. The Republican William McKinley, a committed Methodist, was described as a "Christian gentleman" and a "God-fearing American statesman" who commended the revival meetings of D. L. Moody. His opponent was the Presbyterian preacher, activist, and populist crusader William Jennings Bryan, who was famous for his "Cross of Gold" speech and had argued against the theory of evolution in the Scopes Monkey Trial.[31]

Those men weren't merely practicing Christians; they saw Christianity as indispensable to the nation's flourishing. And it was a bipartisan sentiment. The Republican McKinley declared that "He who serves the Master best serves man best" and that Christianity is "the mightiest factor in the world's civilization." The Democrat Woodrow Wilson, a Presbyterian, framed his policies for world peace in self-consciously Christian terms and framed his justification for the United States' entrance into World War I similarly.[32] The Republican Herbert Hoover, a Quaker, declared that Christianity was "the foundation of economic and social life" and warned that the United States should stay "in tune with the purpose of Almighty Providence."[33] He ran for president against the first Catholic nominated for the office, Al Smith. Franklin D. Roosevelt, who defeated Hoover and served as president through the Great Depression and World War II, quoted Scripture quite often in his fireside chats and his major addresses and was comfortable invoking God as he led the United States through one of her darkest moments. His prayer on D-Day, for example, begged God to bless what he considered America's righteous fight against fascism:

> And, O Lord, give us faith. Give us faith in Thee; faith in our sons; faith in each other; faith in our united crusade. Let not the keenness of our spirit ever be dulled. Let not the impacts of temporary events, of temporal matters of but fleeting moment—let not these deter us in our unconquerable purpose.
>
> With Thy blessing, we shall prevail over the unholy forces of our enemy. Help us to conquer the apostles of greed and racial arrogances. Lead us to the saving of our country, and with our sister nations into a world unity that will spell a sure peace—a peace invulnerable to the schemings of unworthy men. And a peace that will let all of men live in freedom, reaping the just rewards of their honest toil.
>
> Thy will be done, Almighty God.[34]

Harry Truman, the committed Baptist who succeeded Roosevelt, was similarly outspoken in his belief that freedom and democracy are dependent on morality and spirituality. In a speech at the dedication of the New York Avenue Presbyterian Church, he said:

> We talk a lot these days about freedom—freedom for the individual and freedom among nations. Freedom for the human soul is, indeed, the most important principle of our civilization. We must always remember, however, that the freedom we are talking about is freedom based upon moral principles. Without a firm moral

> foundation, freedom degenerates quickly into selfishness and license. Unless men exercise their freedom in a just and honest way, within moral restraints, a free society can degenerate into anarchy. Then there will be freedom only for the rapacious and those who are stronger and more unscrupulous than the rank and file of the people.
>
> If we neglect these truths, our whole society suffers.[35]

Truman's successor, Dwight D. Eisenhower, expressed similar themes in his first inaugural address in 1953: "Rather this change expresses a purpose of strengthening our dedication and devotion to the precepts of our founding documents, a conscious renewal of faith in our country and in the watchfulness of a Divine Providence."[36]

One could continue through the public statements of presidents through the end of the twenty-first century and find similar sentiments. It is no wonder, then, that the British social critic and novelist G. K. Chesterton, upon visiting the United States, remarked that it had the "soul of a church."[37]

There's No Such Thing as Neutrality

The reality is that our current secular society is a historical aberration, not the norm. Why, then, given how deeply Christianity is intertwined with our national story, are many elites so allergic to any kind of civic Christianity? Much of it is obviously animus toward conservative people of faith. But quite a bit of the criticism leaders such as Mike Johnson and others routinely receive comes from a misunderstanding about the nature of American democracy, which in turn comes from a big worldview shift that has happened in the West in the last five hundred years and has perhaps been accelerated in the last few decades by events such as the Supreme Court's ruling on *Obergefell v. Hodges*, which legalized same-sex marriages, in 2015.

The secular view of history that I outlined just now, with rationality defeating superstition, has become so commonly accepted that even many Western Christians take its assumptions as given. One of those assumptions is that religion is a lifestyle choice, an optional addition to the "real" concerns of the secular world.

America, secularists believe, is a secular society or ought to be. The ideal society is free from the taint of faith and governed by pure reason. Appeals to God are unfair. Reason is the only reliable guide that doesn't tip the scales toward one particular constituency in a diverse country. "In a democracy—filled with people of all faiths, as well as non-believers—politics and lawmaking is an emphatically earthly enterprise," wrote one journalist. "No one gets to impose their wishes on others simply by asserting their confidence that heaven is on their side."[38]

The underlying argument is that faith "forces" people to do things, oppresses and reshapes them through the will of corrupt priests. Meanwhile, the apostles of reason use studies and statistics to determine the best arrangements for society.

That seems fair enough, right? Neutrality, pure reason, a public square stripped "naked" of the garments of faith—surely that's the only possible way to create a "fair" playing field. The problem is that society needs a lot more than reason to function; it needs a shared vision of the good life, and reason can only get us so far. Even a supposedly "neutral" or "naked" public square actually operates on the basis of unacknowledged moral assumptions.

As Richard John Neuhaus wrote so eloquently over four decades ago, "When . . . religious values and the institutions that bear them are excluded, the inescapable need to make public moral judgments will result in an elite construction of a normative morality from sources and principles not democratically recognized by the society. The truly naked public square is at best a transitional phenomenon. It is a vacuum waiting to be filled."[39] Consider how the rituals and practices of the LGBT movement have adopted the rites and rituals of civic religion, with high holy days, sacred symbols, and rigid norms enforced by both the state and corporate power. Or the way scientism became a righteous creed during covid.

Humans are inescapably moral creatures. All political actors operate with a vision for the flourishing of the human race founded on moral assertions. What's unusual in a secular society is that only the religious are disallowed from promoting their view of human flourishing. The result of this decision is not to create a neutral public square but to allow the moral terms of public life to be set by irreligious people's priorities that are just as much an assertion of faith as any religious claim can be.

Driving the faithful from public life is also perilous because faith has long been the best bulwark against vice and moral anarchy. The American founders knew that. Classic liberalism, the system of government that guarantees freedom of speech, freedom of assembly, and freedom of worship, wasn't intended by its architects to function without a strong religious influence. In his book *Virtue and the Making of Modern Liberalism*, the Hoover Institution political scientist Peter Berkowitz made a convincing case that thinkers such as John Locke had never intended a morality-free secularism: "Locke maintains that such virtues as self-denial, liberality, justice, courage, civility, industry, and truthfulness are necessary to public life."[40] Locke, an Anglican heavily influenced by British Baptist separatists, assumed his project would unfold in an environment shaped by Judeo-Christian values. He believed that virtue, necessary for a flourishing society, "can only be the Will and Law of a God, who sees men in the dark."[41]

But among the revolutionaries of the eighteenth century, not all were as concerned with faith as were the American Founders. Across the Atlantic, the French were so enamored of their anti-authority philosophy that they went beyond toppling a king; they tried to topple God, too. We all know what happened next. In a few short years, the French Revolution devoured more lives than the Spanish Inquisition had in hundreds.

Atheism on a state level rarely correlates with freedom and prosperity. The ideological descendants of the Jacobins gave us the Soviet Union, Mao Zedong's China, and North Korea. In similar fashion today, many people appeal to the phrase "the separation of church and state," a phrase not found in the Constitution but found in a 1960s reinterpretation of the Founders' intent in the Bill of Rights as a justification for creating a totally secular state. Drawing from a misinterpreted letter Thomas Jefferson sent to Danbury Baptists, the Supreme Court began to create what is often called a theory of "strict separation," starting with the 1962 ruling *Engle v. Vitale*, which struck down state-sponsored Christian prayer in public schools. As a Baptist and constitutionalist who believes that the government shouldn't require the practice of any one religion over another, I think the Court got the ruling right.

I believe the Court was right in that it was not constitutional for state-sponsored schools to demand that nonbelieving students participate in a Christian ritual, such as prayer or worship, just as I'd be nervous, as a Christian parent, if a school demanded that my child participate in a Muslim call to prayer. This is different, of course, from voluntary teacher-led or student-led religious exercises or even the teaching of religious texts as historic documents. So that was a necessary corrective.

In spite of this, I believe that the secularist impulses behind this ruling set a judicial and cultural precedent that sought not merely to keep the government from interfering with religious belief but to attempt to push religion out of the public square entirely. In a dissent in a similar case at the time, Justice Arthur Goldberg shared these concerns:

> But untutored devotion to the concept of neutrality can lead to invocation or approval of results which partake not simply of that noninterference and noninvolvement with the religious which the Constitution commands, but of a brooding and pervasive devotion to the secular and a passive, or even active, hostility to the religious. Such results are not only not compelled by the Constitution, but, it seems to me, are prohibited by it.[42]

Goldberg seemed to appreciate that there's nothing truly neutral about a "secular" state. Just like people of faith, rationalists embrace a number of axioms about human nature that aren't empirically provable. Christians believe that we humans are valuable because we're made in the image of God. Secularists believe that we all have human rights. Thomas Jefferson called those rights "self-evident," but he wasn't merely talking about their existence; he said it was self-evident that those rights came from God.

If you ask someone to use science to "prove" that rights exist, they'll probably appeal to their "obvious nature." But why should their nature be obvious? It's clearly not obvious to many people in Saudi Arabia that women should have the same rights as men. It was clearly not obvious to antebellum Southerners in the United States that a white man and a Black man were of the same value before God.

Even Thomas Jefferson, who did understand the Declaration of Independence as a step beyond "monkish superstition," knew that the rights he proclaimed as being self-evident had no defense absent the robust philosophical framework provided by belief in God. He wrote of slavery, "Can the liberties of a nation be thought secure when we have removed their only firm basis, a conviction in the minds of the people that these liberties are the gift of God? That they are not to be violated but with his wrath? Indeed I tremble for my country when I reflect that God is just: that his justice cannot sleep forever."[43]

Neuhaus wrote:

> Jefferson understood that the naked public square is a very dangerous place. No constitution or written law is strong enough to defend rights under attack. Their "only firm basis" is in their being perceived as a transcendent gift. At the same time, the denial of such rights, as they were denied by slavery, cannot be sustained without invoking the dreadful judgment that follows upon the defiance of that moral basis.[44]

Yet any recognition of this moral law is met with scorn by modern American elites. "For some reason, the most vocal Christians among us never mention the Beatitudes. But, often with tears in their eyes, they demand that the Ten Commandments be posted in public buildings," wrote Kurt Vonnegut.[45]

When Louisiana did just that, there was a collective media meltdown. Axios called it "Christian nationalism on the march."[46] One writer castigated the state, pointing out its numerous failures and the hypocrisy of its leaders: "You have exchanged the Kingdom of God for Christian Nationalism. You want to rule, not serve. You travel around the world to colonize Black and Brown bodies, yet when they convert, you make them twice as much of a child of hell as yourselves." (Never mind that Black Americans are distinctly more religious than the public at large and most of those religious Black Americans are Protestant.)

Many modern opponents of patriotism seem to assume that the only alternative to a neutral public square is a theocracy ruled by just such Pharisees.[47]

The Secular Project Drives Charity from the Public Square

But we don't actually face a choice between neutrality and theocracy. In reality, the most immediate effect of the secular revolution has been to transform the United States into a less charitable country because of the tremendous, invisible support of religious institutions.

Many Americans assume that Christians are characterized by empty words and not real actions. "Posturing, virtue signaling, and forcing religious beliefs on others while not lifting a finger to help the other in daily life is Republicanism, and sadly, defines large swaths of American Christianity," wrote one critic.[48]

However, various studies have shown that people of faith are the most generous givers to charity. One such survey showed that church attenders gave more than four times as much to charity as those who don't attend.[49] Another demonstrated that churches in America provide over a trillion dollars' worth of social assistance.[50]

Some states in the Pacific Northwest have implemented standards in their screening for foster families requiring couples to commit to affirming a child's self-stated LGBT identity, a requirement that makes fostering untenable for orthodox Christians. "Washington's foster-care system services roughly 8,000 children, the majority 10 or younger," reported *The Wall Street Journal* in 2024. "By discriminating against families [who won't affirm LGBT identities] . . . the state is reducing the number of homes available to these children."[51] This is particularly notable in that Christians are more than twice as likely as the American public at large to adopt children.[52]

Our system of government isn't built for theocracy, and vanishingly few Americans even flirt with the idea of a Christian state. The Founders resisted the idea of a state church. James Madison believed that "the Religion then of every man must be left to the conviction and conscience of every man; and it is the right of every man to exercise it as these may dictate."[53] Madison was influenced by Baptist pastors and theologians who insisted on the language included in the First Amendment to the Constitution, which prohibits the establishment of a state church.

The Founders, having surveyed the wreckage of the mostly unholy alliances between state and church throughout history, envisioned a new arrangement that would allow people to worship freely. Baptists had left England for that very reason. They grounded their beliefs about government in their interpretation of Scripture and the idea that Christ, not government, is Lord of the conscience.[54]

Yet a Baptist conception of "a free church in a free state" is not the same thing as the kind of ideological secularism that many people have embraced since the middle of the twentieth century. The historian and scholar Daniel L. Dreisbach was right when he wrote, "The 'high and impregnable' wall constructed by the modern Court has been used to inhibit religion's ability to inform the public ethic, to deprive religious citizens of the civil liberty to participate in politics armed with ideas informed by their faith, and to infringe the right of religious communities and institutions to extend their prophetic ministries into the public square."[55]

Secularists' vision of the naked public square is one banning religious authoritarians from pressing a thumb on the scales of justice. But what this belief often looks like in practice is the restriction of any interaction between the state and religious communities in ways that punish good ministry, such as food pantries, adoption agencies, prison ministries, and educational institutions. One constitutional lawyer called this jurisprudence "search-and-destroy missions to obliterate all things religious from public life."[56]

What has often been applied is the so-called Lemon test, which originates from a 1971 Supreme Court ruling, *Lemon v. Kurtzman*, which broadened the First Amendment's establishment clause beyond what the drafters of the Bill of Rights had originally intended. By this standard, the government can violate it any time it is involved in any religious endeavor that doesn't have a secular purpose. That turned the First Amendment from a positive that prevents the government from meddling in church affairs or establishing a preferred religious practice over another to a negative that pushes any and all religious activity out of the public square.

What secularists imagine these rules will do is chase out a sort of evil Spanish Inquisition that they imagine wishes to rule the country. In practice, the major victims of such legislation are religious groups that genuinely want to work with their local or state governments to help solve real-world problems such as addiction, foster care, prisoner rehabilitation, poverty, and other social ills. Under this regime, ministries must abandon the faith commitments that compelled them to do the work in the first place and are forced to adopt a "secular purpose." The new standard moved beyond neutrality to actual hostility toward religious groups participating in civic life because their good work might nudge people toward religion, just by mere association with a church or faith-based group.

Thankfully, in the twenty-first century, a more originalist Supreme Court has begun to claw back the Lemon test while also maintaining the integrity of the First Amendment. Recent cases include *Kennedy v. Bremerton*, which allows a football coach to lead voluntary prayer; *Fulton v. Philadelphia*, which said that the city of Philadelphia couldn't push evangelical and Catholic social service agencies out of the adoption and foster care process simply because they hold evangelical or Catholic beliefs; and *Trinity Lutheran v. Comer*, which prevented the state of Missouri from discriminating against a Lutheran school that applied for playground improvement grants offered to any institution of education.

But the social costs remain. Today religion is still often considered, especially by elites, as a quaint practice best reserved for private worship. Consider the subtle language shift by progressive politicians from defending "freedom of religion" to "freedom of worship." The legal scholar Ashley E. Samelson wrote, "To anyone who closely follows prominent discussion of religious freedom in the diplomatic and political arena, this linguistic shift is troubling. The reason is simple. Any person of faith knows that religious exercise is about a lot more than freedom of worship. It's about the right to dress according to one's religious dictates, to preach openly, to evangelize, to engage in the public square."[57] Consider the fact that the Obama administration tried to force the Little Sisters of the Poor to distribute abortifacients as part of their health care coverage, even though doing so would violate the tenets of their Catholic faith. Or the way it tried to force Catholic hospitals to perform abortions, even though doing so would violate the tenets of their faith. In other words, progressives argue that there are large swaths of public life in which people are not allowed to be religious.

As a result, society suffers. When the shared moral norms that once bound society together recede, what replaces them is often worse. This is not a wide-eyed nostalgia about a fictional "golden era" of America's past. Civil religion didn't spare Americans from sin. Even in the best of times, our grand experiment is still an experiment by fallen humans. But secularism is not a better social arrangement.

America Is Better When Christians Are Involved

As a Baptist Christian, I am aware that a generic sense of civil religion is not the same as authentic New Testament Christianity. Americans can acknowledge God as the source of morality without committing their hearts to him in saving faith. "In God we trust" isn't eternally salvific, yet the loss of this, replaced by a rootless secularism without transcendence, has not been an improvement. We need to accept that there *is* a moral law in the universe and that it proceeds not from mere reason making up clever systems for flourishing but rather from the nature of reality. If we don't do this, our desire to remake the world will quickly escalate into anarchic revolutions, which we can see in the more secular parts of the country.

C. S. Lewis, in his classic *The Abolition of Man*, called this the Tao, that self-evident sense of right and wrong that humans are foolish to deny. Without it, democracy becomes moral anarchy and ironically leads to a loss of freedom and opens the door to state power. That was Alexis de Tocqueville's stated fear in his otherwise positive commendation of America in *Democracy in America*.

The Founders believed that deeply. They understood human nature and especially the Christian doctrines of total depravity and final judgment. "The notion that God is watching you even when others are not," wrote Jonah Goldberg, "is probably the most powerful civilizing force in all of human history."[58]

Today, many people are recognizing this reality afresh and not merely conservative Christians. The atheist Richard Dawkins, a fierce critic of religion, recently admitted to being a "cultural Christian." In other words, as an atheist, he'd rather live in a country shaped by Christianity.[59] Derek Thompson admitted in a piece for *The Atlantic* that the decline in church attendance in America has had significant negative social costs:

> As an agnostic, I have spent most of my life thinking about the decline of faith in America in mostly positive terms. Organized religion seemed, to me, beset by scandal and entangled in noxious politics. So, I thought, what is there really to mourn? Only in the past few years have I come around to a different view. Maybe

> religion, for all of its faults, works a bit like a retaining wall to hold back the destabilizing pressure of American hyper-individualism, which threatens to swell and spill over in its absence.[60]

The atheist feminist Louise Perry made a similar observation, noting that in pushing religion farther and farther away from the public square, we are "sawing off the branch we are sitting on."[61]

Perry is right. The branch she is referring to is the underlying moral and spiritual foundation that gives us the ideals we champion, such as human rights, fairness, freedom, and the rule of law. Those have to come from somewhere. Dawkins, Thompson, and Perry recognize, even if indirectly, the resources Christianity brings to society as it shapes its conception of the good. That was why the Founders put into the Declaration of Independence the acknowledgment that our natural rights "are endowed by their Creator." As one group of political scientists put it:

> Our constitutional system and political culture would not exist without Christian ideas, nor will they be intelligible or sustainable in the long run if meaningful, orthodox Christian influence disappears. Christianity provided the vision of creation, knowledge, and humanity that made liberal democracy possible. Indeed, any society in which democracy flourishes is drawing water from wells that Christianity dug.[62]

This is an empirical reality. Consider the work of academics and historians such as Tom Holland, whose book *Dominion: The Making of the Western Mind* chronicled the Christian roots of the values secularists claim to champion: human rights, equality, justice. Similar work by scholars such as Kyle Harper and Rodney Stark affirms it.

When people claim, then, that democracy is a secular enterprise, designed to exile ultimate truth claims from its sphere of operation, they're both historically inaccurate and philosophically naive. As we'll see, many of the other maladies in the American body politic stem from just this denial of ultimate reality. A defense of Christian patriotism has to be predicated on a denial of the secular story and a rejection of the hysteria that says that every expression of faith in public life is fascist.

So it's not weird when public officials express their Christian faith. Believers should not be bullied into retreating from the public square. Christian values helped shape our nation's founding ideals, ideals that have helped shape it into an imperfect but exceptional beacon of liberty.

Now that I've outlined why it's normal for Christians to be involved in politics and why it is beneficial for society to have some stated recognition of the supernatural source of our common vision, what does the Bible say about how Christians are to be patriotic?

CHAPTER 2

You Can't Obey God and Hate Your Country

The Christian position is beautifully balanced. On one hand, we don't deify our country. We don't wrap the flag around the cross. For we know that our ultimate citizenship is in heaven, and that's where our ultimate allegiance is. But the only place for expressing that allegiance is in the concrete loyalties God calls us to here on earth—including loyalty to country. We can't love mankind in the abstract; we can only really love people in the particular, concrete relationships God has placed us in—in our family, our church, our community . . . and our nation.[1]

—*Chuck Colson*

THE TRADITIONAL RITUALS OF CIVIC REVERENCE ARE DIFFICULT TO EXplain in a secular, materialist culture. Secularists don't understand that worship and reverence are as necessary to the human condition as are air and water.

When I was eleven years old, my parents packed up our silver Chevy station wagon and drove down the interstate 750 miles from our Chicago suburb to Washington, DC. My kids can hardly believe this, but they planned the trip before the age of the internet. There were no Instagram reels to make us jealous of other families' trips to the nation's capital. There were no apps to book hotels because there were no smartphones. We didn't even have one of those clunky early car phones because they weren't invented yet.

I'm not sure what motivated that trip. Did my parents simply want to create memories for us kids? Were they determined to give us an education in civics and American government? Or maybe a visit to the nation's capital was the fulfillment of a lifelong dream of their own. Probably they did it just because that sort of civic pilgrimage was seen as normal and inevitable. Just as the people who originally erected statues and monuments to presidents and heroes intended, taking such a trip is a process of collective memory and mythmaking.

Whatever motivated them, they couldn't have known that that long and arduous car ride east with three restless kids would be life changing for their oldest son. We toured the Pentagon, the US Capitol, and the FBI building. We got into line before sunrise and waited all day to get through security and visit the White House, where, in the pre-9/11 world, we could step into the Lincoln Bedroom and peer up toward, but not enter, the living quarters that the first President Bush and his wife had just moved into. By far the most emotional moment of that trip was the first time I looked up at the Lincoln Memorial. I specifically remember that moment, walking with my father past the reflecting pool on the National Mall and ascending those sacred steps. I was not old enough to fully understand the weight of history there, but I knew enough to weep a little at the sight of arguably our greatest president. Lincoln's own life, which was lived in constant appreciation of the fragile democracy into which he had been born and had been given in service to hold it together, is a kind of icon of the American experiment. That sight, that trip, was a booster shot for my burgeoning love of America. It's a love that has not faded in the decades since. Civic pilgrimages like that one are hard to explain with secular reasoning. Interestingly, however, secular Americans are very comfortable with a different sort of pilgrimage: the ritual journey of self-flagellation, examining our nation's very real guilt. This sort of introspective learning and remembering isn't alien to the Christian tradition—but it's notable that we are comfortable only with the latter, not the former, today.

You Can't Obey God and Hate Your Country

A few years ago, I was back in Washington, DC, invited, along with a group of other evangelical leaders, to tour the National Museum of African American History and Culture. I was not new to learning about the wicked legacy of chattel slavery and the evils of Jim Crow, having read and studied the civil rights movement and having participated in those kinds of gatherings before. That tour, with its comprehensive look at that painful part of our history, was a vivid reminder of and education in the racial horror that is a part of our nation's complicated history. Millions of men, women, and children were trafficked against their will and forced into labor. Millions more, even after slavery was abolished, were denied the basic rights and freedoms promised by our founding documents. America has made enormous progress, but our original sin still haunts us.

Given that sin, it's easy to dismiss reverence for a great man's statue as a naive self-deception. And many Americans have begun to do just that. According to a recent Gallup Poll, quite a few Americans think patriotism isn't good or necessary. Only 39 percent of Americans are "extremely proud" of their country. When broken down by generation, the survey found, 50 percent of those aged fifty-five and over were "extremely proud," 40 percent of those aged thirty-five to fifty-five, and a meager 18 percent of those aged eighteen to twenty.[2]

It is clear that patriotism is seen as passé in many quarters of American society, as something highly cringeworthy at best and a sin to be repented of at worst. I sense this spirit even among some otherwise conservative Christians, who fear being confused with their flag-waving parents and grandparents. Even many well-meaning Christian books, sermons, and conferences seem to equate any form of patriotism with idolatry. There's also a sharp class divide between the top 20 percent and the rest of us on patriotism. The middle class is patriotic; the elites are not.[3]

These generational and class trends have left many Christians wondering what, at all, we should do about this place where we've been born. The scholar James R. Wood wrote:

> For many Christians in America today such patriotic love does not come easily. Much grade-school public education, university teaching, and even Christian moral theology over the last few decades has trained many to be highly critical of America and any explicit appeal to love for nation. This was true for me. In recent years I have been challenged to reconsider these things through deeper engagement with the Christian tradition but also just thinking through what neighbor-love entails and what effective and responsible governance looks like.[4]

Wood is right. In fact, considering the duty of neighbor love that God gives us, I have come to a conclusion that may strike modern Christians as startling: You can't both obey God and hate your country. This isn't true just of America; it's true of every country and every person.

Many objections, I'm sure, spring to mind. One could be that I'm not doing anything except urging a general sense of good feeling about America's potential, which nearly everyone feels. In certain definitions, that "love of country" could be defined to mean just about anything. In fact, conservatives and liberals both tend to define it according to whatever behavior they support. During the Vietnam War era, the phrase "Dissent is the highest form of patriotism" became a popular rallying cry.[5] By this standard, the historian Howard Zinn could claim to be a patriot, even though few people on the right would see him as such, since it's fairly clear that his idea of dissent includes an affinity for America's enemies. People in the dissent-is-patriotism camp tend to see more traditional patriotism as thoughtless obedience to the ruling class. A nineteenth-century French statesman wryly noted the fickleness of his government when he observed that "treason is a matter of dates."[6]

But few people identify patriotism with disloyalty, so for my purposes, I'll use the more traditional definition: Patriotism is love of country as manifested in loyalty, service, and giving honor to one's country. (A country, roughly, consists of citizens living in a specific place, united by a state, an institution bonded by laws but strengthened by shared memory and culture.)

This is what most anti-patriots mean when they say that a Christian engaging in normal patriotic behavior is somehow compromised or sinful. When Supreme Court Justice Samuel Alito flew an "Appeal to Heaven" flag, a common symbol going back to the Revolution, *New York* magazine ran a piece with the headline "The Christian Nationalist Danger Behind the 'Appeal to Heaven' Flag," attempting to make the case that because January 6 rioters had used the flag, it was now a symbol of hate. This is a comical, bad-faith misunderstanding of patriotism, but if we take a step back, it's easier to understand why people are suspicious of the symbols and rituals of country love.

For one thing, such love seems preferential. By loving one country above others, doesn't it mean that we deny this special feeling to other countries? Relatedly, because it is grounded in a specific place, people, and culture, doesn't that make it exclusive? Isn't it dependent on oppressing others, "othering" outsiders, opposing enemies, and idolizing the status quo? In fact, many of the critiques people have of traditional marriage are echoed by this framework. Aren't we being narrow minded for interpreting love in this narrow way? Isn't it freer, more forward thinking, to erase boundaries, extend our love to everyone, and aspire to a sort of cosmic oneness? On a basic level, many Christians are uncertain about patriotism because it seems to come into conflict with core elements of the Gospel life. How, for instance, can we have a special love for our own country when the Gospel calls us to love the nations? If this world is not our home, why must we be loyal to a temporal kingdom?

This is particularly relevant when younger Christians are, by habit, disaffected and suspicious of love of country. To take America's biggest Protestant group as an example, my friend Trevin Wax wrote presciently in 2014 that, in his experience, "Older Southern Baptists are more likely to see the U.S. as Israel. Younger Southern Baptists are more likely to see the U.S. as Babylon."[7]

The implication for many believers is that we should love Babylon in a different way than we loved Israel. But does that mean that endless "dissent" is our only form of patriotism?

Loving God's Kingdom Doesn't Mean Hating Your Country

The first and most obvious objection to the command to love our country is an understandable one. Doesn't commanding such love risk the creation of deranged jingoists willing to commit any impieties in the name of the flag? Furthermore, doesn't it signal hostility to foreigners? Anyone who has been mistreated by a country is unlikely to look kindly on a command that its people should love it.

Pastor and author Brian Zahnd highlighted an example of exaggerated American nationalism in Washington, DC: "Consider the Apotheosis of Washington painted on the dome of the Capitol rotunda that depicts a deified George Washington ascended to heaven and seated in the place of prominence among the other gods and goddesses. (The risen and ascended Christ is nowhere in sight.)"[8]

We all know examples of people who have taken country love to demonic extremes. In his book *The Four Loves*, C. S. Lewis quoted an old proverb arguing that any "love," taken to an extreme, becomes evil: "Love becomes a demon when it becomes a god." In fact, such love ceases to be love.

Steven B. Smith, in his book *Reclaiming Patriotism in an Age of Extremes*, called this deranged love "nationalism" to distinguish it from patriotism: "Nationalism is not patriotism's exact opposite but a deformation of the patriotic spirit."[9]

I am hesitant to apply the term *nationalism* because it is often confused with patriotism. I think it's important for us to explore exactly what nationalism looks like so we can distinguish it from patriotism.

Christians who are skeptical of patriotism tend to justify this with an appeal to the Christian duty to evangelize the nations. Doesn't wrapping ourselves in our own flag signal an idolatrous indifference to the feelings of foreigners? Isn't that going against Christ's message?

The underlying assumption is this: Love of the familiar is limiting. It is stultifying and incestuous. It needs to be rejected in order for one to flourish as an open-hearted person. Don't love your country, such people argue; you should instead love humanity.

Does this question have a point? After all, a large part of Christ's message was about challenging his disciples to understand that the Gospel would go not just to the Jews but to the whole world.

Let's travel back in time to around 800 BC to consider a man who took country love too far. The setting was near the shores of Galilee in the smaller northern territory of the divided kingdom of Israel. There was a prophet named Jonah, who was something of a folk hero in Israel, having prophesied that the country would experience an extended season of peace, wealth, and expansion (2 Kings 14:23–25). He was a strong ally of King Jeroboam II, who had expanded the borders of the northern kingdom to their farthest reach. Israel was thriving. But all was not well. While the country experienced unprecedented prosperity and peace, Jeroboam led the people of God toward continued idolatry, injustice, and moral degradation. Alongside Jonah were other prophets, such as Amos, who condemned false worship (Amos 4, 5, and 8) and exploitation of the poor (Amos 6).

Hosea was a contemporary of Jonah. Hosea delivered an even more pointed rebuke from God and prophesied that Assyria, Israel's powerful and feared northeastern neighbor, would eventually conquer the northern kingdom.

You could describe Amos and Hosea as the "dissenting patriot" prophets and Jonah as the "loyal patriot" prophet. This was why, when God summoned Jonah, not Hosea or Amos, and commanded him to go to Assyria's capital city, Nineveh, and preach repentance, it was one speaking engagement the prophet wished had never passed through his inbox. God was asking him to go and preach repentance to his enemies. Surely if they repented, they would be blessed. Didn't that represent an unforgivable act of treason on Jonah's behalf?

Israel wasn't simply an underdog in that situation, despite its foretold doom. Scholars tell us that during Jonah's time, while the northern kingdom of Israel was flourishing, Assyria was experiencing turmoil, including famine, military defeats, and populist revolts. There was also an eclipse of the sun, which the superstitious and pagan Ninevites likely viewed as a message from the gods.[10] What's more, Assyrians were a bloodthirsty, cruel people, known for their savagery. Some of it is told in the book of Nahum. Pastor Timothy Keller described it in vivid detail:

> Assyria was one of the cruelest and most violent empires of ancient times. Assyrian kings often recorded the results of their military victories, gloating of whole plains littered with corpses and of cities burned completely to the ground. The emperor Shalmaneser III is well known for depicting torture, dismembering, and decapitations of enemies in grisly detail on large stone relief panels.[11]

You Can't Obey God and Hate Your Country

Jonah had two motivations to resist God's call. First, he was probably scared out of his mind. You would have been scared, too. Assyria was Israel's sworn enemy and, not long after Jonah's death, would fulfill Hosea's prophecy and conquer Israel. Imagine being sent as a missionary to Hamas, ISIS, or Boko Haram.

But fear was not the only thing that kept Jonah from Nineveh. He had political reasons to resist that mission from God. If the message of repentance and salvation was heeded by these bloodthirsty savages, it would mean that Israel's sworn enemies might repent of their bloodthirsty and wicked ways and begin to flourish. Jonah didn't want that. It wasn't that he didn't believe that God could spiritually transform the hearts of his enemies; it was that he didn't *want* God to save them. Jonah not only wanted Israel to thrive, he wanted every other nation to suffer. But that was against God's desire for the nation of Israel, which had been raised up to bless the nations (Genesis 12, 22).

Well, the anti-patriot might argue, this seems like an open-and-shut case. Love of country is in direct conflict with the Gospel. The earthly city and the heavenly city are at war, and we must choose one or the other. But this is the wrong takeaway. Jonah's love of his country was not bad in itself; it was bad because he had made it paramount.

Keller explained how Jonah's politics had become idolatrous:

> As long as serving God fit into Jonah's goals for Israel, he was fine with God. As soon as he had to choose between the true God and the god he actually worshiped, he turned on the true God in anger. Jonah's particular national identity was more foundational to his self-worth than his role as a servant of the God of all nations. The real God had been just a means to an end. He was using God to serve his real god.[12]

Keller is right. We shouldn't be naive to the ways in which we can adopt this nationalist posture of Jonah, perhaps in attitudes and sentiments that have us thinking that Americans are superior to the citizens of other nations or in allowing ourselves an ambivalence about or even disgust at other nations and peoples or ignoring the imperative given to Christians to participate in missionary efforts to all the nations of the world. This posture toward one's country, a temptation today, is what C. S. Lewis labeled *demoniac* or demonic.[13]

Jonah's problem was not that his love for his country was too big, it was that his love for God was too small. And his hatred of the Ninevites blinded him to what God wanted to do: see the people of that nation experience God's love and thus become less bloodthirsty, less antagonistic, and, perhaps, less of an enemy. You can't obey God and hate your country, but you also can't love your country more than you do God's kingdom. Natural affections are good but in their proper place. If they abandon that place, they also lose their nature as affection. They become something else. But in their proper place, such affections shouldn't need to be at war with each other.

For instance, a Brit such as C. S. Lewis might well feel a special kinship with other Brits because of the sound of their voices or the shared sense of cultural memory, as would a Kenyan who ran into another Kenyan in a foreign city. But this kinship is a bond that is nothing to the bond between a Christian and other members of the body of Christ. Rather, it should prepare us for loving those outside its limits, just as loving our siblings teaches us to love the citizens of our city. That was why the Apostle Peter described believers as "a peculiar people" (KJV) and "holy nation" (1 Peter 2:9) and why Paul routinely used familial terms such as "household" to describe Christians (1 Timothy 3:15).

We should picture every person as being like a multivariable little culture (variables such as personality type, habits, culture, and so on) that loves what's familiar first. Thus, we love ourselves first, then our families, then our immediate communities, and then the world. What nationalists such as Jonah seem to miss is that these loves are supposed to escalate. If your goal isn't to ultimately love the world, you're not exhibiting Christian love; whereas the progressives' error is to assume that loving the world means hating or resisting the familiar.

In fact, the path God gives us to love the world is to start with the immediate and move outward. The idea is to love everything, so starting with what's easy to love is pragmatic. But *sticking* with what's easy to love makes that love itself the end, which is idolatry.

A genuine love of God, then, enlarges rather than diminishes our capacity for love. Genuine gratitude for what is near—church, family, country—produces a generosity for what is a little farther out. The most missions-minded Christians I have known have been motivated by gratitude for their own personal salvation. The biggest-hearted Americans desire to help other nations from a well of pride for the goodness of their country.

Thus, in avoiding Jonah's mistake, we should not, as is so often the temptation in this age of American self-loathing, view every expression of patriotism as idolatry. One left-leaning Christian writer bragged about his lack of patriotism and declared, "Prophecy, not patriotism, is what is needed from Christians," as if we must choose.[14] The flag, noted the self-proclaimed "anti-American theologian" Stanley Hauerwas, "represents for many a more determinative sacrifice than the sacrifice of Christ."[15] Perhaps this is true for some people, but it is no reason to dismiss the flag entirely.

Consider, for instance, the words of Ted Landsmark, a Black man attacked by a white man with a flag in an iconic 1976 photo. When given the chance to dismiss the importance of Old Glory, Landsmark said:

> I view myself as an American who has benefited tremendously from the best America can provide. And I also recognize that in the name of the flag some very heinous things have been done to people in this country and elsewhere. . . .
>
> I think that it is a symbol of what we aspire to be as a democracy and that when there's a demonstration that involves the flag, that speaks to how we express our values of democracy and fairness, that it is really an appropriate icon for all of us to look to as to what we want to be, as opposed to what we sometimes have been.[16]

C. S. Lewis, again, is helpful here. In his book *The Four Loves*, penned after the Second World War, he wrote of the importance of not seeing our allegiances as binary choices but understanding how to rightly order our loves, expressing affection for our homeland yet holding that love in such a way that it is always subordinate to our love of God. Lewis was drawing from the fourth-century Church father Augustine, who wrote that "living a just and holy life requires one to be capable of an objective and impartial evaluation of things: to love things, that is to say, in the right order, so that you do not love what is not to be loved, or fail to love what is to be loved, or have a greater love for what should be loved less, or an equal love for things that should be loved less or more, or a lesser or greater love for things that should be loved equally."[17]

Augustine's words came after the fall of Rome, when some Christians were deeply distraught at the demise of the Christian government established by Constantine the Great and other Christians cheered their country's demise. Augustine rebuked both postures and urged believers to see value in earthly governments and nation-states while being mindful of their ultimate allegiance to the Kingdom of God.

Keller is also helpful: "Don't love anything less; instead learn to love God more, and you will love other things with far more satisfaction. You won't overprotect them, you won't over expect things from them. You won't be constantly furious with them for not being what you hoped. Don't stifle passionate love for anything; rather, redirect your greatest love toward God by loving him with your whole heart and loving him for himself, and not just for what he can give you. Then, and only then, does the contentment start to come."[18]

Too often, well-meaning American Christians create a false binary between love of country and love of God. One Bible teacher insisted, "And wherever I may choose in the future to live, I will remember that I am not a patriot or partisan—but a little Christ."[19] But as Lewis, Chesterton, and Augustine showed us, the dichotomy between patriotism and faithfulness is not really a more faithful expression of Christian faith than Christian patriotism is. Consider what Peter wrote to the members of the first-century Church: "Honor all men. Love the brotherhood. Fear God. Honor the king" (1 Peter 2:17, ASV).

Fear God. Honor the king. That's a hierarchy. That's an ordering of loves. It's not God *or* the king, unless the king is telling you to disobey God. As Thomas More supposedly said of King Henry VIII after the king ordered his death, "I die the king's good servant, and God's first." So yes, we can pledge allegiance to the flag, knowing that our fullest allegiance is "under God." We do this in other areas of our lives without thinking about it.

I pledged allegiance to my wife almost a quarter century ago. That vow is underneath my vow to God. But on an even lower level, I pledge allegiance to the cell phone company and the mortgage broker every month when I send off a check to them. Now, if any of those allegiances supersedes my allegiance to Christ, well, then, my life and the posture of my heart are out of alignment with God.

Are there times when love of God and love of country do come down to a binary choice, when we have little recourse? Sure, there are rare moments, such as the situation in the Book of Acts where disciples were ordered to stop preaching the Gospel by the state, or in totalitarian governments around the world, where people of faith have no freedom. Or in the case of someone such as Dietrich Bonhoeffer, who was called to resist the Nazi regime that had overtaken his country.

Still, even this resistance to wrong policies springs from a love of the nation and doesn't truly mean rejecting love of a country so much as rejecting obedience to a bad government. G. K. Chesterton was right: "'My country, right or wrong,' is something that no patriot would think of saying."[20] Because we love our country, we care deeply about whether its government is on the right or wrong path. And we have another Old Testament context to help us understand this.

Love Must Start with Loyalty

Earlier, I mentioned that many Christians see the United States as being like Babylon instead of like Israel. This paradigm, which I happen to affirm, tends to influence how we see our duties as citizens. If we live in Babylon, is there a moral duty for us to be patriotic? You might be surprised. To help answer this question, I will move from the story of Jonah in the kingdom of Israel in the eighth century BC to the pagan kingdom of Babylon in the sixth century BC. Here, another prophet, Jeremiah, is speaking to the people of God.

They were captives in a place they hardly knew, surrounded by pagan rituals, strange foods, and false gods. They were led by despotic rulers who stuffed political enemies into ovens for sport. A few spiritual charlatans were selling them a quick fix: Huddle together, ignore the noise, and soon God would rescue them from that hellscape.

Jeremiah was the only prophet who had the truth, from the mouth of God himself. He came to tell it straight: The Israelites weren't going to get their country back for a long, long time. The grifters promising an immediate and triumphant recovery of their homeland were wrong. The people of God weren't going anywhere. God had placed them in Babylon for at least seventy years. It would be their new home, even if they didn't quite feel at home there.

God had a mission for them in Babylon. Yes, they were exiles, uncomfortable with the prevailing culture, besieged on every side. Yet they needed to see Babylon in a new way:

> Build houses and live in them. Plant gardens and eat their produce. Find wives for yourselves, and have sons and daughters. Find wives for your sons and give your daughters to men in marriage so that they may bear sons and daughters. Multiply there; do not decrease. Pursue the well-being of the city I have deported you to. Pray to the Lord on its behalf, for when it thrives, you will thrive. (Jeremiah 29:5–7)

Only refugees from war-torn places such as Afghanistan, Ukraine, and Syria can fully relate to what the people of God in Jeremiah's day experienced in Babylon. Still, American Christians can relate in some sense, given that we can often feel like outcasts in a world that prioritizes other values. The social mores, the decisions made by our leaders, and the unrighteous messages often preached by corporate brands all have us feeling out of place.

This sense of alienation is not strange. Peter told another marginalized group of God's people, living throughout the Roman Empire in the first century, that the discomfort they felt was normal. He called them "strangers and exiles" (1 Peter 2:11). The Apostle Paul would use similar language when speaking to the members of the Church at Philippi, reminding them that their citizenship was in Heaven (Philippians 3:20), and the writer of Hebrews comforted his audience by commending the saints of the past, who, he said, had been "looking forward to the city . . . whose architect and builder is God" (Hebrews 11:10).

This is often referred to by theologians and Bible teachers as "exilic theology." One theologian described it as "the experience of knowing that one is an alien, and perhaps even in a hostile environment where the dominant values run counter to one's own."[21] It's a great way to think about the ways in which living for the kingdom of God is always going to cut against the grain of the world in some way. Jesus promised that (John 15:18), and the New Testament reinforces it (1 John 2:15–17). In Ephesians, the Apostle Paul says that there are often wicked forces at work, run by "the prince of the powers of the air" (Ephesians 2:2, ASV).

In modern America, this message is often seen as being congruent with a negative view of patriotism. Obedience to God must mean resisting the status quo, the logic goes. We can't love a fundamentally corrupt and compromised system that oppresses marginalized people, goes the left-wing version, and right-wingers would say that we can't love a country that hates Christians and kills the unborn. While neither side may go so far as to say, "Don't love your country," their actions tell a different story when they repeatedly show a tendency to believe the worst of their country. One thinks of something like the 1619 Project, painting our national origins as thoroughly corrupt, or right-wing influencers who always believe the best of foreign dictators but believe the worst of American leaders' motivations.

Some Christian communities tend to withdraw from society entirely because of this. Anabaptists refrain from voting for reasons such as these. One Anabaptist writer summed up this posture well: "The mantra 'freedom isn't free' is a counterfeit of our freedom in Christ" and "The patriotic slogans 'God and country' or 'America first' constantly go unchallenged as contradictions of the Greatest Commandment and Second Commandment." Christians who use such slogans turn politics into an idol, he argued.[22]

So does our status as exiles and strangers imply that we should withdraw from the life of our nation, as some people imply? That we should not at all identify with the United States of America?

In fact, Jeremiah gave the exiles in Babylon the opposite advice. They were to be distinct as the people of God and not absorb the values of a pagan culture. Yet they were also to "seek the welfare of the city." In other words, the Israelites in exile were to be loyal to Babylon and seek her good. How does this connect to patriotism? Ask yourself: Is it possible to seek the welfare of a country you detest? Why would you try to improve, to serve, to protect a place you care nothing about? The first place to start with seeking Babylon's welfare is to do something that must have been a baffling command for a Jewish refugee: Love Babylon.

But doesn't this make us complicit in Babylon's sins? A young professional in Washington, DC, wrote:

> As a millennial believer, I have an interesting career configuration as a defense intelligence contractor and an evangelical Baptist church planter in Washington, DC. Our church preaches the gospel and cares for the poor and vulnerable. We are a diverse bunch of people—racially, educationally, vocationally, and politically. I also care about the security and prosperity of the US homeland and other US interests. I enjoy both pursuits and feel a sense of personal accomplishment and God's satisfaction. Nevertheless, not all of my peers would say these two pursuits are morally compatible for Christians.[23]

The sentiment that writer described is not uncommon. If some people, such as Jonah, are tempted toward a disordered love of country, I sense that in this generation, it's far more common to recoil at any sense of loyalty to America.

No Christian should behave in a corrupt way or sin by abandoning truth or justice. We are to be "exiles" from the world, in that we must not participate in the world's evils or love the world's evils, no matter how popular they may be. This definition of "world" refers to a sort of unholy zeitgeist. But we are also commanded to love like God, and God loves the world, the people of the world. Similarly, resisting the corruption of a country has to start with loving that country. You can't improve a thing you hate.

Richard John Neuhaus argued as much when he wrote that "the affirmation of loyalty to a community is the ticket that grants admission to the critical debate about the meaning of that community." Neuhaus, a fierce opponent of the Vietnam War as well as abortion on demand, nevertheless saw the importance of patriotism:

> The alternative to loyalty is disloyalty. No community knowingly takes its directions from the avowedly disloyal. We are speaking of course about patriotism. The tragedy is that patriotism has become a negative, or at least a shadowed, concept in the view from the left. Effective criticism, however, depends upon rejoining protest to patriotism.[24]

Understanding the temporal nature of our earthly home helps us love it with the proper perspective, but love it we must. And, according to Lewis, exercising this sort of love might even train us in having affection for our future home:

> There is a love of home, of the place we grew up in or the places, perhaps many, which have been our homes; and of all places fairly near these and fairly like them; love of old acquaintances, of familiar sights, sounds and smells. It would be hard to find any

> legitimate point of view from which this feeling could be condemned. As the family offers us the first step beyond self-love, so this offers us the first step beyond family selfishness . . . those who do not love the fellow-villagers or fellow-townsmen whom they have seen are not likely to have got very far towards loving "Man" whom they have not. All natural affections, including this, can become rivals to spiritual love: but they can also be preparatory imitations of it, training (so to speak) of the spiritual muscles which grace may later put to a higher service.[25]

When applied to the story of Jonah, we see the point: Jonah's love of his fellow Jews should have prepared him to love the Gentiles. His love of Israel should not have been diminished or threatened by the call to love Assyria, and the fact that it *was* threatened by God's call indicates how tepid was its true nature. The fact that Jonah couldn't extend his love for a plant to an entire city was God's entire point: It was not wrong for Jonah to love the plant. But it was wrong that he couldn't grow that love beyond its small origins.

In an essay entitled "In Defense of Patriotism," G. K. Chesterton wrote:

> The fundamental spiritual advantage of patriotism and such sentiments is this: that by means of it all things are loved adequately, because all things are loved individually. . . . Patriotism begins the praise of the world at the nearest thing, instead of beginning it at the most distant, and thus it insures what is, perhaps, the most essential of all earthly considerations, that nothing upon earth shall go without its due appreciation.[26]

Both Lewis and Chesterton adapted their ideas from Augustine, who wrote that love of the particular helps us foster love of the universal.[27] This is a notable piece of wisdom because we now see everywhere encouragements to love enormous, nebulous abstractions such as "the world" or "humanity." This can sound like Christian language, but in fact, it tends to end up being a way of sidestepping or diminishing the duty to love the familiar.

Though such calls usually come from the Left, we should also watch out for influencers commanding the love of right-wing abstractions, such as an imaginary, pure country of the past, which diminishes our duty to love the imperfect present neighbor. But because the conservative philosophy emphasizes loving local things and growing out from this base, the Right is inoculated against—though not immune to—losing itself in abstractions.

Neuhaus went so far as to say that a healthy patriotism is "a species of piety."[28] At its essence, to love one's country is to demonstrate gratitude, an essential virtue for a faithful Christian (1 Thessalonians 5:18). John Wilsey described patriotism as "a rightly ordered love of country that comes from gratitude and joy in the good gifts God has freely given by his grace."[29]

Gratitude Starts with Attentiveness

Part of what makes country love easy is that it's natural; it's instinctive. But the love that Jeremiah commanded the Israelite exiles to have in a foreign land didn't come naturally; it had to be cultivated by admiring the virtues of the pagan city, though not deemphasizing its vices. In one sense, that would have been difficult for the exiles, for the sights and smells and sensations of Babylon must have seemed disorienting and unfamiliar and therefore difficult to love. If you grew up in New York City, it's easy to love the busyness and theatricality of a great metropolis, and if you grew up in Arizona, the warm red rocks and deep blue skies are where your heart is. These details are loved because they are familiar, because they are home.

However, even in a place where love should come "naturally," it often has to be cultivated with effort. We all know people who grow weary of home because of that selfsame familiarity. Despite our tendency to love the familiar in our lives, familiarity can also breed ingratitude, because we take a place's virtues for granted and assume that its vices are unique. Even the Shire has Sackville-Bagginses with whom the protagonist must cope.

As I was writing this chapter, a student in one of my classes told me the story of his parents, Christian refugees from Burma, who had immigrated to the United States to escape persecution. "They are the most patriotic people you will ever meet," he told me. "They love the Fourth of July and love this country." Why is that? "Well, because, having lived in a nation without the freedoms Americans take for granted, they see the home we enjoy with fresh eyes." When a free and prosperous America is all we have seen and known, when we have little grasp of history or a world outside our borders, we are tempted to focus on all the ways in which we can't feel proud of the United States. It is easy to lose a sense of gratitude for the things we take for granted, privileges and liberties that most people in human history could only long for and that many people around the world today will never experience.

Don't get me wrong: Things are not good merely because they are familiar. But if we can't see the good in the familiar, it's unlikely that we'll be able to perceive the good that's far away. Instead we'll love an abstraction made in our own image.

Another reason people may lack love for the familiar things of their country is because of an oppressive government's relationship to that place or because there truly are rotten aspects of that place in a fallen world. There are many places around the world where having patriotism isn't even a matter of debate, though because of the nature of that enforced, absolutist "patriotism," it becomes disordered love, replacing God in the minds of totalitarian subjects. It's compulsory, and if one doesn't have a portrait of the nation's leader displayed prominently in the home, if he or she isn't saluted in public, if the mildest criticism of the leader in even the smallest of meetings is expressed, it often results in imprisonment or death. This is true in countries such as North Korea and increasingly in Russia, where Vladimir Putin has had high-ranking executives poisoned or thrown out of the windows of skyscrapers for less.

In this way, evil leaders may poison a person's natural affection for the familiar. Compelled love is easily soured. A bad father often leads an abused child to assume that all other authorities are similarly corrupt. One Christian writer, Jennifer Greenberg, whose father was abusive, had to unlearn his poisoned view of authority:

> In our family, I was taught to honor my father and mother, forgive others, and not gossip, but homes warped by abuse have their own language. "Forgive" meant pretend you're happy, even when you're covered in bruises. "Honor your father" meant obey him, even when you're terrified he might kill you. And we were repeatedly warned not to "gossip," which meant telling anyone the truth.

But learning a Christian definition of love enabled her to recognize that love doesn't mean affirming someone in all they do but helping them reflect God and rejecting their actions when they do not do so. She continued:

> Honoring godly people means building them up in righteousness. Honoring ungodly people means calling them to repent of their sin, encouraging them to do what is right, and preventing them from doing further evil. . . .
>
> In the spirit of the law, I honored my father by refusing to succumb to the damage his sin inflicted. I honored my father by reporting his abuses.[30]

We should be aware that anti-patriots have many different reasons for how they came to that position. The cynicism that results from boredom with or contempt for the familiar should be rebuked, but the cynicism that results from abuse should be met with gentleness.

However, we should also recognize that many hostile actors seek to portray their own boredom and lack of charity as if they were a result of abuse. Just because the congregation of your hometown church sang "America the Beautiful" when you were young doesn't mean you were raised in a cult.

Happily, compelled country love in America is the exception, not the norm. In America, you can viscerally loathe the nation's leader, you can refuse to salute the American flag, and you can publish volumes on the awfulness of America, and not only will you not be punished but you will likely find a decent-size audience.

We should thank God for these freedoms and for our country. To loathe America may be chic, but it's certainly not Christian. At the very least it is a disdain for the home God has given us and a subtle admission that we think he may have made a mistake by placing us here. To refuse to see anything noble in our history, to cringe with condescension at any expression of patriotism, to view the flag and our national symbols with disgust is, in my view, disobedience to our call to "seek the welfare" of the place where we live as citizens of God's kingdom.

How to Be Patriotic

Having established that patriotism is a duty as long as it remains ordered in correct priority to our highest calling, how does one define it? I like Wilfred M. McClay's description:

> Patriotism . . . is an intricate latticework of ideals, sentiments, and overlapping loyalties. Since its founding, America has often been understood as the incarnation of an idea, an abstract and aspirational claim about self-evident truths that apply to all of humanity . . . our shared memories of our nation's singular triumphs, sacrifices, and sufferings, as well as our unique traditions, culture, and land.[31]

This definition helps us understand why ordinary Americans were so disturbed in recent years at the dishonoring of the American flag during public ceremonies. Protestors may have wanted to make a point about particular injustices, but in attacking aspirational patriotic symbols, they shifted the topic from the injustice to the desecration of the symbol. Because to most Americans the flag means something aspirational, attacking it appeared to many to be an attack on that aspiration.

While one can sympathize with those who want to ensure that we never forget the injustices and sins against certain minority groups in America's history, the aspirational Americans were more right about the flag, both philosophically and pragmatically. We should understand our symbols not as representative of our worst impulses but as aspirational and celebratory of America's highest ideals. If anything, the presence of the flag should bring a sober conviction about the ways in which we still fall short of a "more perfect union."

Furthermore, to dishonor the flag dishonors the veterans who have fought and died to preserve our freedoms. In my office, I have a folded flag that was presented to our family at my grandfather's funeral. Herman Yagoda was a second-generation Jewish American and World War II veteran who fought valiantly for American freedom. He fought disease and exhaustion while marching through swamps on Babelthuap Island in the nation of Palau in the South Pacific.

When I see that tightly folded flag, I don't see America's worst sins; I see men like Grandpa who gave up the best years of their lives, who saw their friends die fighting fascism. Grandpa served in service of our highest ideals. He served to protect and honor the home and country he loved.

If you ask patriotic Americans why they revere the flag, they'll probably refer to its symbolic meaning, but if you drill down further and ask why a piece of cloth is more important to them than, say, social injustice, they're likely to struggle to answer. This is not unusual in a secular age. Because we see a natural affection such as patriotism as being arbitrary or socially constructed, it can be difficult to summon up a defense for it.

One word that will likely come up, though, is *sacred*. Because of the meaning of the flag, people hold it sacred. There's something to that. That's not to say it's sacred to the same degree that God's name is sacred. But *sacred* merely means "set apart." The flag, like many other national symbols, has been set apart as a badge of reverence for a good ideal, a pure ideal. When someone burns a flag or skewers a sacred cow, even if they don't think of it this way, they desecrate the ideal, sullying its purity. Human beings react instinctively against desecration because we understand that God created a universe that is full of meaning. Specific objects call for reverence, not out of chance or because culture "told" you to revere them but because of the way God designed the universe. There are obviously many things we should value above a flag, but it's not crazy to see it as something worthy of affection and respect and to see desecrating it as a sign of an iconoclast's immaturity and ingratitude.

Some symbols deserve to go. But our bias should be toward cultivating more gratitude, not less. Eric Patterson, a political science scholar and historian, and Abigail Lindner, a writer, say that honoring the flag can be a form of Christian discipleship:

> The thirteen stripes remind us of the struggle that the thirteen colonies had in protecting themselves from the increasing tyranny of imperial England. The colors—red for valor, white for purity, and blue for justice and perseverance—remind us of sacrifice, noble intentions, and the ongoing struggle to live out the ideals of the Declaration of Independence and Constitution. The field of stars reminds us of unity—the Union—preciously held together during the dissension of the nineteenth century, a civil war, periods of regional injustice, and national growth.
>
> As Christians, these reflections also remind us that our categories of sacrifice, neighbor-love, and justice all originate in God's ordering of this world.[32]

The flag can be a reminder of these virtues, which can point us back toward our faith. This is why I no longer view the presence of a flag in a church auditorium on Sunday as a discordant symbol. It's true that Sunday mornings shouldn't be civic pep rallies for America. Christians need to hear from God every week. Still, a flag can serve as a reminder of the location in which God has called us to serve him. Juxtaposed with a cross, it helps us put our love of God, love of our country, and love of our families into the proper order.[33]

For the record, Americans' embarrassment about displaying flags in church seems to be a uniquely Western neurosis. Miles Smith, writing for the magazine *First Things*, quoted pastors from around the world. An Indonesian pastor said, "When we display the flag in our church, it is not to express idolatry. We want to honor our national identity. It reminds us of our responsibilities as Christian citizens. It's also a sign of gratitude for living in Indonesia." An Egyptian pastor advocated the display of "the flag of my country only and not other countries, as it is a spiritual and not a political orientation." A Jordanian minister said he displayed the flag "in order to show our loyalty as citizens to the country of Jordan. We believe that by doing so, we are a good example and testimony to others and also following the teachings of the Bible."[34]

Notably, these pastors in nonsecular countries easily harmonize their loyalties because they exist in a culture that understands that things and places can deserve and receive honor and loyalty without thereby becoming idols. What is true of created living things can be true of created nonliving things. You shouldn't love, say, your mother more than God, but if you love God, you'll love your mother. The same is true of our country.

What's ironic is that a cosmopolitan young Christian embarrassed about his Baptist grandmother's love of the flag might actually be more out of step with the global norms than she is.

I also feel this way about my children reciting the Pledge of Allegiance every morning in their Christian school. Our ultimate pledge is to the kingdom of Christ, but that doesn't preclude us from making promises and commitments to lesser loyalties. More than two decades ago, I made a vow to love and cherish my wife as long as we both shall live. That didn't imply that my devotion to her would be higher than my devotion to God. The same logic applies to the moments I put my hand on my heart and express my devotion to the United States of America. Both commitments ultimately yield to my commitment to Jesus. Yet I believe that my loyalty to Jesus helps me better fulfill my duties to my country and my family.

There are other Christians who rightly recoil at unnecessary wars or the social policies left-wing American administrations have exported to the world and are embarrassed by the flag. Some even deny patriotism with the argument that our government is a wicked regime.

Yet I come back to Jeremiah's instruction to the exiles to seek her welfare, or *shalom*, in a country far more pagan and bloodthirsty than America at her worst. We might also consider Jesus' commendation of the faith of the centurion in Matthew 5. Here was a man who wore the uniform of a government that was at times brutal and godless, in an environment where sexual perversion was as pervasive as, if not more than, in twenty-first-century America. Still, Jesus commended his faith and, along with Peter's baptizing of Cornelius in Acts 10, didn't require the men to be less Roman upon salvation, even if they were gathered by faith into a new community and a new family and were looking ahead to a better country.

Perhaps it's important for us to understand here that healthy patriotism isn't synonymous with blind loyalty to a certain presidential administration or a blind acceptance of US foreign or domestic policy. It doesn't imply that we should reflexively agree with everything America has done in her history. One of the most deeply patriotic things we can do is express opposition to policies that we believe violate the United States' founding ideals.

That was the perspective of President Theodore Roosevelt, who believed that patriotism requires that we criticize America when she fails to live up to her ideals:

> Patriotism means to stand by the country. It does not mean to stand by the president or any other public official, save exactly to the degree in which he himself stands by the country. It is patriotic to support him insofar as he efficiently serves the country. It is unpatriotic not to oppose him to the exact extent that by inefficiency or otherwise he fails in his duty to stand by the country. In either event, it is unpatriotic not to tell the truth, whether about the president or anyone else.[35]

A healthy patriotism seeks the best for the land in which we live. True patriots work to improve the country where possible; they don't cynically fantasize about her demise. True patriots call America to live up to her promises. It's the difference, really, between peaceful protests and destructive riots, between political activism and political violence, between prophetic words calling for repentance and cynical rejection of the entire American project.

The constructive approach is the one taken by America's greatest prophets. A former slave turned abolitionist, Frederick Douglass, aimed not to destroy the American project but to improve it and called Americans to live up to the statement in the Declaration of Independence that "all men are created equal." Abraham Lincoln took the same approach, pointing back to the Declaration in his Gettysburg Address and urging the country to reject slavery. Dr. Martin Luther King Jr., a century later, made a similar appeal. More on King later.

In a country that had been cruelly unjust to them, Martin Luther King Jr., Frederick Douglass, and countless other Black men and women still saw the idea, the project, the aspiration of America as worth fighting for. They loved a deeply flawed country that didn't always love them back.

I feel the same way about the pro-life movement, of which I am a proud participant. For more than half a century, pro-life activists have joyfully marched in the streets of Washington, decried America's wanton sacrifice of unborn babies, and worked to elect pro-life leaders. Like the civil rights leaders, they understand that changing America will require a long and sustained effort of calling her to live up to her own ideals.

The theologian Richard J. Mouw described patriotism as a sense of "we-ness," separating the government and bureaucracy from a more esoteric sense of the nation:

> We don't sing affectionate songs about, say our national park system or our city's zoning laws. A nation is less easy to define, but we can say this much: a nation is a community of people who experience some kind of unity, based on shared memories of our collective past and some cultural practices and loyalties we

> have in common. As citizens of a nation, we have at least a loosely defined sense of who "we" are. Sometimes, of course, the sense of collective identity is reinforced by perverse notions of what it means to be "we." But at its best, a national identity is based on a common language and a commitment to the ideals of justice and civility.[36]

I'd like to close this chapter with what, for me, was the most vivid recent example of this "we-ness" in action.

Like most members of Generation X, for me the terrorist attacks in New York, Washington, DC, and a field in Pennsylvania on 9/11 were a profoundly formative moment in time. I was a young college graduate and working as writer for a Christian ministry in the Chicago suburbs where I lived and had grown up. That morning, I was listening to WGN Radio. It was about 7:45, and I was on my way into the office. The news anchor broke into the morning talk show and announced that a plane had hit a tower at the World Trade Center in Manhattan. He didn't sound alarmed. We weren't alarmed. I thought perhaps it was an amateur pilot who lost control of his aircraft.

A few moments later, as I swung into a parking spot, the newscaster broke in again, this time his voice a bit more grave: "Another plane has hit the other tower at the World Trade Center." He knew. I knew. It wasn't normal. *It was . . . a terrorist attack.* I ran inside and watched television with my colleagues, shocked, stunned, and emotional as we watched the towers fall, the streets of New York filled with dust, the Pentagon in flames, and a nation reeling.

When I look back on 9/11—and I make sure every year to spend time reading about, listening to, and meditating on what America experienced—I grieve for the precious lives lost. My heart aches for the families whose lives were forever changed. I weep for the children who grew up without moms and dads. But I am also able to reflect on that season with some joy at something beautiful that emerged from September 11. It was a season—however brief—of genuine, meaningful, galvanizing patriotism.

I'll never forget the sight of our congressional leaders—Democrats and Republicans together—gathered on the steps of the US Capitol singing "God Bless America" in unison. Tears streamed down the faces of bitter partisan foes. I'll never forget the steady leadership of President George W. Bush in the immediate aftermath, standing atop the rubble of the Twin Towers, embracing the brave first responders, and shouting, "I can hear you! I can hear you! The rest of the world hears you. And the people who knocked these buildings down will hear from all of us." I'll never forget Bush's first pitch at Yankee Stadium in the World Series not many days after, nor his uplifting words of courage and compassion at National Cathedral. I'll never forget the biblical words of solace from America's aging pastor Billy Graham.

I also treasured much smaller encounters with ordinary people across the country. I was in college and took a planned trip to Florida with a friend. As we drove, every sign on every establishment said, "God Bless America." There was an outpouring of social and civic generosity, including blood drives, financial donations, and even an increase in young people joining the military. Police officers and firefighters from around the country drove to New York to help with the rescue efforts. One local church, New York's Redeemer Presbyterian, became a hub for the care of the many spiritually and physically wounded.

Phillip Yancey, writing in *Christianity Today* after visiting Ground Zero, wrote of his own surge in patriotism:

> September 11 changed my attitude. I choked up . . . when the Buckingham Palace guard played "The Star Spangled Banner," and when firemen told corny stories about their fallen comrades, and when a solitary bagpiper played "Amazing Grace" in Union

> Square . . . and when Dan Rather had to be comforted by David Letterman, of all people. I felt a sudden surge of loyalty and unity with my country that was new to me.[37]

What Yancey was recognizing was a nation returning to sacred symbols and repledging its allegiance to the ideals for which it stands. In a strange way, the common terrorist enemy helped strip away the superfluous things that often divide Americans and helped us rally to appreciate the country we thought we were in danger of losing. As Yancey put it, "Patriotism is not based on a blind belief that the United States has no need to change . . . our love for America rests on the belief that the changes needed are more likely to occur than anywhere else in the world."[38]

What Yancey saw was a healthy expression of gratitude for and appreciation by US citizens for their country. Even though the gratitude was occasioned by an outside attack, it was not fundamentally grounded in "othering" the enemies of America but in glorying in her virtues. It was not idolatrous love but proper piety. It was loyal first but not blindly so. It was a rejection of cynicism and an embrace of attentiveness. Those patriots honored their country for her virtues and honored their enemies by opposing their evil.

Familiarity doesn't have to be stultifying. In fact, it should be *preparatory*. The solution to Jonah's problem wasn't to start hating Israel or to make a habit of tearing his country down in a cynical way. Rather, it was that he should have been able to extrapolate from love of the immediate—like a plant—to love of the external—like a city.

"The more I love humanity in general, the less I love man in particular," says one character in *The Brothers Karamazov*. "As soon as any one is near me, his personality disturbs my self-complacency and restricts my freedom. In twenty-four hours I begin to hate the best of men: one because he's too long over his dinner; another because he has a cold and keeps on blowing his nose."

Chesterton mocked this same "love of humanity" in a poem:

Oh, how I love Humanity,
With love so pure and pringlish,
And how I hate the horrid French,
Who never will be English!

The International Idea,
The largest and the clearest,
Is welding all the nations now,
Except the one that's nearest.

Christians in every nation should love their country enough to try, if possible, to seek the welfare of their country, but it is the recognition that loyalty and love isn't blind, and isn't intended to stay small, by Phillip Yancey that makes patriotism a bit more possible. Loving America is not ignoring her flaws, but recognizing the possibility of positive change is more likely. Why is that? It could be, in part, due to the unique influence of Protestant Christianity on our founding ideals—an influence many people want us to forget.

CHAPTER 3

Why Christians Should Be *More* Involved in Politics

I must study Politicks and War that my sons may have liberty to study Mathematicks and Philosophy. My sons ought to study Mathematicks and Philosophy, Geography, natural History, Naval Architecture, navigation, Commerce and Agriculture, in order to give their Children a right to study Painting, Poetry, Musick, Architecture, Statuary, Tapestry and Porcelaine.[1]

—*John Adams*

Therefore, if you see that there is a lack of . . . constables, judges, lords, or princes, and you find that you are qualified, you should offer your services and seek the position, that the essential governmental authority may not be despised and become enfeebled or perish. . . .

Here is the reason why you should do this: In such a case you would be entering entirely into the service and work of others, which would be of advantage neither to yourself nor your property or honor, but only to your neighbor and to others. . . . In this way the two propositions are brought into harmony with one another: at one and the same time you satisfy God's kingdom inwardly and the kingdom of the world outwardly. . . . The gospel does not forbid this; in fact, in other places it actually commands it.[2]

—*Martin Luther*

IN HIGH SCHOOL, I INTERNED IN THE ILLINOIS STATE CAPITOL, HANGING out in the offices of members of the Illinois General Assembly. That was back when Republicans still held power in what is now one of the bluest states in the Union. My first political crush (not yet abated) was George W. Bush, for whom I volunteered in a futile attempt to put my home state into the red column.

In my professional life, I've advised candidates, been in many greenrooms, and met quite a few elected officials and celebrities. A couple of years ago, I attended a meeting of pastors and Christian leaders at the White House. I remember sitting in my chair during an informational session when all of a sudden, I saw a stirring in the corner. Members of the media started filing in. Aides began shuffling things around onstage. And then it hit me: The president of the United States was about to enter the room. My chest tightened. I texted every friend and family member I could think of. I had serious disagreements with that president. And yet . . . when he walked in, I was overcome by the majesty and grandeur of the office.

That evening, as we finished our meetings, I remember walking back from the White House thinking how amazing that this son of a plumber had been within ten feet of the most powerful man in the world. It was intoxicating. The desire to do whatever it takes, make whatever compromises, and use any shortcuts in order to be back in rooms like that is real.

Authority is dangerous. But what I experienced there was more than being swept into the sensation of power; there was also a sense of reverence around the very idea of the office. Was I merely transposing the honor due to God onto a human prince? Or was there something healthy and good in the wonder of earthly power?

Politics holds promise, but we must be honest that it also invites peril. Nobody understood this more than the late Chuck Colson, once known as Richard Nixon's hatchet man, who admitted that he would have run over his grandmother if it would have given him political advantage.[3] Colson went to prison for crimes committed in the Watergate scandal but emerged a changed man. He founded the ministry Prison Fellowship and became a courageous, compassionate voice for the Christian worldview. While urging believers to engage in the public square, he warned of the seductive temptations that prey on those close to power. He often told a story about the impact of a visit to the Oval Office.

> I took all kinds of groups to see the president, from friendly cattlemen to sophisticated educators enraged over budget cuts or the Vietnam War. It was always the same. In the reception room they would rehearse their lines and reassure one another, "I'll tell him what's going on. He's got to do something."
>
> When the aide came to escort us in, they'd set their jaws and march toward the door. But once it swung open, the aide announcing, "The president will see you," it was as if they had suddenly sniffed some intoxicating fragrance. Most became almost self-conscious about even stepping on the plush blue carpet on which was sculpted the Great Seal of the United States. And Mr. Nixon's voice and presence—like any president's—filled the room.
>
> Invariably, the lions of the waiting room became the lambs of the Oval Office. No one ever showed outward hostility. Most, except the labor leaders, forgot their best-rehearsed lines. They nodded when the president spoke, and in those rare instances when they disagreed, they did so apologetically, assuring the president that they personally respected his opinion.
>
> Ironically, none were more compliant than the religious leaders. Of all people, they should have been the most aware of the sinful nature of man and the least overwhelmed by pomp and protocol. But theological knowledge sometimes wilts in the face of worldly power.[4]

Colson's advice wasn't for Christians to abandon politics; in fact, he urged the opposite. His strong admonition, however, was for believers always to hold politics in its rightful place as a useful vehicle for human flourishing and not as an ultimate prize.

When I write about the temptation to worship at the altar of politics, I'm writing first to myself. Though my primary calling has been Christian ministry, I've been interested and involved in politics my entire life. From the time I could read, I read the three newspapers that arrived at the bottom of our driveway every morning: *Chicago*

Tribune, *The Chicago Sun Times*, and *The Daily Herald*. I begged my parents to subscribe to newsmagazines such as *U.S. News & World Report*, *World Magazine*, and *Newsweek*. In high school, I paid for my own subscriptions to *National Review* and *The Weekly Standard* and volunteered in the reelection campaigns of Representative Phil Crane, who attended our church. My earliest political memory is from 1988, when our family bent our ears over the radio and waited for the presidential election returns, hoping that George H. W. Bush would defeat Michael Dukakis. My heroes were Colson, William F. Buckley Jr., and Ronald Reagan.

Not everyone who works in the White House or is in a position of influence in the government is there because they left their integrity at the door. I know many good men and women who do good, faithful work at the highest reaches of government out of a desire to serve their country and glorify God. This is a way they serve us, their neighbors. In Scripture, we see men such as Daniel and Joseph serve leaders who would make our worst presidents look like Mother Teresa.

Still, we should be wary of the temptation to hold on to power at all costs. And this doesn't merely affect those within reach of the Oval Office. Today there is a great temptation to maximize our influence by taking shortcuts. Perhaps a bit more faux outrage online, we think, will ramp up the clicks and fundraising. Perhaps a careful massaging of core Christian truth will help secure a coveted position. Perhaps a friendship can be sacrificed for the sake of career advancement.

We should see political power, however, for what it is: temporal. I like the Apostle Peter's framing in 1 Peter 2:17 (ASV), in which he instructs the people of God to "honor all men. Love the brotherhood. Fear God. Honor the king." Though we fear the king and respect authority, we ultimately and only fear God.

Some people have suggested that because the world is so troubled, it is incumbent on us to break the rules and take whatever means are necessary to advance policies and win cultural battles,[5] but winning at all costs is, as Carl R. Trueman rightly observed, "a transvaluation of Christian values."[6] Consider the admonitions of Apostles Peter and Paul, both of whom faced a much more sinister and hostile culture than anything we face in twenty-first century America. Peter urged believers to "rid yourselves of all malice, all deceit, hypocrisy, envy, and all slander" (1 Peter 2:1), while Paul urged believers "to slander no one, to be peaceable and considerate, and always to be gentle toward everyone" (Titus 3:2, NIV). Christian virtue doesn't require us to abandon important arguments, nor does it preclude conducting healthy debate or making a strong and forceful argument against evil. Yet we are not called to achieve good outcomes with evil means (Romans 3:8).

The Bible isn't interested merely in the fact of our engagement in the world but also in the way in which we engage. Not only are we called to bring truth to bear on the policies that affect our neighbors, but we are tasked with conducting ourselves in a distinctly Christian way.

1 Peter 3:15–16 reminds us that we are to "give a defense to anyone who asks you for a reason for the hope that is in you," but we are to do so with "gentleness and reverence." In other words, courage and civility are not enemies but friends. We represent another world, not merely by the policies we champion but by the way in which we champion them. Even as we oppose what is evil and hold fast to what is good, we do so in a way that recognizes the dignity and worth of even our most entrenched ideological foes. Exercising kindness is a command, not a tactic. Sometimes it will open doors and open hearts. At other times it will do nothing to mollify the animus folks have toward our positions. We should periodically ask if we face opposition because we are standing up for truth or because we are acting in ways that are antithetical to Christian witness (1 Peter 2:20).

Courageous kindness is not the same as "niceness," where we fail to speak out because we are scared to offend. It is the deliberate and careful use of words; it is speaking truth in love; it is seeing those who disagree with us as image bearers and not as monsters. In fact, Peter is saying that kindness is a type of courage, the willingness to firmly believe and declare something with the confidence that we don't need to rely on demeaning rhetoric to make the case.

If it is good and proper to love our country, doesn't it follow that Christians have a responsibility and stewardship to "seek the welfare of the city" in our unique and special republic? Yes, we do. Thus, the remaining chapters of this book will lay out several areas where the people of God can concretely express their rightly ordered patriotism in both preserving and renewing America. This will often involve—you guessed it—politics.

There is much angst and confusion among many American Christians about their place in our political system. It doesn't help that the media, as I've highlighted, often hyperventilates when conservative believers have the audacity to exercise their rights of citizenship. Breathless news reports lump the worst and most toxic Christian voices with ordinary Christians who engage in the process. Ironically, most evangelicals not only are not sending dank memes or peddling conspiracy theories but are fairly sheepish about engaging at all. There is a large percentage of Christians who don't even vote.[7]

Reacting against the small minority of the hyperobsessed, many well-meaning Christian leaders communicate the message that getting involved in politics at all is at odds with the mission of God. Just look at the titles of some bestselling books come election time: *The Party Crasher*, *American Idolatry*, *The Politically Homeless Christian: How to Conquer Political Idolatry, Reject Polarization, and Recommit to God's Greatest Two Commandments*, *The After Party: Toward Better Christian Politics*, *Exiles*. There is a whole genre of academic studies that examine the civic engagement of conservative Christians as if they were some dangerous and strange species from another planet. Even some Christian thinkers such as Stanley Hauerwas, Shane Claiborne, and Brian Zahnd condemn most conservative political engagement as being complicit with supporting "empire."[8]

To be sure, it is easy for politics to become an all-consuming idol, especially in a secular age where political power often seems to ordinary people to be the most "real" power, yet I think the net effect of pastors' encouraging a sort of political Gnosticism is not to keep hyperobsessed politicos from being hyperobsessed but to dampen the civic involvement of good-hearted, faithful Christians.

Many modern commentators seem to take as given the idea that power is something that always corrupts and that the only pure existence is one of noncoercive, nonviolent, Gnostic harmony with the world around us. Yet no one actually lives like this. Our modern world is full of bullies, micromanagers, swaggering influencers, and shrill bureaucrats using money, cameras, intelligence, and political power to get their way even as they portray themselves as victims. Consider how often tremendously powerful people portray themselves as the most powerless people in the world.

Pretending that power can be avoided won't make it go away; it'll just leave it in the hands of people who don't know how to use it well. Christians have to have a theology that accepts the possibility of using power well; otherwise we hand the philosophical car keys over to nihilists who want to outlaw driver's licenses.

There are some Christians who need to step away from the internet and the 24/7 news cycle and reorder their spiritual priorities. But I don't think the problem, even in these instances, is the mere fact that they are involved in politics but with the way they practice politics. As I mentioned earlier, progressive Christians are way more politically involved than conservative Christians are, and the sort of "cultural

Christians" who make the biggest noise in the political sphere tend to be nonbelievers embracing Christianity as an aesthetic.

The question I want to discuss in this chapter is this: Is it illegitimate for believers to roll up their sleeves, join a political party, and try to get people elected who share their values? Given the long history of Christians misusing power, isn't the better solution to retreat, submit, surrender, and take up our cross? Do Christians—especially American Christians—worship the power of the sword?

Is Politics Too Dirty for Christians?

First, let me make a right-wing point with a left-wing frame. Let's acknowledge that the entire conversation of "Should we or shouldn't we?" when it comes to engagement in the public square is a privileged one, because we live in a free nation. All of the arguments American Christians have about politics pale in comparison to the moral dilemmas people have to face in authoritarian countries. The reason our questions are low stakes, for the most part, is because other people faced those moral dilemmas in the generations before us. Let's recognize that we are able even to have this conversation—you are able to read this very book—because previous generations of Americans, in some form or fashion, cared about politics. This is John Adams's thesis at the beginning of this chapter. He studied politics so his sons could study math and philosophy.

Nobody in a North Korean gulag or a Moscow jail cell or at the point of the Taliban's sword complains about partisanship. Christians in China, Rohingya Muslims in Bangladesh, and dissidents in Cuba would love to come here and experience our politics. Deciding to engage in or withdraw from the public square is a luxury we owe to the freedoms we enjoy, freedoms that many others fought and died for. Even as we grow weary, every election cycle, of robocalls, political texts, and mudslinging, we Americans enjoy a privilege afforded few people in human history. With great privilege comes great responsibility.

What is politics? Put simply, politics is the business, the affairs of the *polis*, the city. Andrew T. Walker, a Christian theologian and ethicist, defined it this way:

> Politics is fundamentally about how we, as human beings, go about the process of organizing our lives around common goods, goals, and values in whatever setting we are in, including, of course, government. When God calls human beings to be fruitful and exercise dominion over creation (Gen. 1:28), that is God's call for human beings and human societies to order themselves for the purpose of cultivating God's creation.
>
> Some may not consider themselves political in the sense of being overly engaged in the day-to-day events of what is happening in government, but every single person has a vested interest in making sure that our society is organized in such a way that individuals are provided every opportunity to flourish.[9]

Every single person has a vested interest in politics. Because we live and work in a specific place with specific policies and ideals that shape the way we live together as a people, there is no way to avoid it. To be specific, engaging in politics does mean employing power. Some critics of Christian nationalism, such as Kristin Kobes Du Mez, point out that the Right is power hungry and fear driven (usually implying that the Left isn't). Even well-meaning conservative folks may wonder if engaging in politics taints Christian witness.

Of course, Christians should not idolize power or live in a spirit of fear, and the Right is not free of these sinful tendencies. But the progressive Du Mez's implied solution to the desire for power is a sort of power-free utopia where coercion doesn't exist or one where conservative Christians don't just joyfully bear up under suffering but refuse to do anything to prevent it when it occurs.

One left-wing Christian musician illustrated this conceptual shift when she rewrote the lyrics of "Battle Hymn of the Republic," an ode to Christian martial virtue: "Mine eyes have seen the glory of the coming of the Lord / You are speaking truth to power, you are laying down our swords. . . . Dismantling our empires 'til each one of us is free / Your peace will make us one."

To refresh your memory, here's how the original goes:

Mine eyes have seen the glory of the coming of the Lord;
He is trampling out the vintage where the grapes of wrath are stored;
He hath loosed the fateful lightning of His terrible swift sword;
His truth is marching on. . . .

In the beauty of the lilies Christ was born across the sea,
With a glory in his bosom that transfigures you and me;
As he died to make men holy, let us die to make men free,
While God is marching on.

There is, of course, something Christian about a vision of a world in which swords have been discarded and oppressive structures dismantled, but it's one that requires us to assume that the earthly city *already is* the heavenly city. (The vision also exaggerates the heavenly vision to, à la John Lennon, "imagine there's no countries." In fact, Revelation imagines a globe full of nations united in worship of the Lamb but distinct.) In this way, anti-patriots accidentally end up hallowing nature as much as the nationalists they oppose do.

Of course, anti-patriots impose this standard inconsistently. Left-wing policies are portrayed as power-free, noncoercive servant love, even if they result in obvious uses of force. Consider state schools hosting speakers who force students to pray to the earth, as happened at UCLA in 2024, or the government punishing small-business owners who refuse to bend the knee to woke pieties. When Christians define marriage as being between a man and a woman, they are imposing a superstition on the country, the logic goes, but when transgender activists in government revoke parental custody of gender-confused children, they are "supporting love."

"If we have read the Bible well, we know that a moral movement will never persuade the powerful to establish God's kingdom here on earth as it is in heaven," wrote one left-wing Christian. But he also wrote:

> A moral movement must push both parties to address issues that impact women, children, the poor, the undocumented, and the environment—the vulnerable in our communities whom the prophets will not let us forget. There is nothing partisan about insisting that everybody has a right to live, to learn, to enjoy the fruit of their labor, to have access to healthcare, and to receive equal protection under the law. To call policies that deny our neighbors these basic rights "conservative" is not only an act of violence against them; it is a misrepresentation of conservatism.[10]

Force seems to magically become "care" when employed by the Left and "the sword" when employed by the Right.

The Christian Gospel itself is deeply political. In the first century, when Christianity was a new and fledgling movement within the Roman Empire, followers of Jesus were political just by the way they lived their lives, bumping up against the ritual cult practices of the empire. Those first Christians didn't have the agency and opportunity American believers have today, yet even when they engaged in the simple practice of gathering, often in secret, for Sunday worship to declare that an itinerant rabbi put to death by the Romans was the resurrected Lord of the universe, they were, by inference, declaring that Caesar was not. When the early Christians resisted the sexual practices of the age by ordering their families through a covenant of marriage and respect for the dignity of women, they were unavoidably political. When they stayed in the cities and lived intentionally alongside their neighbors during a pestilence or plague, declaring that no human beings were disposable, they were unavoidably political. And in many places in the New Testament, first-century believers are urged to participate as good citizens, except when they are asked to violate their Christian beliefs (Romans 13; 1 Peter 2; 1 Timothy 2).

Faith Can't Be Private

It's impossible to not have a public theology. As I wrote elsewhere, "Even the most pietistic answer to the way humans should order their lives and communities is a public expression of the way humans should order their lives and communities."[11] Scripture portrays faith as an inescapably public exercise, from the declaration in Genesis that "It is not good for the man to be alone" (Genesis 2:18) to Cain's rejected excuse for murder, "Am I my brother's keeper?" (Genesis 4:9, ASV), to Jesus's prayer in John 17 declaring that he has not taken Christians "out of the world." The twentieth-century apologist Francis A. Schaeffer declared that "Christianity is not just involved with salvation, but with the total man in the total world."[12]

Three passages from Scripture help illuminate this. First, we must revisit the passage from Jeremiah I discussed in the first chapter. If you remember, Jeremiah spoke to the exiles in Babylon. They'd been snatched from their homeland. They were living in a place that was foreign to them in every way, from culture to language to way of life. False prophets were whispering in their ears that their sojourn would be temporary and that they'd soon get their country back.

They wondered, "How can we sing the song of the Lord in a strange land?" (Psalm 137:4, NLV). God's answer in Jeremiah 29 was an emphatic yes.

God wanted the exiles to engage with their strange new world. In fact, he wanted them to act not like exiles but like citizens. "Seek the welfare of the city," the prophet instructed, "for in its welfare, you will find your welfare" (Jeremiah 29:7, ESV). The word "welfare" derives from the meaning of the Hebrew word *shalom*, which means "wholeness."[13] Even in a place much more hostile to religious freedom than America, where the people of God found themselves with very little influence, they were not to retreat from doing what they could to help improve Babylon.

Twenty-first-century Christians can apply this verse because, in the New Testament, Peter declares God's people to be strangers and exiles (1 Peter 1:1–2). Peter, like Jeremiah, was writing to first-century Christians, who similarly found themselves with little influence. Yet where they could, when they could, he directed, they should help advance the wholeness of their communities. We are to be exiles to the world as regards engaging in its sins, but it is clear from Scripture that engaging in politics at all is not inherently compromising but rather is a command. Thus, when Christians seek to use political power to make the city of Earth more like the kingdom of Heaven, they're not sinning.

Jesus boiled down the responsibility of a Christian to two basic instructions: Love God and love our neighbors. This is a consistent theme throughout the Bible. Our devotion to God is measured, in part, by the way we treat those made in God's image. Loving our neighbors can encompass a lot of things, such as communicating to them the good news of the Gospel and helping to meet their material needs, but in a representative democracy like ours, could it not also include working to shape policies that will encourage our neighbors' flourishing?

To speak more pointedly, can we truly love our neighbors if we eschew all work that involves wielding power? Let's ask this in a historical context. Imagine you are in the antebellum South in the 1800s. You are a Christian who reads Jesus' words in the Gospels. Your neighbor is an enslaved Black man who is separated from his wife, who is also enslaved. Do you not speak up for your Black neighbor's freedom?

Or imagine you're in the civil rights era. Wouldn't it be simpler to avoid the strain and compromise of politics and say that the Gospel is a private matter?

Believe it or not, that was what many Christians did. They often advocated a kind of piety that "didn't want to play politics." Billy Graham, for example, initially allowed segregation at his rallies and thought that the civil rights movement was too focused on politics. "For Graham, the Bible had a clear message for Christians living in what he believed were humans' last days on earth," summarized a piece in *The Guardian*, disapproving of Graham's indifference to political power. "Individuals alone can achieve salvation; governments cannot. Conversions change behaviors; federal policies do not."[14]

The source of this criticism is interesting because it's unlikely that a writer for *The Guardian* would have approved of Graham's using political power to oppose abortion or to further other socially conservative aims. But the underlying point makes obvious how morally necessary politics is for Christians who wish to improve the world. Graham himself came to understand that, speaking out about the importance of civil engagement. He took the courageous step of desegregating his rallies and inviting civil rights leaders onto the stage. He also spoke against abortion on demand.

Martin Luther King Jr. addressed this tendency in his "Letter from a Birmingham Jail." He started by affirming a place for God in politics: "How does one determine whether a law is just or unjust? A just law is a man made code that squares with the moral law or the law of God. An unjust law is a code that is out of harmony with the moral law. To put it in the terms of St. Thomas Aquinas: An unjust law is a human law that is not rooted in eternal law and natural law."

Then he condemned those who rejected political action or disruption under the assumption that justice will come about over time, without the need for human engagement. "Human progress never rolls in on wheels of inevitability," he wrote, rejecting what was ironically a progressive view of history then being advocated by some conservatives; "it comes through the tireless efforts of men willing to be co workers with God."[15]

If King were to make these comments today, he would be accused of being a Christian nationalist. "The thing that unites . . . Christian nationalists," said one journalist on MSNBC in 2024, "is that they believe our rights as Americans and as all human beings do not come from any earthly authority. They don't come from Congress, from the Supreme Court, they come from God." While she later walked the comment back, its ignorance of thousands of years of precedent was striking.[16]

Today, could we say, for instance, to our unborn neighbors, our immigrant neighbors, our trafficked neighbors, our impoverished neighbors that we had had opportunities to speak up for their welfare or to implement laws defending them but had been too sheepish to do so? This is an especially important question in a republic in which, unlike the people of Jesus' or Jeremiah's day, we actually have some measure of influence. Can we fully obey the Great Commandment if we withdraw from public debates over policies that will impact our neighbors?

I don't think we can. As I was going through the final edits of this book, I had the opportunity to travel to Poland and visit the Auschwitz concentration camp, where millions of Jewish people were sent to their deaths by the Nazi regime. The horror I saw will never, ever leave me as long as I live. I'm thankful, though, for Christians such as Dietrich Bonhoeffer, who stood against the Nazi regime. And the Ten Boom family, who sheltered Jews in their homes at the cost of their lives. How can we not, in our own time, raise our voices against evil and injustice in our day? How can we not use our influence to speak up for our vulnerable neighbors? Scripture tells us that we should "speak up for those who cannot speak for themselves" (Proverbs 31:8, NIV).

In her book *Jesus and John Wayne: How White Evangelicals Corrupted a Faith and Fractured a Nation*, Kristin Kobes Du Mez made a few astute criticisms of the cultural blind spots of Southern evangelicals. But she seems to be not as aware of her own. Accusing evangelicals of morphing Jesus into a John Wayne–esque tough guy, she intimated that he was more like Mr. Rogers.[17]

In fact, Jesus was like neither figure and like both figures. He spoke with authority and in alarmingly uncompromising absolutes, promising division and a life of trouble to his followers that would require perseverance and virtue. He also lifted up the vulnerable, cared for children, wept for Jerusalem like a mother, and willingly underwent disenfranchisement, powerlessness, weakness, and death.

The paradox is that he was both. He used and exemplified power, but his idea of kingship upended people's conceptions of worldly success. Given this reality, how should Christians think about power?

Might Doesn't Make Right, but Right Can Use Might

What about the temptations to power? This is one of the chief objections to Christians' being engaged in politics. As we will see over the next few pages, getting close to power can be an intoxicating drug. It is what fuels a lot of political ambition. But does this mean *all* power is bad?

It's tempting to believe this and, looking at the powers that be that exist in our world now, easy to believe it. Everywhere we see that power goes hand in hand with arrogance, lust, vanity, exploitation, and cruelty. "You can take up the sword of Caesar or you can take up the cross of Jesus," Brian Zahnd told the journalist Tim Alberta. "You have to choose."[18]

"Culture is changed not through the coercion of the state, but through the powerful witness of a people living a way of life that challenges ideologies that drive a culture's injustice," wrote David Fitch in *The New Yorker*. "The work of God, by the Spirit, on the ground, [comes] through a people's non-violent witness to the work of Christ as Lord, not through imposition via the legislative branch and the courts."[19]

Exercising godly power precludes using political power, this logic goes. "Power tends to corrupt," wrote Lord Acton, "and absolute power corrupts absolutely." But Lord Acton was also Catholic. He believed that the Gospel was the coming of a new power, which was a good thing. "The liberties of the ancient nations were crushed beneath a hopeless and inevitable despotism, and their vitality was spent," he wrote, "when the new power came forth from Galilee, giving what was wanting to the efficacy of human knowledge, to redeem societies as well as men."[20]

In fact, in the very letter in which he coined his famous dictum, he was comparing earthly powers to divine power and finding them wanting. His point wasn't that all earthly power was bad or that power can only be bad but that it is extremely easy to forgive kings things we wouldn't forgive ordinary men, because human beings tend to think that might makes right. Might doesn't make right, but right does use might.

Romans 13 is the main text in the Bible that many Christians use as the central governing principle of their political theology. Here, the Apostle Paul is addressing first-century Church members, who were increasingly marginalized in the Greco-Roman world. The tiny but growing minority was viewed with suspicion by many of their friends and neighbors. They refused to participate in the ritual cult practices of the empire in favor of worshipping a God who was not "made by hands" (Acts 17:24–28) but was worshipped "in spirit and in truth" (John 4:24). Increasingly, they were seen as a subversive threat and eventually became victims of systemic and cruel persecution for several centuries.

Romans 13, therefore, was written at a time when leaders had become absolutely corrupt in the way Lord Acton describes. Caesar was a terror to Christians not because they were thieves or murderers but because they worshipped a God that was not Caesar. The Christians Paul was addressing were wondering whether they must submit to the Roman government, considering their newfound allegiance to the kingdom of Christ. Paul helped them see that even the pagan government was accountable to God:

> Let everyone submit to the governing authorities, since there is no authority except from God, and the authorities that exist are instituted by God. So then, the one who resists the authority is opposing God's command, and those who oppose it will bring judgment on themselves. For rulers are not a terror to good conduct, but to bad. Do you want to be unafraid of the one in authority? Do what is good, and you will have its approval. For it is God's servant for your good. But if you do wrong, be afraid, because it does not carry the sword for no reason. For it is God's servant, an avenger that brings wrath on the one who does wrong. Therefore, you must submit, not only because of wrath but also because of your conscience. And for this reason you pay taxes, since the authorities are God's servants, continually attending to these tasks.

> Pay your obligations to everyone: taxes to those you owe taxes, tolls to those you owe tolls, respect to those you owe respect, and honor to those you owe honor. (Romans 13:1–7)

Paul commanded that Christians in Rome be good citizens and submit to the governing authorities. That wasn't, of course, to be a blank-check submission. In other places in the New Testament, believers resisted when required to violate their faith by the state (Acts 5:9). However, Christians in Paul's day could be good citizens not because they liked Caesar but because they understood that even Caesar had been appointed, in the inscrutable mystery of providence, to hold power by God. Connecting God to all earthly authorities in this way means less that all authorities are good than that they are modeled on God's authority. While Paul was commanding obedience to even that corrupt authority, he was also implicitly creating a map for what good governance should be.

That word from Paul was reassuring because it let the increasingly persecuted Christians know that regardless of their circumstances, God was ultimately in charge. Despots and dictators have an expiration date. Caesar would one day be gone from the scene, but the kingdom of God would endure forever. And Paul, like every other martyred believer, would rise again one day at the end of the age.

So this passage from the Bible is, in one sense, a warning for those who hold power. God is watching, and the sword that public officials wield is only delegated temporarily by God. Rulers are to be "his servant for good" and are held accountable by the Almighty.

But what does that mean in a democracy like ours, where, in Lincoln's immortal words, we have a government "of the people, by the people, and for the people" and with a governing document that begins "We the people"? Does it not imply a sober responsibility of governing not merely for those who hold elected office but also for those who have the power to put them into office? In the American system of government, citizens share power and thus are also accountable for it to God.

This means we can't escape our political responsibilities so easily. The governments we have, the policies we see put into place, the debates that take place are, in a sense, our government, our policies, and our debates. There can be no washing of hands. The hands are always dirty.

The people to whom Paul was writing, of course, did not possess this power. The Jesus followers of first-century Rome wouldn't have voted for Nero. They could only take comfort in God's sovereignty over the wickedness of the evil empire and live in faithful obedience to God. In fact, they could pray only for the kind of freedom we enjoy (1 Timothy 2). Christians in America, however, have greater political agency. We have a voice and a vote. We have resources and influence. What will we do with it? Michael R. Wear explained it this way:

> Christians care about politics because we care about our neighbors and our communities. And political decisions impact the well-being of our neighbors. As a citizen, you do not choose to have political influence; you already have it. Politics is within your kingdom. Therefore, sitting out of politics does not absolve you of blame for the state of our politics; your sitting out is your choice about how to steward the responsibility you have been given.[21]

Yes, politics is, in some sense, an exercise in seeking power: for the ones who run for office, for the coalition that votes for them, and yes, for Christians who vote and organize. But if we read Romans rightly, *this power is going to be delegated to somebody.* Should we abandon the public square to those who might hold power but have different values than we do?

Andy Crouch, in his book *Playing God: Redeeming the Gift of Power,* wrote that power is not something Christians can or should avoid but is a reality, something to be stewarded for good ends:

> Remove power and you cut off life, the possibility of creating something new and better in this rich and recalcitrant world. Life is power. Power is life. And flourishing power leads to flourishing life. Of course, like life itself, power is nothing—worse than nothing—without love. But love without power is less than it was meant to be. Love without the capacity to make something of the world, without the ability to respond to and make room for the beloved's flourishing, is frustrated love. . . . Power at its worst is the unmaker of humanity—breeding inhumanity in the hearts of those who wield power, denying and denouncing the humanity of the ones who suffer under power. . . . This power ultimately will put everything around it to death rather than share abundant life with another. . . . Power, the truest servant of love, can also be its most implacable enemy.[22]

This is why the American Founders' vision was so prescient. They didn't pretend that political power didn't exist. They wisely diffused it among three branches of government and to the states so that ultimate power—that which can corrupt in a fallen world—is never held by any one entity. You might even argue that the necessity of Christians' getting involved exists in order to ensure that the federal government will stick to that vision, that it won't accumulate more power than it should, and that it will use its power for the flourishing of her citizens.

In a sense, it's impossible to escape becoming involved in political power in a system that gives us a choice. Not to vote or not to engage is, in and of itself, a decision to engage. It is to strengthen the status quo. One pastor wrote correctly, "Not to speak *is* to speak. Not to act *is* to act. To do nothing when a house is burning is to do something.

It is to let the house burn. To say nothing when a country is burning is to say something. It is to say something."[23]

So perhaps a better question than "Should American Christians participate in politics?" is "What kind of politics should American Christians practice?"

Christian Political Engagement Is as Varied as the Body

What exactly would it look like if more believers engaged in politics? This is a complicated question, of course, because Christians have varied gifts, resources, and opportunities. Active citizenship will not look the same for everyone. We have varied callings. Some, like me, enjoy writing, teaching, and speaking publicly. Others feel compelled to either run for public office or serve in important roles as public officials. Still others are engaged in quiet but active work in their communities.

At a baseline level, I believe that every Christian has a responsibility to vote in elections, both locally and nationally. This doesn't mean that you are required by God to vote for certain politicians or parties. Sometimes you'll be faced with two unbelievably bad choices. Even the rare act of leaving one line on your ballot blank while doing your best to choose for the other offices is a way of stewarding your citizenship and asking your party for better choices.

But beyond voting, it is essential for every American Christian, regardless of calling, to think carefully about politics and how best to steward our influence in our families, our communities, and the life of our nation.

What about joining a political party? Is it okay to pick a side? Often we will hear, in a political season, that it's wrong for believers to be involved in one party or the other, and then we will hear, often from the same voices, how bad the parties are. In one sense, a believer's ultimate allegiance must transcend a political party because our values should be shaped not by pundits and politicians but by Scripture. Yet in another sense, in our system of government, engagement in important policy debates and public service almost always requires at least engaging in and organizing with the most like-minded folks. Political parties, in our system, are temporal but necessary institutions.

So it's not idolatrous if a Christian, by necessity, identifies as a member of one party or another. Again, Andrew Walker is helpful:

> While it is fine for a Christian to identify with a particular political party, there are limits to such identification. A political party and its platform can change, so a Christian should always keep a loose affiliation with parties and not allow partisanship to unduly influence them. Furthermore, we should expose ourselves to a diversity of viewpoints and media resources in order to prevent ourselves from being in a silo. This is not because all viewpoints are equal, but only because if we become unwilling to read viewpoints that do not favor our own, we can become intellectually fragile.[24]

I'll be transparent: I'm a Republican and have been my entire life. Of course, I'm first a Christian, then an American, then a conservative, then a Republican. This ordering matters. I try to engage viewpoints across the spectrum, so I'm not intellectually fragile. But the most hospitable place for my views has been the GOP.

As counterintuitive as it sounds, I think we need *more* Christians involved in party politics than less. Political parties are institutions that need reformation and renewal. Some well-meaning Christians advocate "political homelessness" as a way of being detached from the more toxic elements of both parties.[25] I don't think that being politically independent is an altogether bad choice.

Yet there is a sense in which well-meaning bromides about transcending both parties often lead to disengagement from the way in which candidates are selected, party platforms are established, and laws are put in place. Spirit-filled, faithful Christians' retreating only makes our political parties more toxic, not less. It cedes these important institutions to the most unhinged, unchurched, Machiavellian forces in society.

I often watch with dismay as the candidate for president I prefer loses an important primary. I'm even more dismayed when I look at the paltry turnout numbers. For instance, in 2024, only 13 percent of registered Republican voters turned out to vote in the primaries. Who made up that 13 percent? The most obsessed, hard-core voters. Yet at the same time, I saw scores of evangelical leaders, many of whom I deeply admire, decry the choices the primary voters had made and criticize their complicity with toxic candidates. But what if instead of blasting away at party officials from the safe redoubt of social media, these leaders and influencers were to work behind the scenes to build a coalition and elect good candidates?

In a sense, you might argue that Christians are not engaged enough in party politics. Imagine if evangelicals were to get serious about nominating good, virtuous candidates and do the hard trench work of retail politics to make sure those candidates get a fair hearing. Instead of washing their hands in the process, what if they were to lean in a little more and ensure that the shrillest and most toxic voices are not the only ones heard when it came to choosing nominees? They might still lose a particular fight or primary, but they would be recognized as a viable constituency that can't be ignored. When we retreat, we allow a very narrow slice of the electorate to determine our future. Former Indiana Governor Mitch Daniels lamented that in a recent primary, the major-party nominees had been chosen by only 5 percent of the voting population in his state.[26]

Again, for some people, being an independent is the best choice.

But there is a smug wash-my-hands-and-judge-the-world kind of faux purity that curses the darkness but never tries to penetrate it with light. We can't really complain about the direction our parties take if we've not done the work to influence them in the first place or if we've sat on our hands whining about the politics from which we deliberately disengaged.

Of course, if we choose to be a part of these institutions, we should join them in a healthy way. Being a Republican or a Democrat doesn't mean that you shouldn't ever disagree, often loudly, with your party. Parties, by nature, are coalitions of varied people and interests. You'll never get everything you want in a party, yet you can, by your presence, speak up for the things you believe that party should champion.

Michael Wear wrote, "We belong to political parties because we believe things. We shouldn't believe things because we belong to political parties."[27] We should never uncritically embrace everything that is popular within our movement. I became a conservative in my formative years, mainly because I am pro-life and believe we need laws against abortion. I'm also a conservative when it comes to the family, which, as you will see in a later chapter, is a foundation of a healthy society. I also happen to believe, perhaps less strongly but no less confidently, in a healthy national defense and free-market capitalism. This mix of issues leaves me with the Republican Party as the best home. This doesn't mean that I don't think Democrats always have bad ideas or that Republicans have a corner on the truth.

At times I disagree with Republicans, strongly and vehemently. I'm willing to take flak within the conservative movement if I think the movement is embracing policies that I believe are wrong. And when I decide to vote for a particular candidate, I don't feel compelled to always defend that candidate, especially their misdeeds and deficits of character. My vote is not a lifetime public relations contract. What's more, I believe that a candidate must always earn my vote. Even if they are in the party that I prefer. Nobody should be browbeaten into voting for a candidate simply because the other guy is worse. We should make our candidates work hard for our votes by making a positive case for their own policies.

At the moment, there are a few things I disagree with the current Republican Party about. I don't like the creeping isolationism, the softening of the pro-life language in the platform, and some of the protectionist economic policies. I wish the party were more welcoming of refugees who flee political and religious persecution.

Political parties provide an opportunity for us to revisit the ordering of our loves and allegiances mentioned in chapter 1. My allegiance is first to Christ, then to my family, and then to the family of God. This means that with every institution I join, in every temporal partnership or coalition, there will always be some dissonance, some discomfort, some distance between the kingdom of God and the short-term kingdoms of men.

This gap is sometimes wide and sometimes narrow. Yet good work can be done within these flawed institutions and temporary arrangements. As a friend who works in DC once said to me, "We should see our political parties as a mission field, not a home base."

Is the Solution to Combine Politics with Church?

I have resisted using the increasingly elastic term "Christian nationalist" because it is often used today to apply to any Christian who actively advocates for policies that reflect his or her values or who rightly understands America's Christian roots. Yet there is a small but influential cohort of academics and thinkers who willingly accept this moniker and fantasize about a return to some version of the explicitly theocratic forms of government similar to church-state arrangements in Europe during the medieval era.

Among Catholic thinkers, leading voices include Notre Dame political science professor Patrick Deneen, the author of *Why Liberalism Failed* and *Regime Change: Toward a Postliberal Future*; Harvard Law School professor Adrian Vermeule; and the editor of *First Things*, Rusty Reno. Among Protestant thinkers, voices include those of Stephen Wolfe, the author of *The Case for Christian Nationalism*, as well as Andrew Torba, the author of *Christian Nationalism: A Biblical Guide for Taking Dominion and Discipling Nations*.

It's worth noting that few Americans share their sentiments. One poll showed that a mere 11 percent claim to be Christian nationalists and only about 5 percent hold beliefs that would actually qualify.[28] Another survey asked Church members in the largest evangelical denomination about their views of the Church and the state, finding that 92 percent believe that religious liberty should apply to all persons and all religions.[29] There is a raging debate, but it's mostly an academic and online conversation, even as it is gaining some purchase among younger Christian leaders.

Though some of these nationalist commentators make good arguments about the moral confusion brought about our receding shared moral norms, I'm convinced that in a fallen world, our system of ordered liberty is the most desirable arrangement. With Winston Churchill, I believe that "many forms of Government have been tried, and will be tried in this world of sin and woe. No one pretends that democracy is perfect or all-wise. Indeed it has been said that democracy is the worst form of Government except for all those other forms that have been tried from time to time."[30] Christians should commit to working within our current system, however imperfect, to bring about improvement rather than champion undemocratic ideas. We should do this for both theological and practical reasons.

Theologically, I don't find a strong justification in Scripture for an explicitly Christian state in the period of salvation history in between Christ's first and second comings. Christian nationalists wish to apply the specific arrangement God had with the nation of Israel in the Old Testament to apply to all nations always. But God's dealings with Israel as a theocracy were temporal and not prescriptive. Old Testament Israel was meant to be a specific and temporary witness to the nations and to serve as the vessel from which God would bring his Son into the world to save sinners and renew and restore His creation.

In his fine book *Politics After Christendom: Political Theory in a Fractured World*, the scholar David Van Drunen made a persuasive case that we should look at the covenant God made with Noah in Genesis 9 after the worldwide flood. Unlike every other covenant God made in Scripture, that one didn't merely involve those who follow him in faith but governed the entire human community. That is why he was fairly modest in his expectations for human government as opposed to his expectations for the redeemed members of God's kingdom community. This is echoed in the way God instructed the exiles in Babylon to live and flourish in their own pagan society (Jeremiah 29) as well as the way Romans 13 and 1 Peter 2 lay out a vision for human government, as delegated by God. Nowhere in these texts is there the expectation that human governments must be explicitly Christian. There is an understanding and expectation that communities and nations will comprise both believing people and unbelieving people and certain standards of justice should govern them all.

Andrew Walker, a Baptist scholar, says that standards of right and wrong are derived from natural law, the idea that certain moral truths are self-evident and written on men's hearts, even if men don't acknowledge their source in God: "Natural law supplies the world with a minimal moral standard that it must honor or else society will fall apart" (Romans 1:18–32).[31]

Furthermore, Scripture teaches us that the role of the Church and the role of the state should be distinct. The Church is made up of the Christian community, those who have put their faith in Christ as Lord and are being sanctified by the Holy Spirit (1 Corinthians 1:2). Nations are made up of both believers and unbelievers. A nation that demands Christian belief for citizenship is going against its God-given role, which is to be "God's servant for . . . good" (Romans 13). Stephen Wolfe, a proponent of Christian nationalism, blurs these lines in his call for a Christian prince "who would suppress the enemies of God and elevate his people; recover a worshiping people."[32] But this is not the role of the government. Preaching the Gospel, evangelizing, combatting false teaching—this is the role of the Church, God's outpost of the kingdom of God.

Wolfe also called for a Christian Caesar who would punish false teaching.[33] But again, this is not the role of the government but of the Church, which is tasked with "contend[ing] for the faith that was delivered to the saints once for all" (Jude 3). Isaac Backus, an influential Baptist preacher in the Founding era who influenced the passage of the Bill of Rights and specifically the First Amendment, wrote that "God has appointed two kinds of government in the world, which are distinct in their nature, and ought never to be confounded together; one of which is called civil, the other ecclesiastical government."[34]

A government that can barely manage a post office or a healthcare website is not equipped to make decisions between right and wrong belief. It is Christ, not government bureaucrats, who is tasked with separating "the sheep from the goats" (Matthew 25). When Jesus declared that the people of his day should render unto Caesar what is Caesar's and unto God what is God's (Mark 12), he was declaring that there are some things—the conscience in particular—over which the state has no jurisdiction. Congress got it right when it passed the Religious Freedom Restoration Act in 1993, prohibiting the government from infringing on religious practice unless there is a compelling state interest to do so, such as extreme cults that have practices that may violate human dignity. Subsequent Supreme Court decisions have upheld this delicate balance.

So no, I don't think that theocracy is the answer. But lots of ink has been spilled critiquing conservative Christians for seeking to "protect" God when they defend, say, traditional marriage. They're just living in fear, the critics allege, rather than welcoming persecution when it comes. For many Christians, this message comes off like "There's nothing to be afraid of," instead of "Trust in God." Of course, we should trust in God and not fear, but we shouldn't gaslight people and pretend that bad developments are good things or that we should not steward our power to try to prevent such things.

Ask Yourself: Why Do You Want Power?

There are a lot of motivations for entering politics: ambition, the thrill of the crowd, a desire to hold power and a title, a desire to see meaningful policies enacted that will advance the common good, a sense of calling to give back to one's country. From the least civically involved Christian to the White House staffer who has made politics a career, most of us have a complicated combination of motivations.

Hunter Baker, a political scientist and former political candidate, wrote:

> When we [Christians] deal with politics, then, we should approach the subject with the greatest sobriety and a strong sense of the stakes involved. It is entirely inappropriate to treat politics and government as though these things are the stuff of college football where we cultivate silly hatreds and rivalries. Politics lies on [the] other side of war. If we want to talk about loving our neighbor, let's think about being very careful before we apply the force of government against them.[35]

Followers of Jesus should periodically ask ourselves why we are doing what we are doing. This is where the rhythms of spiritual formation are really important for the life of a Christian engaged in the world. In James 1:27, Jesus' brother and the pastor of the church at Jerusalem offered a pattern for public engagement in the world. "Pure and undefiled religion," he wrote, "is this: to look after orphans and widows in their distress and to keep oneself unstained from the world." In the first century, widows and orphans were the most vulnerable group of people. It was Christians who rejected society's discarding of them as unwanted and appealed to the Christian doctrine of human dignity. If you had been doing any kind of activism and advocacy (what little you could in the Roman Empire), it would have been in service of widows and orphans, for whom there was no public safety net.

The thesis of James's letter is that a conversion to Christianity is demonstrated by a life lived in service toward others. "Faith without works is dead," he declared in chapter 2. But it's important to understand the inside-outside dynamic at work in the apostle's instructions: action (assisting widows and orphans) *and* holiness (remaining unspotted by the world). Just as a life of mere piety that has no discernable change in our actions toward our neighbors is fraudulent, so, too, is a life of activism that neglects the deeper work of the heart.

In many ways, I think that spiritual formation is what is often missing in our conversations about Christianity and the public square. But we will be ineffective advocates without the weekly rhythms of church attendance, the daily rhythms of Bible reading and prayer, and a life lived in community with other Christians. Your life in the world is only ever as good and effective as your life with God is. Most important, a soul untethered from God will quickly grow malnourished and empty.

The command to be Christ's hands and feet in the world has

empowered many of the great Christian social reformers. Dietrich Bonhoeffer, the courageous pastor who resisted the Nazi regime, wrote eloquently about the importance of the inner life with God and the life in community with the people of God. His book *Life Together* still inspires Christians today. William Wilberforce, who spent his life working to defeat the slave trade in Great Britain, was in regular fellowship with his pastor, John Newton, the author of the hymn "Amazing Grace."

Without spiritual formation, activism becomes an obsession, a near religion, an object of worship. This is one reason why our politics is often so fractious; it is easy to let our work *for* God get ahead of our life *with* God.

In this digital age, we can easily become catechized by the steady stream of political content that competes for space in our brains.[36] We let pundits and politicians shape the way we think, speak, and see the world. We maximize small differences and let everything become political, even the areas of our lives that shouldn't be.

I've seen too many brothers and sisters who neglected the care of their souls and allowed the tribal demands of politics to reorder their priorities, often resulting in failed marriages, moral compromises, and a worldly way of engaging in politics. At the same time, I've seen admirable leaders who have resisted this with the power of the Spirit and are the same people in private as they are in public.

Tending to the spiritual disciplines also tempers our political engagement, as we recognize our limits and reset our expectations. It allows us to fear God more than mere mortals and to treat even our ideological foes as humans worthy of respect and dignity. At its heart, public service should be service on behalf of our neighbors. Walker wrote, "At the deepest level, there will always be disagreement between Christians and non-Christians about what is truly good. Nonetheless, Christians should be motivated at their core by a God-honoring desire to see everyone in their community thrive."[37]

Serving our neighbors helps us work to accomplish some good, rather than using a cause merely as a platform for self-advancement.

There is a difference between performative activism and effective advocacy. Much of what we call politics is a theater of the absurd. It's not actually designed to make meaningful change but to rile up an audience, raise money, and score cheap political points. The real work of getting things done happens by building coalitions and alliances, hammering out differences, and finding common ground.

This is one of my frustrations with Congress. It has become increasingly more difficult to pass legislation because members of Congress, in order to win their seats, have to promise more than they know they can deliver. And they are hounded by advocacy groups who demand perfection and punish any attempt at compromise. Yet successful politics is, as Otto von Bismarck wrote, "the art of the possible, the attainable—the art of the next best."[38]

There is a time for using sharp rhetoric and opposing destructive and evil policies. There is a time to just say no. But Christians in public office should advocate, as much as possible, for as much good policy as they can possibly drag across the finish line and not allow the ideal to be the enemy of the good. We live in a very divided nation. It's very rare that an elected official will be able to get every single item on his wish list accomplished. Politics is also about prudence, timing, and the wise use of political capital.

Passing legislation often involves negotiating with people who disagree with you in small or big ways. I'd rather have 60 percent of something good than 100 percent of nothing. Sadly, today's politics are optimized less on the basis of accomplishment and more on performative outrage. Genuine humility should allow us to triage between issues of moral seriousness such as the sanctity of human life, the structure of the family, and religious liberty, about which Scripture is earnest and clear, and issues where we agree on the problem but might disagree on the solution.

Hunter Baker is helpful here: "Consider issues such as immigration, the environment, taxes, the size of government, education, and a host of others. We can debate these things at great length. Why? The answers are often not immediately obvious. Loving our neighbor matters in the context of politics, but much of loving our neighbor has to do with figuring out how we can accomplish the common good."[39] I happen to come down on the conservative side of most of those issues, but in seeking solutions to real problems, I can acknowledge the wisdom of those who disagree and be willing to be less strident. Christian humility helps us understand that we are not always right and have room to learn and grow.

Most of you reading this are not in elected office and don't have to take difficult legislative votes. Still, in your advocacy and your voting decisions, you should not demand of your leaders more than they can possibly deliver in a divided nation in legislative bodies with multiple perspectives. Compromising, after fighting as hard to get as much as we can, is not always a dirty tactic.

Spiritual formation can also bring focus to our political engagement. It allows us to see where the real important battles are and where we can best apply our efforts. There is a role for speaking publicly on social media, writing columns, and participating in punditry, as I often do. Shaping the public discourse matters.

However, we tend to reduce politics to being mad at the same time on the same platform over the same news story. Instead, it might be more prudent to put our energies into building relationships with our local public officials, perhaps even running for office, helping on a political campaign, or working for a nonprofit or an advocacy group. Serving in this way can be a noble, God-honoring calling.

When we rightly order our priorities, we understand that even though we can do much good, we cannot solve every problem, we cannot save the world. Only Jesus can. As we walk in obedience to him, there is, however, much good we can do.

This moment in America needs more Christians who possess a politics of hope and not fear, a politics motivated by love for our countrymen, not a hatred toward those with whom we disagree. Even in a time of great moral questions and vexing social problems, we can demonstrate courage as we remember Jesus' words: "Be of good cheer; I have overcome the world" (John 16:33, ASV).

CHAPTER 4

Aren't National Myths Just Made Up?

History, I like to think, is a larger way of looking at life. It is a source of strength, of inspiration. It is about who we are and what we stand for and is essential to our understanding of what our own role should be in our time. History, as can't be said too often, is human. It is about people, and they speak to us across the years.

Our history, our American story, is our definition as a people and a nation. It is a story like no other, our greatest natural resource.[1]

—*David McCullough*

IN MY CONVERSATIONS WITH MY STUDENTS, WITH COLLEAGUES, AND with friends about the proper shape of American patriotism, a question inevitably comes up: How can we properly love our country when we know it has allowed, even perpetuated, injustices?

This doesn't have to be a partisan question. Very few people seriously disagree with the fact that America has committed great sins, though some may disagree on the exact list of sins. But sometimes it may seem as if patriotism involves embracing a rosy view of our country when we all know that every government has done monstrous things, whether it admits it or not.

How often do we see young people roll their eyes when their grandparents wax nostalgic about America's past? Doesn't Grandma know that we live in a fascist authoritarian empire? This is a somewhat comical example. Yet young, naive people aren't the only Americans who feel profoundly disillusioned with their country.

One friend who served a few tours of duty overseas is disillusioned about US military might and failed wars. He frets about the supposed "military-industrial complex" and finds it harder to beam with pride when he hears the national anthem played at a ball game.

Another friend, a member of a minority group, feels the weight of slavery and Jim Crow on his family and asks how he can be proud of a country that first enslaved and then disenfranchised an entire group of people simply because of the color of their skin.

Yet another, a conservative, recoils at the half-century-long legacy of *Roe v. Wade* and the tens of millions of babies killed[2] as well as the exporting of the sexual revolution, with all of its perversions, to other countries: "I don't know if I can be proud of my country when I think of the wicked and ungodly policies we've often championed."

Love can take a person only so far when a nation, a person, or a place is thoroughly corrupt. What does it mean to command the love of country to people who see or have suffered its abuses? How far can we demand forgiveness or the overlooking of sins, especially when we're not the victims of those sins? Thankfully, Christians have the intellectual tools to consider such things and come to solid conclusions.

Reading History as a Christian Means Starting with Love

There's great wisdom in the command to love even an imperfect country and to let that love color our approach to history. The historian John Wilsey, summarizing an essay by Beth Barton Schweiger, wrote:

> The Christian historian has a duty to love the historical subjects she studies, who are now dead. This love is not sentimental, nor does this love absolve the subjects of their sins. Loving the dead

> means we tell the truth about them, as far as it is possible given our limitations and the complexities of the past. . . . The dead are at our mercy—they cannot come back and offer their explanations, their justifications, their apologies, or their acts of restitution.[3]

Elsewhere, he wrote eloquently:

> If human nature is found in a tension between human dignity (Psalm 8) and human fallenness (Isaiah 59.1–2; Romans 3.23), then reckoning with American identity has to start with biblical anthropology. And if we care about who we are as Americans, we have to know our history as human persons, as fallen yet dignified.
>
> We have to think virtuously about history, exercising faith, hope, love, prudence, justice, wisdom, and courage as we labor to make sense of our past. Coming to grips with American nationality is hard work, but it is the work of the American citizen. Christian American citizens have a special responsibility in this work, because we believe that the tension between dignity and fallenness in human nature has been resolved through the Incarnation of the Lord Jesus, and his substitutionary work in redemption on the cross and the resurrection. The place of the American federal democratic republic is to set the conditions for American Christians to argue for and demonstrate a rightly ordered set of loves in which God is our first love, but love for country is eminently appropriate as a form of neighbor love.[4]

I have found, in recent years, that many American Christians are confused about how to interpret US history. Understanding our country's history is not merely an exercise for history nerds like myself but a necessity for all believers who wish to rightly seek the welfare of the country to which God has called them. We can't fully understand where we are going until we have a good understanding of where we've come from. What's more, I fear that we are often misled by wrong approaches to US history. The assumption is that there are only two options: Either one must consider our country to be irredeemably racist, founded specifically for the purpose of prioritizing one group of people over the other, or we must think that our country's sins can be explained away and she has not committed these and other grievous injustices.

In reality, both of these positions on history represent un-Christian sentimentality. On the one hand, those who view the story through rose-colored glasses are quick to believe anything good about the country, no matter how implausible. Anti-patriots, on the other hand, are quick to believe anything bad about the country, no matter how implausible.

Hagiography and iconoclasm about America are not only the wrong way to understand our country's story but the wrong way to think about the story of any nation. To think about history Christianly is to believe both that human beings are made in the image of God and have the capacity for good and that human beings are sinners who have the capacity for evil, so we shouldn't hew to a hagiographic bias or an iconoclastic one. In our minds, it should be just as plausible that people in our nation's history could sin as it is that they could do righteous deeds. Christians shouldn't feel threatened by acknowledging our country's sins, nor should they assume that the presence of those sins renders a country despicable in a fallen world.

The Westminster Confession of Faith rejects hagiography by explaining that "from this original corruption, whereby we are utterly indisposed, disabled, and made opposite to all good, and wholly inclined to all evil, do proceed all actual transgressions."[5] Yet Christians also believe that humans, while being corrupted by the fall, are not *utterly* depraved. We believe that humans also have capacity for good, by virtue of their creation in the image of God.[6] While we believe that humans can't fully exercise good until they are regenerated from within by the Spirit of God via the saving death of Christ, we also believe in a concept called *common grace*, whereby even those who express no belief have some capacity for good.

The Founders believed this to be true. In *The Federalist Papers*, James Madison wrote this about the human condition:

> But what is government itself, but the greatest of all reflections on human nature? If men were angels, no government would be necessary. If angels were to govern men, neither external nor internal controls on government would be necessary. In framing a government which is to be administered by men over men, the great difficulty lies in this: you must first enable the government to control the governed; and in the next place oblige it to control itself.[7]

So any history of any people requires us to square our assumptions with reality. We are dealing not with bots or beasts but with people created by God who have agency and will. This is true about the American story; though the country was shaped by Christianity, it has its share of evil in its history because it was built, inhabited, and shaped by fallen humans. Loving our country does seem to involve uniting around positive stories, though. Can a Christian do this with integrity? I argue that yes, we can, and indeed, in most circumstances, we must.

Let's be clear: When I say "uniting around positive stories," what I mean is something more like "choosing a charitable interpretation of events" rather than "always believing that the best version of events happened." Roosevelt Montás was wise when he wrote in *Rescuing Socrates: How the Great Books Changed My Life and Why They Matter for a New Generation*, "'In what way are they right?' is almost always a more productive and a more difficult question [about historical figures] than 'In what way are they wrong?'"[8] This is a matter of being charitable to and grateful for the lives of the dead, who cannot defend themselves.

G. K. Chesterton rejected optimism out of hand as blind loyalty and charted a third Christian position in the consideration of history. We're to be patriots, not optimists or pessimists. But, the pessimist might object, isn't that because you don't want to admit that our position is the true one? Chesterton dismissed that logic:

> What is the matter with the pessimist? I think it can be stated by saying that he is the cosmic anti-patriot. And what is the matter with the anti-patriot? I think it can be stated, without undue bitterness, by saying that he is the candid friend. And what is the matter with the candid friend? There we strike the rock of real life and immutable human nature.
>
> I venture to say that what is bad in the candid friend is simply that he is not candid. He is keeping something back—his own gloomy pleasure in saying unpleasant things. He has a secret desire to hurt, not merely to help. This is certainly, I think, what makes a certain sort of anti-patriot irritating to healthy citizens.[9]

I mentioned in chapter 1 the emotional experience of touring the National Museum of African American History. The only proper response to the history of slavery and Jim Crow is deep remorse for and anger at the violation of human dignity. Millions of men and women were brought to these shores against their will, trafficked, sexually assaulted, and sold as property. Once the Civil War ended, there was another century of Jim Crow racism and segregation. No American should be ignorant of this shameful history. It is America's original sin, whose ripple effects are still haunting us today.

We must also lament the mistreatment of Native Americans by colonial settlers and unjust actions such as the Indian Removal Act, signed by President Andrew Jackson, as well as the shameful internment of Japanese Americans during World War II. There should be no sugarcoating of these and other evils that are a part of our history. Today a Christian might lament our ongoing legacy of abortion on demand and the government sponsorship of harmful sexual mores and gender fluidity.

Thinking about history Christianly means also to believe that faith and history do not run on separate tracks because God is the author of history and is gathering all of it toward his final purposes and kingdom. The scholar David Dockery was right when he stated, "A Christian worldview has implications for understanding history. We see that history is not cyclical or random. Rather, we see history as linear, a meaningful sequence of events leading to the fulfillment of God's purposes for humanity."[10]

In previous generations, the temptation to glamorize history or distort it to paper over injustices was a significant one. This is still true in some places and is something believers should avoid. But the more contemporary temptation is the concerted effort on the left to erase everything that came before, to radically rewrite America's story in a way that has caused many younger generations to hate the country. There is a reason for this. Karl Marx said, "Take away a nation's heritage and they are more easily persuaded."[11]

This is the root of much of the far-left social justice movement's push to remove or at least problematize genuine American heroes such as Abraham Lincoln and George Washington. It's one thing to (rightly) reconsider the false mythology of Confederate leaders whose lives were devoted to preserving the institution of slavery and committing violence against the Union through the Confederacy; it's an entirely different exercise to make everyone who was born before the age of the iPhone a villain. This is pernicious.

Is it correct to say that the injustices that happened in America are the *only* story worth telling about America or, for that matter, any nation in the history of the world? Is it accurate to state, as some do today, that America didn't just allow slavery, even empower slavery, but was *founded specifically to facilitate slavery*? This is the prevailing view of many since the work of historian activists like Howard Zinn, whose bestselling text *A People's History of the United States* is standard issue in many high school and college history courses. One reviewer described Zinn's recasting of American history this way:

> A *People's History* presents a relentlessly dark tale of xenophobia, brutality, racism (foisted on poor white laborers by the master class), poverty, hardened inequality and class divisions, misogyny, imperialism, corruption, and always and everywhere, capitalist greed papered over with hypocrisy. It offers more than a revisionist version of American history. A *People's History* lays out a radical recasting of the American past.[12]

More recently, the critically acclaimed 1619 Project, published by *The New York Times*, has a similar thesis: that the folks who first came to the shores of this country in the late seventeenth century had one purpose in mind: the propagation of chattel slavery. That, the editors declare, was also the catalyst for the American Revolution. Many historians criticized[13] the project, both for significant historical errors and for the premise itself.[14] Allen C. Guelzo, one of the United States' most celebrated historians, wrote of the 1619 Project's faulty theses and sloppy scholarship:

> Finally: the 1619 Project is not history; it is evangelism, but evangelism for a gospel of disenchantment whose ultimate purpose is the hollowing out of the meaning of freedom, so that every defense of freedom drops nervously from the hands of people who have been made too ashamed to defend it. No nation can live without a history, and no free nation can flourish without a history

> that affirms—in Ralph Waldo Emerson's words in 1856—"that the evil eye can wither, that the heart's blessing can heal; that love can exalt talent" and "overcome all odds." What the 1619 Project offers instead is bitterness, fragility, and intellectual corruption—not history.[15]

Why does this matter? Should we care that many people in America feel that the country is irredeemable and can be characterized only by her worst sins, that she was founded not as an experiment in ordered liberty but as a vehicle for the execution of egregious injustices? It matters more than you think, because "the gospel of disenchantment" has real-world implications for the flourishing of the nation.

Hagiography Isn't Our Biggest Problem Right Now

Most anti-patriots will claim that the biggest problem in our country is a too-rosy understanding of our history. But look at the people smashing windows at the Capitol and think: Is reverence the real problem here? Does this look like a surplus of gratitude?

The Right needs to do the same thing the Left does: reject sentimentality and embrace truth. And the truth is, America is a nation that's full of beauty. It's worth our gratitude.

I believe that the way we view America's history does matter for several important reasons. Just as an overly romantic view of our founding and a minimizing of historic evils can cause us to repeat those same mistakes in the future, so, too, can an overly cynical view of history blind us to the progress we've made by appealing to the high ideals at the heart of the American experiment.

There is no excusing the practice of chattel slavery. It was wicked to the core. Unfortunately, the practice wasn't unique to Americans when the first European settlers came to our shores. East Africa, for instance, had often been raided for human capital since 1580 BC.[16] Even the Native American populations that the European colonialists encountered in America often practiced forms of slavery after conquest in war.[17] Slavery has been a sad and tragic reality for much of human history.[18] Abolitionist movements began to emerge in the West in the 1800s, fueled somewhat by Christianity, the Industrial Revolution, and the Enlightenment's emphasis on people's natural God-given rights.

When the Founders gathered in Philadelphia in 1776, they understood the contradiction at the heart of their experiment.[19] The majority of them owned slaves, a practice that cannot be defended. Yet most of them wrestled with the fact that the documents they were drafting, the country they were forming, the ideals they were espousing directly contradicted their own practices.

But talking about the Founders as though they were one monolith of white supremacy is incorrect. Consider Benjamin Franklin: He owned a few slaves between 1735 and 1781. However, he was personally convinced that the practice was evil and released them. He later joined the Pennsylvania Society for Promoting the Abolition of Slavery, and for the Relief of Free Negroes Unlawfully Held in Bondage and eventually became the president of the society.[20] Two months before his death, he added his name to a petition urging the complete abolition of slavery in the United States.[21] Or consider John Jay, the nation's first Supreme Court chief justice. He signed a law, as governor, that led to the gradual outlawing of slavery in his native New York State and served as the president of a New York–based antislavery society.[22] Or Benjamin Rush, a doctor and member of the Continental Congress, who wrote a pamphlet decrying slavery.[23]

Consider also the words of Patrick Henry, a slave owner who nevertheless knew the inherent contradiction he was living. "Is it not amazing," he wrote a friend, "that at a time when the rights of humanity are defined and understood with precision, in a country above all others fond of liberty, that in such an age and in such a country, we find men professing a religion the most humane, mild, gentle, and generous, adopting a principle [slavery] as repugnant to humanity, as it is inconsistent with the Bible, and destructive to liberty?"[24]

George Washington expressed his distaste for slavery in a letter to a fellow Founder, Robert Morris: "There is not a man living who wishes more sincerely than I do, to see a plan adopted for the abolition of [slavery]."[25] Washington would free his slaves after his death through his will.

The Founder with perhaps the most contradictions was Thomas Jefferson, who seemed to vacillate back and forth between his conscience, which told him that slavery was evil, and his material interests, which required slavery. Thomas S. Kidd captured the essence of Jefferson's double-minded life in his book *Thomas Jefferson: A Biography of Spirit and Flesh*. It was Jefferson who penned the words "All men are created equal," yet he not only owned slaves but fathered children with a slave woman, Sally Hemings. Kay S. Hymowitz wrote poignantly, "Consider that as the American Founders pondered the design of their new country in the 1770s, they were caught between two worlds—a past where human servitude was an unremarkable fact and a future, just taking shape, that condemned the idea as grossly immoral."[26]

We should be wary of chalking up that indifference to slavery as men like Jefferson simply being "men of their time." The wanton exploitation of fellow human beings is evil in any generation. However, it's important to understand that the project those flawed men created was bigger than their sins and that this understanding of the American founding was one shared by leaders of many political stripes until about five minutes ago.

The late civil rights leader John Lewis declared, "We knew [about

Jefferson's faults]. But . . . His words were so powerful. His words became the blueprint, the guideline for us to follow."[27] Jonah Goldberg asserts what is unique about American slavery "against the backdrop of the last 10,000 years . . . is not that it existed but that we put an end to it."[28]

Both the ideals of ordered liberty as set out in the Declaration of Independence and the words of Christian Scripture that influenced it were like rocket fuel that eventually led to the demise of slavery and the coming of freedom for more and more people. Hymowitz again: "It wasn't until the eighteenth century that anti-slavery sentiment became enough of a moral force to exorcise the practice on a large scale in the West. Historians generally trace the origins of this revolution to two forces: first, secular, Enlightenment notions about the natural rights of man; and second, religious fervor among Quakers and later on, evangelical Christians."[29]

First, the words of the Declaration were more powerful than even the Founders might have imagined. When those men met in Philadelphia and created the document, they didn't know that the phrase "All men are created equal" would become a stubborn social creed that would refuse to go away. Consider the way Abraham Lincoln, in his Gettysburg Address, appropriated the Declaration in the fight to end slavery: "Four score and seven years ago our fathers brought forth on this continent, a new nation, conceived in Liberty, and dedicated to the proposition that all men are created equal." Lincoln's message was not that the United States was irredeemably bad but that she had yet to live up to her lofty ideals, those words penned by conflicted and flawed men. America, in Lincoln's thinking, couldn't claim to believe those words if she didn't extend the promise of liberty to everyone. That was the same approach taken by Lincoln's contemporary, the former slave turned abolitionist and Christian prophet Frederick Douglass. In his magisterial address "What to the Slave Is the Fourth of July?" he wrote, "Are the great principles of political freedom and of natural justice, embodied in that Declaration of Independence, extended to us?"[30]

Those men did not let the perfect be the enemy of the good. They chose gratitude instead of cynicism and chose to see what was good in the founding, since a life of gratitude is wiser than one of ingratitude.

A hundred years later, Martin Luther King Jr. appealed to the Declaration as a reason to extend civil rights protections to Black people:

> When the architects of our republic wrote the magnificent words of the Constitution and the Declaration of Independence, they were signing a promissory note to which every American was to fall heir. This note was a promise that all men—yes, black men as well as white men—would be guaranteed the unalienable rights of life, liberty and the pursuit of happiness.
>
> It is obvious today that America has defaulted on this promissory note insofar as her citizens of color are concerned. Instead of honoring this sacred obligation, America has given the Negro people a bad check, a check which has come back marked insufficient funds.[31]

Lincoln, Douglass, King, and many others who fought for justice viewed the American experiment as a good one. This is a markedly different attitude from that of cynics today, who see the country as both founded on racism and irredeemably sinful. Why does this matter? It matters because without that fixed point, without the words of the Declaration as a north star, there is no agreed-upon foundation on which to base the fight for a nation where people will no longer "be judged by the color of their skin but by the content of their character."[32]

Again, it's more practical to love a concrete, albeit imperfect, reality than to hold out for an abstract ideal. In Scripture, the praise of "heroes" of the faith in Hebrews 11 doesn't add a caveat listing their sins; not because it's trying to conceal those sins—they're enumerated clearly in the Old Testament. But the deeper principle is that, in memory, we should start with gratitude and not cynicism. The deeper principle still is that what makes these heroes heroic is their faith. In the same way, though on a lesser scale, that heroes of faith deserve credit for what, by faith, they did, national heroes deserve reverence to the degree that they reflect the character of God, whose character is the model for righteous leadership.

When we admire a hero, we admire their virtue, not for their sake but for the sake of their creator. In a real way, Christians are free to have heroes because we admire them but don't worship them. Heroism is like beauty in this way, as C. S. Lewis wrote:

> The books or the music in which we thought the beauty was located will betray us if we trust to them; it was not in them, it only came *through* them, and what came *through* them was longing. These things—the beauty, the memory of our own past—are good images of what we really desire; but if they are mistaken for the thing itself, they turn into dumb idols, breaking the hearts of their worshippers. For they are not the thing itself; they are only the scent of a flower we have not found, the echo of a tune we have not heard, news from a country we have never yet visited.[33]

There is a marked difference between the nihilism of the 1619 Project and the idealism of those who fought for equality. Frederick Douglass, even as he rebuked America for her sins of slavery, extolled the American founding. The Founders, he said, were "wise men . . . brave men," the Declaration of Independence was a "ring-bolt to the chain of your nation's destiny" containing "saving principles." On the Constitution, he heaped praise: It is, he said, a "glorious liberty document."[34] At least one leading historian seems to agree:

> The Revolution . . . became a major event in the history of antislavery in the Western world. . . .
>
> The nation's founding, beginning in 1776, has a special significance for all Americans. As Abraham Lincoln recognized and Frederick Douglass came to appreciate fully, the founding and its documents, especially the *Declaration of Independence*, are among the most vital adhesives that hold the diverse American people together, amid the continuing struggles to redeem the principles those documents express.[35]

The nihilist view of the founding leaves us without the "adhesives" that helped fuel abolition and the civil rights movement, as well as opening up suffrage for women, reversing the policies that led to the shameful internment of Japanese Americans during World War II, and hopefully, one day, to the outlawing of the shameful practice of abortion on demand.

Slavery, at its core, was not a feature of our nation's founding ideals but a direct contradiction. It's thoroughly anti-democratic. The historian Allen C. Guelzo wrote that "democracy and slavery are so unalike that those who want to live in a democracy cannot, ultimately, reconcile that desire with the buying, owning, and keeping of slaves."[36]

Americans' continued moral blindness about race was what made the Frenchman Alexis de Tocqueville nervous about American democracy in his otherwise optimistic eighteenth-century assessment.[37] It was what grieved the Christian theologian Dietrich Bonhoeffer about his time in America.[38] It is in the contradiction between democracy and slavery where the fight for racial justice has been fought. But hypocrisy doesn't demolish an ideal; it merely underlines its importance. If we reject every idea or institution built by people who didn't live up to their promises, we'll be left with precious few ideas or institutions. We'll also foolishly deprive ourselves of learning from what those in the past got right.

C. S. Lewis said that the modern tendency to disdain the past as outdated and irreparably corrupt is naive. "Every age has its own outlook. It is specially good at seeing certain truths and specially liable to make certain mistakes," he wrote. "We all, therefore, need the books that will correct the characteristic mistakes of our own period. . . . None of us can fully escape this blindness, but we shall certainly increase it, and weaken our guard against it, if we read only modern books. . . . The only palliative is to keep the clean sea breeze of the centuries blowing through our minds and this can be done only by reading old books."[39]

We are well guarded against the vices of the past by our own virtues. We should not deprive ourselves of learning about other people's virtues, because in doing so, we lose a source of wisdom on how to solve our own problems.

It's not only incorrect to think of America only in terms of her sins, to consider the stain on our history the whole history; it's also fundamentally bad for the very problems this new history seeks to solve. Without our ideals, there are no arguments that we are failing them. We are left with moral chaos, no uniting principles, no arguments that can help us alleviate the racism and prejudice that keep people from experiencing liberty.

Is the Bible Just a Prop for a Corrupt Society?

If the incongruence between American democracy and slavery was glaring, so, too, is America's identity as a nation influenced by Christianity. This is where many people want to blame Christianity for condoning slavery. It is true that many Christians justified slavery throughout American history. But were they hypocrites denying Scripture or faithful exegetes? It's true that some Bible verses seem to support their position. Many preachers used texts in the New Testament such as Colossians 3:22–24, 1 Timothy 6:1–2, and Titus 2:9–10, in which Paul urged slaves to obey their masters.

There has been a theological debate over these passages throughout Church history. Most scholarship points to the significant difference between slavery in Greco-Roman times and the race-based chattel slavery of the eighteenth and nineteenth centuries in America.[40] The New Testament scholar Murray J. Harris wrote:

> In the first century, slaves were not distinguishable from free persons by race, by speech, by clothing; they were sometimes more highly educated than their owners and held responsible professional positions; some persons sold themselves into slavery for economic or social advantage; they could reasonably hope to be emancipated [freed] after 10 to 20 years of service or by their thirties at the latest; they were not denied the right of public assembly and were not socially segregated (at least in the cities); they could accumulate savings to buy their freedom; their natural inferiority was not assumed.[41]

Was Paul accepting the status quo, no matter how corrupt, by neglecting to advocate for abolition in his own time? First, as a matter of accuracy, we must note that the slavery Paul referred to in the New Testament, while far short of the ideal of human rights and liberty idealized in America's founding documents, was clearly not the same as the inhumane and evil slave trade practiced in the antebellum South. Christian leaders, many of them our heroes, tragically used these Christian texts to advocate for the preservation of the system of chattel slavery that exploited human beings, perpetuated injustice, and upheld notions of white supremacy that were egregiously wrong.

Far from justifying slavery, the New Testament gives agency to those in bondage, even in a system less oppressive than the one that held many Americans in chains. When Paul urged slaves in a Greco-Roman context to work cheerfully for their masters, he was allowing them full agency. What's more, he was speaking to a distinct minority in a culture where they had no ability to change the laws.

Still, when considering the whole of Scripture, we see a distinct theory of human value that fundamentally contradicts the logic of enslavers. From the Genesis depiction of every human being as being made in the image of God to the Psalms' careful narration of the Creator's involvement at each level of development of every human being to the Great Commandment given by Jesus to "love your neighbor as yourself" (Mark 12; Matthew 22), there is no way to wedge the ownership of human beings into a faithful reading of Scripture, even if many otherwise exemplary Christian leaders did so.

In the law given to Israel, "man stealing" was prohibited (Exodos 21:16), and in Paul's letter to Timothy, he listed "enslavers" in the list of heinous sins that invite God's judgment (1 Timothy 1:8–10, ESV).

Sadly, my own denomination, the Southern Baptist Convention, was formed in part to protect white slave owners in the mid-1800s. Like many other denominations, Baptists were more caught up in the spirit of the age than in holding faithfully to Christian witness about human dignity. Thankfully, in 1995, the SBC adopted a resolution apologizing for and lamenting that decision, and it has continued, slowly and painfully, to work toward racial reconciliation in the years since.[42] This episode in American history should cause us humility and reflection on the ways even Christians can be silent or complicit in the face of evil and the ways in which the faith can be co-opted by cultural forces.[43]

Are we, then, to embrace the view of anti-patriots who claim that biblical Christianity or white Christianity is just a cloak for the ruling elites' will to power? Kristin Kobes Du Mez alleged in her book *Jesus and John Wayne: How White Evangelicals Corrupted a Faith and Fractured a Nation* that many American evangelicals are interested in the Bible only insofar as it supports their claim to a "white racial identity." Are these evangelicals' commands to respect authority, maintain the nuclear family, and obey God just covers for power seeking? If this is provably the case for many, does it render the commands illegitimate? Du Mez seems to think so, using the historical record of evangelical compromise to set up a stark binary between a world of corrupt believers pushing biblical inerrancy, traditional families and masculinity, and respect for the military with a world in which all of those things have been deconstructed.

Yet as shameful as the capitulation of many Christians on the issues of slavery and segregation is, it's not the only story when it comes to orthodox Christianity in America. Christians were also at the heart of the movements that opposed racism, slavery, and Jim Crow. Consider John Wesley, the founder of Methodism. Wesley, in contrast to his fellow evangelist and preacher, George Whitefield, virulently opposed slavery. Wesley wrote a powerful denunciation entitled "Thoughts upon Slavery." One scholar wrote about it:

> Wesley identified slavery not only as a moral defect in individuals but as a structural sin infecting society as a whole. He didn't attempt to justify it morally or economically, as Whitefield had done. Instead, he denounced it in his preaching, in pamphlets, in speeches, to anyone and everyone. He refused to baptize slave owners and appealed to the image of God reflected in all the ethnicities of Adam's race to discourage the denigration of nonwhites.[44]

Charles Grandison Finney, an American evangelist whose revival meetings were caught up in what historians describe as the

Second Great Awakening, was a vocal voice against slavery, speaking out against it at public meetings, even participating in the Underground Railroad.[45] The female evangelist Harriet Livermore was another vocal crusader against slavery.[46] They joined people such as the Beecher family and other Christians who formed anti-slavery societies, fought against slavery in the Civil War, and opposed the dehumanization of people based on the color of their skin.

What's more, it was the message of Christianity that fueled the Black Church in its darkest days. The language of freedom and liberation found in the pages of Scripture was used as both inspiration and an ethic by which leaders such as Frederick Douglass, Sojourner Truth, Harriet Tubman, and many others helped awaken Americans' conscience and urged them to live up to the lofty words of the nation's charter.

As the historian Mark A. Noll wrote in *The Civil War as a Theological Crisis*, Christians were on both sides of that national debate. Lincoln said as much in his Second Inaugural Address, calling believers to humility and repentance:

> Both read the same Bible, and pray to the same God; and each invokes his aid against the other. It may seem strange that any men should dare to ask a just God's assistance in wringing their bread from the sweat of other men's faces; but let us judge not, that we be not judged. The prayers of both could not be answered—that of neither has been answered fully.[47]

A hundred years later, distinctly Christian language would be the catalyst of the civil rights movement, in which Martin Luther King Jr., John Lewis, and others appealed to Christian Scripture and the American ideals laid out in the Declaration of Independence to push the country to move past segregation, white supremacy, and Jim Crow.

Indeed, Du Mez did admit that American Christians have been on both sides of many issues:

> Across two millennia of Christian history—and within the history of evangelicalism itself—there is ample precedent for sexism, racism, xenophobia, violence, and imperial designs. But there are also expressions of the Christian faith—and of evangelical Christianity—that have disrupted the status quo and challenged systems of privilege and power.[48]

If this is the case, which of the two groups was right? Du Mez avoided the question by transforming the evangelical movement from an ideological into a sociological phenomenon defined entirely by the actions of its practitioners:

> Despite evangelicals' frequent claims that the Bible is the source of their social and political commitments, evangelicalism must be seen as a cultural and political movement rather than as a community defined chiefly by its theology. Evangelical views on any given issue are facets of this larger cultural identity, and no number of Bible verses will dislodge the greater truths at the heart of it.[49]

As one reviewer pointed out, it is impossible to argue with her thesis, because any critique of corrupt people based on theology can be waved away. It doesn't matter what people *say*, just what a significant number of their fellow travelers *do*.

But if we surrender to the idea that Scripture can be defined by any corrupt cherry picker's words, we give up on the idea of truth at all. The truth is, the view of humanity we see in Scripture can't be squared with things such as the transatlantic slave trade, theft of property, betrayal of treaties, and slaughter of innocent life. We cannot and should not brush away America's sins, nor should we look past the ways Christians have twisted Scriptures in the name of injustice. Our sins are part of our history. This is why it's important for every generation to know and study our history: the good, the bad, and the ugly. We should visit museums. We should read books. And we should endeavor to learn lessons from our history so we don't repeat the mistakes of those who came before.

Yet we should recognize that our sins are only one part of our history and were always deviations from, not fruits of, our country's founding ideals. It has always been both of those fixed points—Christianity and the ideas of ordered liberty in the Declaration of Independence—that help make the case for racial equality and freedom. Glenn C. Loury, a professor of social sciences at Brown University and the author of several books on the history of race and civil rights, put it this way:

> It shouldn't have taken 100 years; they shouldn't have been slaves in the first place. True enough. But slavery had been a commonplace human experience since antiquity. Emancipation—the freeing of slaves en masse, the movement for abolition—*that* was a new idea. A Western idea. The fruit of Enlightenment. An idea that was brought to fruition over a century and a half ago here, in the United States of America, liberating millions of people and creating the world we now inhabit.
>
> This great and historic achievement surely would not have been possible without philosophical insights and moral commitments cultivated in the seventeenth and eighteenth centuries in the West—ideas about the essential dignity of human persons and about what makes a government's exercise of power over its people legitimate. But something new was created here in America at the end of the eighteenth century. Slavery was a holocaust out of which emerged something that actually advanced the morality and the dignity of humankind—namely, emancipation. The

> abolition of slavery and the incorporation of Africa-descended people into the body politic of the United States of America was an unprecedented achievement.[50]

The progress the United States has made toward the ideal of "a more perfect union" is an unprecedented achievement and stacks up well in the annals of history. As wicked as American chattel slavery was, it was not the first time in history one group of powerful people enslaved another. What made America unique was not that it had slavery but that it reckoned with its existence through the bloody sacrifice of the Civil War and, appealing to her unique ideals of freedom and liberty, overcame the evil and become a beacon of freedom for enslaved and oppressed people everywhere.

Any consideration of American history should also see where the country has done enormous good. It's no exaggeration to say that much of the world would be under the grip of fascist totalitarianism had it not been for the involvement of the United States in pushing back Adolf Hitler, Benito Mussolini, and Emperor Hirohito during World War II. Or consider how many people across Europe are free today because of the United States' fierce opposition to communism. We've liberated nations. We've sent lifesaving relief to those in peril. We've given those who immigrate here freedom and opportunity. This, too, is our history. This, too, should swell our pride when we see the flag and hear the national anthem played.

Studying history honestly requires both gratitude and humility. And it disabuses us from the modern tendency to consider ourselves more enlightened than those who built this nation, as if we, in their time, would have been more righteous. Timothy S. Goeglein wrote that history provokes introspection:

> Looking at it from within their present moment, as best we can, the question is more difficult and provides better insights into our

> own day. How are good and evil tangled up in the justice movements of our own day? What broken systems are we propping up for the sake of other goods, as the Founders did? What evils are so intrinsic in our culture that we cannot see them for what they are?[51]

We should treat our history and the people who lived as we'd want ourselves and our present moment to be treated in our own time, with our own blind spots, sins, and frailties.

Rather than succumb to the Marxist impulse to erase history and tradition, as if it didn't exist, we must think about America's past Christianly, reminded that even the best governments under the most ideal conditions will always fall far short of perfection because governments are inhabited by fallen sinners and, in our case, elected by sinners. America is not the kingdom of God, but this is still a great nation and we can say so without reservation.

This is still a place where the average person can succeed and enjoy prosperity beyond what many people around the world enjoy. We can still worship in freedom without the fear of government interference. America is still the place where churches overflow with attendees, with an embarrassment of theological riches, and is still a hub for missions, evangelism, and humanitarian assistance around the world. In other words, America is a nation worth defending, a nation worth preserving. What we need is both humility about our history and a determination to renew our great country.

CHAPTER 5

The Case for American Exceptionalism

France was a land, England was a people, but America, having about it still that quality of the idea, was harder to utter—it was the graves at Shiloh and the tired, drawn, nervous faces of its great men, and the country boys dying in the Argonne for a phrase that was empty before their bodies withered. It was a willingness of the heart.[1]

—F. Scott Fitzgerald

THE LATE COMEDIAN NORM MACDONALD ONCE CRACKED A JOKE ON *Saturday Night Live* about Oprah Winfrey's longtime boyfriend, Stedman Graham, who had recently released a book entitled *You Can Make It Happen: A Nine-Step Plan for Success.* In his typical deadpan manner, McDonald said, "Step number one? Become Oprah Winfrey's boyfriend."

In a certain sense you can say that about the key to success in life. Step number one: Be born in America. It's hard to deny the reality that for the vast majority of people, to be born here is an immeasurable gift. It's the sentiment that drives the immigrant parents of my students to wonder why native-born Americans don't appreciate what they have.

I was overjoyed recently when my teenage daughter asked, "Dad, do you know how blessed we are to be Americans?" She is so right. Ironically, even though America in 2025 is arguably more free and prosperous than ever before, fewer and fewer Americans believe that it is a blessing to have been born in their own country. Many even threaten to move to Canada or Europe if an election doesn't go their way.

Beyond gratitude, which is essential for a Christian, it's right to ask, "Is there something special, perhaps even God blessed, about our country?" This is often called the doctrine of American exceptionalism, communicated throughout our history from the words of a sermon by the Puritan pastor John Winthrop, who described America as a "city on a hill,"[2] echoing Matthew 5:14, all the way up to President Biden's declaration: "We are by far the greatest, powerful, decent nation in the world."[3]

How should Christians think about the "specialness" of America? Some leaders are repulsed by the idea, such as one Christian professor who suggested, "Teaching children that America is the most exceptional nation in the world is religious indoctrination. It's also idolatry."[4]

Is American exceptionalism idolatry?

American Arrogance or American Exceptionalism?

In his book *American Exceptionalism and Civil Religion: Reassessing the History of an Idea*, the historian and theologian John D. Wilsey explored this topic in depth and put American exceptionalism into two categories: closed American exceptionalism and open American exceptionalism. "The fundamental and defining difference between the two . . . is the difference between exclusivism and inclusivism."[5]

The first category, closed American exceptionalism, holds not only that America is unique and special but that, in many ways, Americans themselves are superior to every other people. At times this kind of superiority was a catalyst for territorial expansion, espoused by some American leaders as "Manifest Destiny."[6] Most prominently, that thinking led to American expansionist warfare during the Mexican-American War, fueled by the presumably God-given mandate to settle territory and "civilize" it. In recent years, this kind of thinking has fueled a sort of well-meaning but misguided desire to make other countries like our own, nations whose own history and tradition preclude them from mirroring American-style democracy.

Followers of Jesus who love their country should be careful with this. Though we rightly love our nation and may believe that we are unique in the history of the world, we must always believe what we are taught in Scripture and Christian tradition that sees all peoples of the world as made in the image of God.[7] If American exceptionalism means that Americans are somehow more valuable and talented than any other people, we've gone well beyond truthful gratitude to unbiblical hagiography. If we take seriously both the Great Commission, which calls every one of us to share the good news of the Gospel with all nations and groups of people (Matthew 28:16), American Christians cannot consider ourselves superior simply because of where we were born. This is what Chuck Colson rightly rebuked as a "triumphalist" mindset.[8]

But the opposite of this is not what Wilsey also rightly decries as a kind of globalist, cosmopolitan mindset that sees no borders, nations, or distinct traditions. He termed triumphalist exceptionalism to be "closed exceptionalism," contrasting it with an "open exceptionalism," which is consistent with Christian witness. He described it this way:

> At the heart of what it means to be an American is the act of calling America back to faithfulness to its first principles motivated by authentic patriotism . . . we affirm that America is different because it is a nation in which dissent is not only allowed; it is a

> virtue. Dissenting colonists in the eighteenth century, after all, birthed the nation. Open exceptionalism opens the door for citizens to acknowledge, to address and to rectify real American flaws because, in so doing, citizens express true love for country.[9]

A healthy American exceptionalism is not arrogance but an appreciation of the blessings of freedom, liberty, and prosperity. It's a recognition of the uniqueness of the country. Southern Baptist scholar Richard Land explained it as a matter of stewardship:

> To whom much is given, much is required. No nation or people have ever been as blessed as the citizens of the United States. A blessing by definition is undeserved. I believe we have an obligation to be the friend of freedom and the defender of human dignity whenever we are asked and whenever we can. We can't address all the world's ills, but when we can make a difference, we should.[10]

In this way American exceptionalism is a humble gratitude for our unique blessings. Scripture tells us that "every good and perfect gift is from above" (James 1:17). Yet some Christian leaders scoff at this. One pastor rolled his eyes. "You'll have to excuse me if I don't get too excited about Greco-Roman-British-American Exceptionalism—or any other geopolitical claim to exceptionalism. (There really is a big difference between being truly exceptional and merely the latest in a long line.)"[11]

I disagree. Followers of Jesus can hold two things in tension. We can both believe that America is a good gift from God and recognize that America is not Zion, is not the end of history, and that we must ultimately look for a city whose builder and maker is God (Hebrews 11:10). In its proper place, loving our country above the rest is a way of expressing gratitude for our home.

Okay, but America Really Is Exceptional

But what of the specific claim that America is exceptional, that something special happened here that is rare in human history? Is this claim true? A few years ago, I took my daughter on a tour of George Washington's home, Mount Vernon. One of the most important artifacts is the rolltop desk in Washington's study. The tour guide explained that the presence of the desk signified that Washington, then the most powerful and popular man in the newly free colonies, intended not to use his conquest over Great Britain to gain power for himself but resigned his commission as commander in chief of the Continental Army. He intended to return home, back to that desk. He intended not to be a king but to give up power. The artist John Trumbull painted a famous rendering of the scene before the Continental Congress that is displayed prominently in the US Capitol.

That was an extraordinary act by Washington, virtually unheard of in the annals of history. Winning generals don't normally give up power; they accumulate it. When King George III, the vanquished king of England, heard about it, he said, "If he did he would be the greatest man in the world."[12] Washington did it again when, after being summoned by his countrymen to be the United States' first president, he refused the lofty titles suggested by John Adams, his vice president, insisting on being called "Mr. President."[13] He set a precedent by voluntarily stepping down after two terms. Today the practice of giving up power is common in democracies, but in the late 1700s it was something new in the history of governments.

How can we look at this great act of humility and not see something noble in it? His self-renunciation wasn't self-erasure or the Gnostic denial of power's existence; rather, his heroism lay in his willingness to humble himself for the greater good. Obviously, we all wish he had been more Christlike in other areas of his life, but how many of us, given the possibility of lifelong kingship, would choose to walk away from it?

Revolutions are common in history, but the American one, fought by a ragtag army of untrained farmers, cobblers, and merchants against the world's greatest fighting force at the time, was fought on the basis of something unique. Revolutions come and go and often replace existing tyrannies with new ones. But the Americans overcame betrayals, poor equipment, lack of resources, and losses because they were fighting for something different from mere power for power's sake.

As the historian David McCullough rightly wrote, "Never, ever, anywhere, had there been a government instituted on the consent of the governed."[14] The columnist George Will wrote, "America had an exceptional revolution, one that did not attempt to define and deliver happiness, but one that set people free to define and pursue it as they please. Americans codified their Founding doctrines as a natural rights republic in an exceptional Constitution, one that does not say what government must do for them but what government may not do to them."[15] The historian Thomas S. Kidd wrote that "the declaration [is] the most resounding statement of human equality the world has ever known" because of "its theological character."[16] Jonah Goldberg wrote that American-style democracy and our founding ideals are not only unique but unnatural (meaning that they're improbable). He described its development as a miracle:

> Capitalism is unnatural. Democracy is unnatural. Human rights are unnatural. The world we live in today is unnatural, and we stumbled into it more or less by accident. The natural state of mankind is grinding poverty punctuated by horrific violence terminating with an early death. It was like this for a very, very long time. . . .

> All states prior to the Miracle were designed for the betterment of the tiny slice of humans at the top. Everywhere around the world, rulers saw the masses as little more than instruments of their will. . . . The Founders were creating something new in the world.[17]

It's hard for those of us who have grown up in the United States, where basic freedoms and relative political stability are the norm, to understand just how unique the vision of the Founders was. Though the Magna Carta was the seed of American-style democracy, the Declaration of Independence and the Constitution were, as Goldberg put it, "something new in the world."

That was why Lincoln fought so hard to preserve the Union during the Civil War. Yes, he and the abolitionists were determined to see slavery, that great constitutional contradiction, eradicated from America. But more important, he understood that if the fledgling American democracy didn't hold, it would send a signal to the rest of the world that that kind of arrangement doesn't work. It is, after all, unnatural.

But the United States did hold and has become a model, however imperfect, for the rest of the world. Don't just take the word of American observers and patriots; listen to those who have observed the country as visitors. G. K. Chesterton, the eccentric Catholic writer and philosopher, waxed eloquently about American exceptionalism:

> America is the only nation in the world that is founded on a creed. That creed is set forth with dogmatic and even theological lucidity in the Declaration of Independence; perhaps the only piece of practical politics that is also theoretical politics and also great literature. It enunciates that all men are equal in their claim to justice, that governments exist to give them that justice, and that their authority is for that reason just. It certainly does condemn

> anarchism, and it does also by inference condemn atheism, since it clearly names the Creator as the ultimate authority from whom these equal rights are derived. Nobody expects a modern political system to proceed logically in the application of such dogmas, and in the matter of God and Government it is naturally God whose claim is taken more lightly. The point is that there is a creed, if not about divine, at least about human things.[18]

Unlike other nations, America is, as Chesterton so rightly observed, founded on a creed, a sort of idea that has the aspirational, universal quality that a church's creed would. Like a church, it is structured in such a way that it can more easily assimilate new members than can other nations with, say, more race- or culture-based foundational ideas. This is why America is the place to which people from around the world come, bringing both their ethnic identities and a desire to be free, to be American. He was joined in that assessment by the nineteenth-century French aristocrat and philosopher Alexis de Tocqueville, whose *Democracy in America* described the young nation as a rare place that "exhibits in her social state a most extraordinary phenomenon. Men are there seen on a greater equality in point of fortune and intellect, or, in other words, more equal in their strength, than in any other country of the world, or in any age of which history has preserved the remembrance."[19] The late British historian Paul Johnson remarked, 150 years later, that the "great American republican experiment is still the cynosure of the world's eyes."[20]

Our country's uniqueness is why, every day, thousands of people try to breach our borders and enter the United States. It's why a US visa is one of the most coveted possessions in the world. Not because of blood or soil or because the people born in this nation are any more exceptional than people born anywhere else in the world. No, America is exceptional because of her unique ideals.

Senator Marco Rubio, whose parents emigrated from Cuba, explained that his father, a bartender, who had fled to US shores and made a life here, taught him to believe "how different America is from the rest of the world."[21]

Why did that revolution stick? I always ask myself that, especially after touring some of America's historic places, such as Yorktown, where in 1781, Americans defeated, with the help of the French, Cornwallis's seven-thousand-man army. I think about it when I'm in Boston, where the first shot of the Revolution occurred at the Old North Bridge in Concord. I think about it as I read about the fragile moments when history could have gone another way.

Though we cannot ignore the many current problems and issues that face our country—solutions for which I'll explore in the next section—rather than be surprised at what's not great in America, we should be awestruck that this experiment in human liberty still exists, even if it's rickety, needs some oil, and will require enormous work to preserve it for our children and grandchildren. It's not nostalgic to claim that America is exceptionally free, prosperous, and implausibly successful.

Perhaps the most salient theory for why the American experiment worked while almost every other revolution in history has failed is that the motivation for what our Founders did was different from the reason most movements overthrow governments. Os Guinness, a historian, Christian apologist, and keen observer of America, pointed to a key difference between what happened in America and what transpired in France a little more than a decade later:

> The differences between the two revolutions are extreme. Obviously, they have different sources. One, the Bible, the Torah, the other, the French Enlightenment, Diderot, Rousseau, Voltaire. They have different views of humanity. The American Revolution based on biblical ideas has immense realism. . . . The French

Revolution is utopian. Man is born free, Rousseau says, and everywhere is in chains.[22]

The 1789 French Revolution was about freedom for freedom's sake. There was no coherent moral principle on which to base the foundation of a new society. The 1776 American Revolution, on the other hand, was a unique mix of reason and religion, liberty and virtue. When the war was over, the men who gathered to form a new government were statesmen who understood that freedom is not just mere self-actualization but that our rights come from God. In many ways, American democracy was about government relegating power to its proper place with all of the country's citizens, rather than centralizing it within the state, thus creating a government that recognized its own limits. This system may allow more vice in some ways, but it also doesn't micromanage virtue, which the Founders considered to be the greater danger of government. Their success speaks for itself.

Why Does It Matter?

Why is it so important for Americans to believe our own story and understand our uniqueness? First, I believe we must if we are to demonstrate gratitude. Aldous Huxley was right when he wrote that "most human beings have an almost infinite capacity for taking things for granted."[23] Christian Americans, of all people, should be the last to fail to recognize the gifts God has given us, especially the gift of a free and prosperous nation. Gratitude is a trait that should mark followers of Jesus (Psalm 100:4), regardless of our circumstances.

It often strikes me that in my few trips to developing countries, I found more joy and gratitude in believers who possess far fewer blessings than the average American. I often find deep gratitude in immigrant communities who are overjoyed to live here and understand the contrast between their new home and the one they left.

Understanding how exceptional America is isn't a Pollyannaish exercise that papers over our many problems. It shouldn't blind us to injustices in our society. But it should help us realize the privileges we enjoy simply by being an American.

American exceptionalism is also important as a matter of Christian stewardship. Rather than making us arrogant or making us think that we are superior to people in other nations, we should soberly and prayerfully consider what we might do with what we've been given. Gratitude for blessings shouldn't make the receiver more proud of himself but more humbly committed to sharing those gifts with others. Jesus taught his disciples that to whom much is given, much is required (Luke 12:42–48). In what way might American Christians use their freedom and prosperity on behalf of others?

Christians believe that rights imply duties and that we learn those duties from God. Rights merely give us negative freedom. "Negative freedom is freedom from—freedom from oppression, whether it's a colonial power or addiction to alcohol oppressing you," wrote Os Guinness.[24] But Christians understand that negative freedom in itself doesn't produce the good life. Negative freedom is needed to escape from tyranny, but without an accompanying commitment to be free from sin, this "independence" is just another form of slavery. Guinness continued, "You need to be freed from negative freedom. Positive freedom is freedom for, freedom to be." This is analogous to spiritual freedom, provided in salvation in Christ. Christians are not merely saved from the power of sin; they are saved for a purpose, to glorify God with their lives (Ephesians 2:10).

The American system hinges on the idea that the state tends to be a poor steward of individuals' positive freedom and therefore it is wiser to diffuse power and disperse that freedom widely among the citizenry. Obviously, this works only with a generally moral citizenry, which is where the Church comes in.

American Christians have a kind of double freedom: freedom from the power of sin and freedom from political tyranny. We should ask ourselves how well we are stewarding these gifts. This, I believe, is one of the reasons why the United States continues to be the hub of mission and humanitarian activity around the world. American Christians continue to leave the comforts of their home and go to some of the most difficult places in the world to share God's love in both word and deed.

But we are also capable of losing this gratitude and can succumb to both materialism and a kind of inward focus. In recent years, some conservative Christians have questioned why America continues to send relief and aid to developing countries. Perhaps we should worry about rebuilding and renewing what we have here, they say. As I write this book, we are mourning the tragic death of a young couple in Haiti. There, young, vibrant, gifted Christians gave their lives to try to bring hope and healing to a troubled people.[25] Some people, even some Christians, wonder if their lives were a waste. Why go and give of yourself in your prime years to a country that seems to have no hope of stability or prosperity? The couple did so because they desired not to hoard their gifts of salvation in Christ and US citizenship and instead sought to invest them in the lives of others. It's the same motivation that moved Jim Elliot and his four comrades to go to a tribe in Ecuador in the 1950s, which cost them their lives. "He is no fool who gives away what he cannot keep, to gain what he cannot lose" was Elliot's battle cry.

Few of us will be asked by God to pay this ultimate price. Yet understanding the goodness of what we've inherited as American Christians can motivate us both to thank God for our gifts and to live lives of purpose and meaning for the glory of God.

Does the Bible Command Isolationism or Interventionism?

A healthy love of country and recognition of our unique blessings can help us shape our politics. If we know what makes the United States uniquely successful, we can work hard to preserve those values against those who seek to reshape it according to different values, perhaps more like the revolutions, French or otherwise, that have ultimately failed. This is not about going back to a mythical golden era but about applying the wisdom of the Founders to contemporary challenges.

What's more, seeing the blessings of liberty and prosperity as a stewardship can help us understand America's unique role in the world. Mark Tooley, the president of the Institute for Religion and Democracy, says that this is a duty of every American Christian:

> The young and the comfortable in today's America too often assume their security and ease are the human historical norm. They don't know that war, genocide, tyranny, extreme poverty, and oppression are far more common to the human experience. What America, despite its countless sins, has achieved for its own people and for billions around the world directly and indirectly can only be called blessed and providential.
>
> Are America and its civilization morally worth defending? Yes, because the alternatives are too bleak to consider. And thoughtful, public-minded Christians, who are called by their Lord to care and contribute towards justice, humanity, and the common good, cannot be indifferent to America and its central role in the world today.[26]

Today, a growing number of Christians on both the left and the right want to withdraw from the world. But if America is truly exceptional, a unique incubator of democracy and freedom, shouldn't we take the idea of stewardship seriously when it comes to how we interact with other countries around the globe? Does "to whom much is given, much is required" apply to the United States' role in the world?

I think it does. But figuring out exactly what this looks like is difficult. We can't claim that our blessings give us perfect wisdom to solve problems for other people. To be sure, American exceptionalism has, at times, led to hubris when it comes to fighting wars and getting involved in other nations' disputes. Though the United States can be an "arsenal of democracy" in helping other nations be more free, we have often felt that because we were the greatest nation in the world, we could do no wrong or that we could force American-style democracy on every other nation. But complicated conflicts such as those in Vietnam, Iraq, and Afghanistan have kept us from thinking that we can do so everywhere.

Opposition to poorly planned wars is one thing, but in recent years this justified caution has transformed into a sort of neo-isolationism. In some cases, this is the result of selfishness or sloth, but in others, it's the result of a naive belief that the world's most powerful nation only makes things worse by getting involved or that it is somehow "uninvolved" when it doesn't act.

Yet history shows that America doesn't really have the option to shrink into itself and ignore the rest of the world. We're involved whether we want to be or not, and what we don't do is just as important as what we do. When you have power, there's no true retreat. Our strength and wealth give us negative freedom—freedom *from* the world—but they also mean that we are obligated to seek positive freedom—freedom *to* bless others.

As in a family, the United States' first duty is to her own citizens, but every good family has a responsibility to the neighborhood and community, to do what it can to make it a better place to flourish. Similarly, nations, especially rich, powerful, free ones, can't afford to ignore the community of nations.

We learned this lesson in the lead-up to World War II. Weary after World War I, Americans watched as the fascist dictators Adolf Hitler, Benito Mussolini, and Emperor Hirohito marched across Europe and Asia and even threatened the survival of Great Britain. President Roosevelt found ways to help arm our allies in the United Kingdom, but it wasn't until Japan attacked us at Pearl Harbor that the sleeping giant of America awoke to the encroaching world danger. President Ronald Reagan, on the fortieth anniversary of D-Day, spoke of the folly of retreat:

> We in America have learned bitter lessons from two World Wars: It is better to be here ready to protect the peace, than to take blind shelter across the sea, rushing to respond only after freedom is lost. We've learned that isolationism never was and never will be an acceptable response to tyrannical governments with an expansionist intent.[27]

Today, unfortunately, many political leaders are repeating the same mistakes. We should avoid, of course, becoming involved in foolish entanglements that are not in America's best interests. We can't be the world's policeman. The first duty of our government is, of course, to protect "life, liberty, and the pursuit of happiness" here at home. Still, by virtue of our country's prosperity, uniqueness, and status as a superpower, our leaders can use their power for good where we can and, more important, communicate that we are on the side of those who yearn for freedom. Given our country's uniquely Christian roots, given our unprecedented prosperity, can we deny that God has lifted America into a unique role in the world? Unfettered interventionism and absolute isolationism are both sentimental visions of foreign policy, assuming respectively that national power can do no wrong and that national power can avoid doing wrong by doing nothing at all. Both are mistakes.

Richard Land, who served as the chief Southern Baptist ethicist, an adviser to presidents, and an appointed member, for eleven years, of the United States Commission on International Religious Freedom, told me that the United States was often the only nation that cared about the plight of people around the world who are jailed or killed merely because of their religious beliefs: "It is the United States and sometimes the UK." I don't know about you, but this fills me with enormous pride as an American.

Over a decade ago, I took a trip to eastern Europe to attend a family wedding and visit with some missionaries. Two experiences burned into my memory the importance of America's attempts to do good in the world, to stand on the side of free people and aid those who are vulnerable.

The first experience I remember is a conversation with a gentleman from a country in eastern Europe. He was lamenting to me the Obama administration's policy of "leading from behind," that is, pursuing a policy that had the United States apologizing for itself and diminishing her story as a unique nation. In the view of my guest, that was a well-meaning but misguided way to see the world. As a citizen of a nation vulnerable to oppression by wicked regimes and bloodthirsty tyrants, he told me that when the United States retreats from the world stage, other less virtuous powers fill the vacuum. He was right. That was true in the lead-up to World War II and is true now as Russia, China, North Korea, and Iran seek to influence other countries and threaten our democratic allies. While we pause and gaze at our navels, tyrants seize power.

Charles C. W. Cooke, a British immigrant to the United States, had a similar awakening after 9/11:

> Before September 11, it had never occurred to me that the stability of global trade, international peace, and the integrity of transnational communications were in some regard the product of a

> naval supremacy that the United States silently inherited from the British. It had never occurred to me that the world would look dramatically different if another country or axis enjoyed this power, and that it was in my interest to ensure that this never happened. I had never considered, in other words, the importance of the *Pax Americana*. From now on, I would never forget it.[28]

I had another experience that shaped me as well: I visited Hungary, a nation that like many of its eastern European allies was finally enjoying freedom after being misruled by first the Nazis and then the Russians during much of the twentieth century. In Budapest's Liberty Square stands a statue of President Ronald Reagan. It thanks our fortieth president for opposing communism and helping tear down the iron curtain that kept so many people in bondage.

Reagan's leadership against the Soviets is an example of using our uniqueness and our strength for good. His rhetoric against communism was often criticized, and even today, many historians roll their eyes at Cold War rhetoric. But when he decried the East Bloc's oppressive system of government as "an evil empire" and when he told the leader of the Soviet Union to "tear down this wall" dividing Berlin, his words were like a balm to many dissidents in Soviet gulags and labor camps. We should not hesitate to use our rhetoric and our might this way today. We should let the impoverished people of North Korea, the student movement in Iran, the Muslim Uyghurs in China, and oppressed people everywhere know that the United States of America is firmly on their side.

We can do this and take care of our domestic issues as well. In fact, they go together. A strong, prosperous, free United States is a deterrent to evil and aggression around the globe. This is what was meant by Reagan's doctrine of "peace through strength." Often, by engaging this way in the world, we can help avoid war and create the conditions for peace. Deterrence is a lot cheaper than war.

We have not always gotten this right. We've often made grave mistakes. Sobriety, realism, and humility should govern the way Christian Americans think about the world. Yet we can look with pride on the many times when we have used our power for good, from the windswept beaches of Normandy, where a generation of young men gave their lives to help free a continent from tyranny, to our support of the miracle that is the modern state of Israel to nations of eastern Europe whose citizens no longer live under Communist rule. Not to mention the many times the United States has rushed with aid and resources to places where famine, natural disaster, and war have left people vulnerable and bereft. Or the welcome we've often given to refugees from the world's most dangerous places. These should be seen as sources of pride. They are examples of our extending our blessings outside our borders, of giving back a measure of what has been given to us.

Good Christians will, of course, differ on the specifics of foreign policy. We should not be eager to engage in conflict. We should be sober about our limits. Yet as a steward of God's blessings on our nation, as inheritors of liberty that previous generations fought and died for, we should work to both preserve what makes us free at home and stand on the side of freedom-loving people everywhere. This is the heart of good stewardship. Again, I think the words of Reagan are true today: "Can we doubt that only a Divine Providence placed this land, this island of freedom, here as a refuge for all those people in the world who yearn to breathe freely."[29]

Despite what you may have been encouraged to believe, it's not un-Christian to wax patriotic about America and it's not un-Christian to be proud of the reality that this is a unique and special country. Rather than making us arrogant, that fact should motivate us to not only teach the American story to our children but work, in our generation, to preserve it for those who will follow.

Part II

IT IS NOT GOOD FOR MAN TO BE ALONE

CHAPTER 6

Christianity Won't Abide Lone Rangers

> To be sure, the world crisis is not basically political, economic or social, but religious and moral, and only Christ's redemptive dynamic is able to activate humanity to the highest levels of ethical achievement. To press God's claim upon the masses, regenerate Christians must confront the world *now* "with an ethics to make it tremble, and with a dynamic to give it hope." We must offer a new evangelical world-mind whose political, economic, sociological and educational affirmations reflect the Christian world-life view. We must reach for "a baptism of Pentecostal fire resulting in a world missionary program."[1]
>
> —*Carl F. H. Henry*

IN THE FIRST HALF OF THIS BOOK, I TALKED ABOUT THE IMPORTANCE of patriotism, the uniqueness of the American experiment, and the importance of Christianity to our democracy, as well as why Christians should be involved in renewing and restoring our great country. In this second half, I'd like to think through the specific domains outside politics where Christians can do the most good to renew it. If the first half was about the importance of political power, the second half will be about its relative unimportance compared to other spheres of action. I've been discussing these matters through the lens of Augustine's theory of ordered loves. In the coming chapters, I'll talk about the more important loves and how they relate to politics. After all, while love of country is important, it's pretty far down on the totem pole in the greater scheme of things.

Let's revisit the words of John Adams, who understood that it is well away from the boardrooms, courtrooms, and White House Situation Room that the strength of American democracy lies:

> Because We have no Government armed with Power capable of contending with human Passions unbridled by . . . morality and Religion. Avarice, Ambition, Revenge or Galantry, would break the strongest Cords of our Constitution as a Whale goes through a Net. Our Constitution was made only for a moral and religious People. It is wholly inadequate to the government of any other.[2]

Avarice, ambition, revenge, or gallantry will break the strongest cords of our Constitution. Without the reformation of the human soul, without the transformative power of heart change, even the greatest countries descend into moral chaos and confusion. Almost two hundred years later, Ronald Reagan made essentially the same point:

> Without God, there is no virtue, because there's no prompting of the conscience. Without God, we're mired in the material; that flat world that tells us only what the senses perceive. Without God, there is a coarsening of the society. And without God, democracy will not and cannot long endure. If we ever forget that we're one nation under God, then we will be a nation gone under.[3]

Without God, we are a nation gone under. Many of the most powerful leaders in the world have understood that the source of America's greatness is, as Alexis de Tocqueville said, in her goodness—the goodness that runs through human hearts.

Despite this fact, many modern American Christians seem to denigrate the very institution through which Christ makes himself known in the world: the Church. You'll hear different good-sounding reasons for Christians to retreat from churches. The left-wing version usually starts with an excess of care. As John Pavlovitz put it:

> Church-less Sundays can bring a great deal of guilt, especially if you grew up in organized religion. When you find your spiritual life being defined outside of the local church, you can tend to feel like you're doing it wrong, or that the experience is somehow counterfeit—less spiritual. You either hear an alarm go of [*sic*] in your own head, or from well-meaning church friends or from pushy pastors that you *need to get back to church*.
>
> Well, you may and you may not. You may just need to stay right where you are.

He went on to say that you can encounter God anywhere, from out in nature to with friends, and that "the idea that we need to travel to sit in a space with strangers and consume religious entertainment is not at all Biblical."[4]

The right-wing version of this wears different clothes but is no less suspicious of gathering together or submitting to pastoral authority. In 2024, the right-wing commentator Tucker Carlson told a wild story of being attacked by a demon in his sleep. His response to the incident, he said, had been to be "seized with this very intense desire to read the Bible." He made a point of buying one without study aids, free of "editorializing," because "I've very low levels of trust for Christian pastors."[5] His story has a number of commonalities with right-wing Church-skeptic narratives: personal mysticism, a Gnostic approach to the Bible (the idea that it's a secret message that's been gatekept by the powers that be), and cynicism about Christian leadership.

Outside of political skeptics, other Christians have started to see going to church as a consumer activity or an entertainment and question the necessity of weekly gathering. Pastor Skye Jethani wrote, "I talk with Christians regularly—particularly millennials, for whom digital content is native—who ask me why Sunday morning church attendance is important. They don't recognise the value of a large group gathering built around a 35-minute Bible lesson when they have access to (often superior) sermons 24/7 via their smartphones."[6]

Underneath these beliefs is the idea that one's relationship with God is something that can, and perhaps should, happen in isolation, uncorrupted by institutions. Some left-wing Christians claim that evangelism is colonization[7] and that "organized religion" is out to suppress true faith. Christians are too stuffy in their ancient rituals and don't love the world enough, the logic goes.

Some right-wing Christians tend to impose political purity tests, complaining about pastors who they perceive to not be partisan enough in the pulpit. These pastors really, the logic goes, just want to be loved by the world.

A lot of these narratives succeed in the popular imagination because of media incentives. Increasingly isolated people turn to social media for news and instead get ragebait. In the Nashville suburb where we lived for nine years, there was one crazy pastor who did crazy stunts to get attention and at least two dozen other pastors who simply worked together to serve the community. Guess which one consistently made the headlines? Hint: It was never ever the faithful guys garnering media attention.

The Bible is unequivocally clear: Churchgoing is not optional. Christianity possesses both a worldview and the transformative power of the Gospel that takes hardened hearts and makes them tender: tender toward God and tender toward their neighbors. A few years ago, a sociologist named Robert Woodberry studied the impact of Christian missions in the world, often derided by the Left as a destructive, colonizing force on vulnerable populations. His massive research study of civilizations into which Christianity entered and made inroads found the opposite to be true:

> Areas where Protestant missionaries had a significant presence in the past are on average more economically developed today, with comparatively better health, lower infant mortality, lower corruption, greater literacy, higher educational attainment (especially for women), and more robust membership in nongovernmental associations.[8]

Christianity, for the most part, enhances the societies in which it is practiced. That was the thesis of a talk Tim Keller gave before the British House of Commons, in which he argued that the values that most people seem to yearn for—human rights, women's suffrage, justice, the elimination of poverty, and so on—all hail from Christianity. What's more, he argued, it is the simple story of Jesus' life, death, and resurrection that transforms people, who then can transform societies.[9] The work of historians such as Tom Holland, Rodney Stark, and others only underscores this truth.

Often this apologetic is in defense of Christianity's usefulness to a country, yet we Christians must ourselves believe it to be true. We must believe our own story. As important as political engagement is—and I hope I've persuasively argued that Christians cannot in good conscience abandon political engagement—the most important work all Christians do begins on Sunday in their local churches.

Why, for Christians, should the Church be the starting point for the renewal of American society? Because, unlike every other institution, the Church is the only place where God has promised to locate himself as the center of his mission in the world. It's the one enduring organism that Christ promised to build throughout the ages. "I will build my church," he told his disciples, "and the gates of hell shall not prevail against it" (Matthew 16:17–19, ESV).

Chuck Colson reminded us that while political activity for a Christian is imperative, the locus of our activity should be centered in the Church: "Through the centuries, when Christians have lived out their faith . . . they have renewed, restored, and on occasions, even built new cultures. They have literally turned the world upside down."[10] The scholar Stephen O. Presley wrote this of the early Church:

> They were simultaneously citizens of the country in which they resided and foreigners whose identity was rooted in Christ as King.
>
> Not that they then retreated or denied their citizenship. . . . Simply put, they were active citizens embedded in the life of their communities. They did not confuse their earthly citizenship with their heavenly one, or reject the world and live in isolation, but sought the welfare of the city. The early church had no designated "Christian" country; rather, with Paul, it accepted political authorities as appointed by God and "obey[ed] the established laws." Yet this form of citizenship was qualified by their commitment to Christian doctrine and practice and their understanding that all earthly political rulers were provisional and temporary.[11]

For the Christian, Going to Church Isn't Optional

I'm not arguing merely for the goodness of Christianity in a society; I'm arguing that Christians who care about their country should first make attending a faithful, Bible-believing church a priority. This is more important than being involved in politics, having hobbies, doing sports. In fact, disordered manifestations of the latter activities often stem from the neglect of this greater duty.

Believe it or not, there is a growing class of Christians, particularly on the right,[12] among conservatives, that professes to believe in the orthodox beliefs of Christianity but does not attend church consistently.[13] I've even met some leaders who speak out publicly about Christian values but tell me privately that they are not active members of a Christian congregation. I once emceed an apologetics conference where the main speaker admitted that he was so busy defending Christianity that he didn't have time to attend church locally. This is getting it backward.

For some of those who have stopped attending church, the rhythms of the political life fill a spiritual void. But politics, while a useful vehicle for human flourishing, cannot fulfill what only genuine spirituality can. I plead with my fellow American Christians not to make this mistake and to consider prioritizing your relationship with God above your relationship with your political party.

The way to make our politics more Christian is neither to withdraw from politics nor to put politics first but to first center yourself within the life of a local church. As the Methodist scholar and thought leader Mark Tooley noted, "America will be more Christian when more Americans take Christianity seriously, a task for which politics is profoundly ill-equipped."[14]

Prioritizing the Church matters not merely for the effect it has on the life of the nation but because, for a Christian, it is essential for obeying Christ. John Stott, the late British theologian, was right when he wrote, "The church lies at the very center of the eternal purpose of God. It is not a divine afterthought. It is not an accident of history."[15]

Put simply, in the New Testament, there is no version of Christianity that doesn't include the weekly rhythms of Christian community. Not only did Jesus declare "where two or three are gathered together in my name, there am I in the midst of them" (Matthew 18:20, ASV), but the letters that form the New Testament were written to congregants of local churches around the known world.

The Baptist scholar Gregg R. Allison explained it this way:

> The church is the people of God who have been saved through repentance and faith in Jesus Christ and have been incorporated

> into his body through baptism with the Holy Spirit. It consists of two interrelated elements; the universal church is the fellowship of all Christians that extends from the day of Pentecost until the second coming, incorporating both the deceased believers who are presently in heaven and the living believers from all over the world.[16]

The Church is therefore both local and global, the growing family in Heaven and on Earth who know God by faith in Jesus Christ.

Often I hear from well-meaning conservatives who are rightly concerned about the degradation of America that because the times are so bad, the countercultural weekly rhythms of preaching, singing, praying, and reciting ancient creeds are not fit for such a time of ongoing cultural warfare.

But what if it turns out that that this is exactly what our moment needs? The writer of Hebrews, addressing first-century Church members increasingly besieged by an oppressive Roman government, says to them, "Let us hold unswervingly to the hope we profess, for he who promised is faithful. And let us consider how we may spur one another on toward love and good deeds, not giving up meeting together, as some are in the habit of doing, but encouraging one another—and *all the more as you see the Day approaching*" (Hebrews 10:23–25, NIV; my emphasis). Paul was saying that the darker the times, the more important it is for Christians—the light of the world—to gather.

This is why corporate worship is modeled in the New Testament, including the public reading of Scripture (1 Timothy 4:13; Colossians 4:16), listening to preaching and teaching (1 Timothy 4:13), the sacraments of the Lord's Supper and baptism (1 Corinthians 11; Acts 22:16), shared singing and praise (Ephesians 5:19), praying together (Acts 2:42), and public confession (1 Timothy 6:12).

These are corporate worship experiences. God wired his people for regular, meaningful, worshipful community gathered around the Word, worship, and the sacraments. Technology has, in many ways, enriched our worship experiences and made it possible for those who physically can't attend worship to enjoy at least some of what constitutes a church service. For most of the body of Christ, at least those who are physically able, there is the expectation in Scripture to gather and worship weekly.

There is something about assembling with others who are God's people that forms our souls. When the Church is at its best, there is a grace-filled accountability, a togetherness. We are encouraged and strengthened. Think about Paul's words in Ephesians 5:19. He says to speak to one another "in psalms, hymns, and spiritual songs." When we sing, we are singing to God and to one another. We preach the Gospel to one another because we need to be reminded of the great truths of who Christ is and who we are. When we partake of the sacraments together, we remind ourselves that we've been invited back to God's table in fellowship, made possible by the shedding of Jesus' blood and his resurrection.

There is something powerful about God's people from all walks of life joining together in unity, acknowledging that Christ is the King, Savior, and Lord. There is something uplifting about moving through a passage of Scripture together over long stretches of life. There is something enriching about joining hands through struggle, lament, triumph, and grace.[17]

As you know from the previous chapters, I'm not arguing for a pious Christianity that eschews politics but for a politics that begins, first, by prioritizing what is eternal. It's a paradox, really, but when we consider that the nation we love is temporal and the kingdom to which we've pledged ultimate allegiance is eternal, we become better patriots, because we love things in proper proportion to what they deserve. We render unto Caesar what is due to Caesar and don't overburden him with the love we owe to God.

I think our politics will improve when faithful, churchgoing, spirit-filled believers enter the fray, knowing their limits, understanding the temporal nature of our times, and desiring to love our neighbors by influencing policies that will help them flourish.

Erick-Woods Erickson, a Christian talk show host, urges this even as he daily engages in political and cultural skirmishes: "Christians in the early church drew people to them not by wielding power, but by wearing a smile in the face of adversity. They loved their neighbors, earned their trust and turned a pagan empire into a Christian kingdom."[18] Clearly Erickson by his actions demonstrates that he doesn't mean that we should totally divest ourselves from the political world or from using power but must recognize that the thing that draws people to us is our ability to offer them not a physical good but an eternal one.

Six Ways the Church Can Help Renew America

The mission of the Church, says the theologian Trevin Wax, is to be

> a sign and instrument of the kingdom of God, a people united by faith in the gospel announcement of the crucified and risen King Jesus. The mission of the church is to go into the world in the power of the Spirit and make disciples by proclaiming this gospel, calling people to respond in ongoing repentance and faith, and demonstrating the truth and power of the gospel by living under the lordship of Christ for the glory of God and the good of the world.[19]

How can the Church, by fulfilling this mission, bear witness in the nation we love? I believe that there are six key ways in which congregations can seek "the good of the world" in this country.

1. Tell the Full Truth

Christians are called, in every culture, to "not be conformed to this world" but to "be transformed by the renewal of your mind" (Romans 12:1–2, ESV). The philosopher and apologist Os Guinness declared that there is "a social tension required by the Way of Jesus."[20]

That was the anthem of the fourth-century church leader Athanasius of Alexandria, who famously said, "If the world is against the truth, then I am against the world." It sounds somewhat paradoxical. How can we be good American citizens if we are against, in some aspects, American society? This isn't to be confused with extreme withdrawal, such as separatist societies and cults such as the Amish or weirdos who build religious compounds in remote places in Idaho. Christians in every age must engage with their world but do so with countercultural truths that will help lift people out of their bondage to falsehoods that enslave.

Christians should do this not to merely be contrarian or out of spite for those who disagree with them but from a place of love. This is how we can both "love not the world, neither the things that are in the world" (1 John 2:15–17, ASV) yet, like Jesus, love the people of the world (John 3:16). Our fellow citizens don't need, in our churches, more of the same confusion, tribalism, and destructive ideas they hear throughout the week from pop culture, social media, and other voices. Churches should do this as a faithful steward and herald of the truth as it is revealed by God in His Word.

What America most needs is for Christians to be distinctive for being Christian—which is to say, for being Christlike. Timothy says about the Church that she is "the pillar and ground of the truth" (1 Timothy 3:15, ASV). This is to say that there is a body of truth that is true in all times and all seasons. It's a body of truth that, when lived and practiced, helps advance human flourishing.

America desperately needs faithful preachers who consistently preach God's word, without reservation. Chuck Colson, writing decades ago, was never more prescient:

> The time is ripe for a message that the social peace and personal fulfillment people really crave are available only in Christianity. The church has stood unshaken through the ebb and flow of two millennia. It has survived the persecutions of the early centuries, the barbarian invasions of the Middle Ages, and the intellectual assaults of the modern era. Its solid walls rise up above the ruins littered across the intellectual landscape. God forbid that we, heirs of saints and martyrs, should falter at this pivotal moment. . . . This is the time to make a compelling case that Christianity offers the most rational and realistic hope for both personal redemption and social renewal.[21]

To speak the truth in love requires courage. One of the most central truths we declare is that of the created order: we affirm the goodness with which God has ordered the world, the way he has created humans in his image (Genesis 1:26) with care and precision (Psalm 139) with unique value above the rest of creation (Psalm 8:5–8). God's design for gender, male and female (Genesis 1:27; Matthew 19:4–6), and his design for human sexuality in the covenant of marriage between men and women (Matthew 19:4–6; Ephesians 5:31) are not strange but beautiful. Christians have a unique vision of human dignity that serves as a stark alternative to the confusion of our day.[22] This shouldn't be the only thing Christians hear on Sundays, but pastors shouldn't shy away from repeating these truths just because they go against the grain of modern fashions.

There has been relentless pressure for the Church to give up what has made it distinctive: its "strangeness." Many voices have urged conservative evangelicals and Catholics to soften this good news or even change the historic Christian doctrines.[23] However, the Christian ethic, which seems so countercultural and offensive, will become an apologetic for the faith. Consider the women's rights activist Ayaan Hirsi Ali, who converted from atheism to Christianity because she saw it as the "only credible" option to unite the West in opposition to "great-power authoritarianism," "the rise of global Islamism," and "the viral spread of woke ideology."[24] Or Paul Kingsnorth, another former opponent of Christianity who saw in the ancient faith that "freedom was no freedom at all, but enslavement to the passions: a neat description of the first thirty years of my life. True freedom, it turns out, is to give up your will and follow God's."[25]

The true reason to speak countercultural truth is not that it will eventually age well, but we should take comfort in the fact that it will. The reason that we can, in J. R. R. Tolkien's words, "fight the long defeat" is that we are aware of "final victory." But we should also be aware that anti-nature fads are just that; nature will come roaring back sooner than we think.[26]

Consider the current "vibe shift" in American culture around these issues. Some who have yet to "give up their will and follow God's" are nevertheless looking afresh at Christianity *because* of its worldview, not in spite of it. The British journalist Louise Perry, a religious skeptic, nevertheless wrote a book titled *Against the Sexual Revolution* that lauded the distinctiveness of Christianity as refreshing:

> Whereas the Romans regarded male chastity as profoundly unhealthy, Christians prized it and insisted on it. Early converts were disproportionately female because the Christian valorization of weakness offered obvious benefits to the weaker sex, who could—for the first time—demand sexual continence of men. Feminism is not opposed to Christianity: It is its descendant. . . .

> What if . . . we understand the Christian era as a clearing in a forest? The forest is paganism: dark, wild, vigorous, and menacing, but also magical in its way. For two thousand years, Christians pushed the forest back, with burning and hacking, but also with pruning and cultivating, creating a garden in the clearing with a view upward to heaven.[27]

Christians should resist the pressure from disgruntled or left-leaning people to deemphasize or silence Christianity's unfashionable truths and lean into its fashionable ones. We should instead clear the forest of deception by giving our communities, our cities, and our country a clear testimony of what God has given us in his word and has embedded in nature as a reality of how he ordered the universe. Recently, former skeptics such as Elon Musk, Richard Dawkins, and Jordan Peterson have made similar observations.

A Church that preaches the truth without reservation is a bulwark against confusion, insanity, and chaos in society. God promises that his word reverberates and will not "return void." Faithful pastors in large cathedrals and tiny country churches, in suburban megachurches and rented gymnasiums, are doing the most important work in society by faithfully preaching from Scripture and applying that truth to the real-world challenges their parishioners face. And those Christians, equipped on Sunday, can gracefully declare that truth in the places where they live, work, and play.

But it's not merely propositional truth that we must declare with power. In other words, we mustn't speak merely for the rhetorical effect of our words. We must share the transforming power of the Gospel to change hearts. Only the life, death, and resurrection of Christ have the power to transform lives racked by loneliness, despair, and addiction. Even in our supposedly secular age, there is a growing hunger and yearning for the transcendent. The truth we preach is not only about how the world was designed by God to work but about the message of salvation offered by the One who gave his life so that sinners might find grace and truly live.

Some of those who most vociferously oppose Christianity today may be our brothers and sisters in Christ tomorrow, having experienced, as we have, their own road to Damascus. This requires, however, a humility of a heart softened by our own story of redemption. We, like Jesus, must see those around us, confused and corrupted, as people whom God loves and who desperately need their own encounter with God. Christianity is not merely a set of principles—though it is that—but a relationship with a person, Jesus. Churches must not waver in exhorting, summoning, and persuading people to "come to me, all of you who are weary and burdened, and I will give you rest" (Matthew 11:28).

The constant barrage of negative news headlines may condition us into thinking that perhaps the nation is too far gone, too darkened by confusion and sin, to experience revival and renewal. But we have seen that it was historically in times of the greatest tumult in America that there was a spiritual awakening. Consider the tumult of the 1960s and 1970s, which included three political assassinations, the Watergate scandal, the Vietnam War, the sexual revolution, and upheaval in the Middle East. Yet out of that time emerged the Jesus Revolution (through which my father was converted). That era also produced the Reagan Revolution, which, while an imperfect movement, represented a renewal of our politics and national identity as a country.

Christians should not yield to despair but should double down on church planting, evangelism, strong preaching, discipleship, and community outreach. Os Guinness notes that "the story of Christian reformation, revival, and renaissance underscores that the darkest hour is often just before the dawn, so we should always be people of hope and prayer, not gloom and defeatism. God the Holy Spirit can turn the situation around in five minutes."[28]

Revival doesn't look like a sudden surge of emotion in a formless space—at least not for very long—but like hard work and institutional growth. The award-winning American historian Allen C. Guelzo described the conditions that led to the Second Great Awakening, arguably one of the moments in US history with the most concentrated Christian presence. From the end of the eighteenth century to the middle of the nineteenth, there was significant growth in conversions, church attendance, and other signs of spiritual fervor.

But what sustained that great revival of the Spirit in America was that "people did extraordinary amounts of work which was blessed by the spirit of God but they set to it with their shoulders to the wheel of moving people's hearts and minds and the growth of those churches and institutions was extraordinary."[29] This, Guelzo asserts, is what contemporary Christians should do, while not neglecting the important work of politics.[30] An insightful observation from a leading American historian.

Faithful pastors should tether their sermons not to the headlines but to the text of Scripture that is relevant to the world their people live in. Christians should believe that we were made for this moment in history and should put our shoulders to the plow, evangelizing, discipling, and church planting. It is this kind of Gospel work that helps seed and prepare our communities for the kind of spiritual revival our country has experienced and desperately needs at this hour.

2. Be Honorable

If the church is, as pastor Mark Dever asserted, "the gospel made visible,"[31] it follows that in order to be influential in our communities, cities, and country, our churches must seek to be not merely truthful and transformational but honorable.

It's no secret that Christians have experienced quite a few scandals in recent years, as daily headlines are filled with stories of institutions and leaders embroiled in scandal. Nothing hurts the witness of the Church more than when Christians fail to live out what they believe. Paul urged the church at Ephesus to "walk worthy" of the calling (Ephesians 4:1) and explained that we should care about our integrity and reputation before a watching world (1 Timothy 3:7). When pastors or Christian leaders are caught in financial or moral sin, it further erodes trust in the Church and causes many people to become disillusioned with Christianity.

Our churches should pursue integrity in every way. Christians should pay careful attention to both our lives and our beliefs (1 Timothy 4:16). We dishonor Christ and hurt our witness when we either fail to live out what we believe or abandon the beliefs Christians have held for all of Church history.[32]

At the same time, Christians shouldn't yield to the cheap cynicism about Christianity that is so popular these days on both the left and the right. On the left, there is hardly a hotter genre than the anti-evangelical screed, usually in the form of a memoir, that lumps the worst actors with everyday believers living out their faith. Producing such books has become a cottage industry.

Consider this quote by Kristin Kobes Du Mez: "For conservative white evangelicals, the 'good news' of the Christian gospel has become inextricably linked to a staunch commitment to patriarchal authority, gender difference, and Christian nationalism, and all of these are intertwined with white racial identity."[33] While this criticism has a kernel of truth in it, as we saw in chapter 4, it's also blinkered about history and unhelpfully mixes sins that orthodox Christians condemn with beliefs that she dislikes for her own reasons.

If we're not careful, we'll be catechized by headlines instead of understanding that most pastors and most Church members are trying, imperfectly, to live out their faith in their communities, giving sacrificially so that the poor and vulnerable can find relief, and raising their families. On the right, especially the online right, there is increasingly an incentive to accuse faithful Christian institutions of being captured by wokeism. When a faithful, conservative, Bible-preaching pastor such as Tim Keller is accused of being left wing, the plot has been lost.

The gravest danger is when Christians stop believing our own story: that God is working through his local church in this age. The Church has always been a messy but sure work of God, from the dysfunctional Corinthian congregation in the first century to the several churches in Revelation subject to the Lord's rebuke through fissures, scandals, heresies, and wars. Colson, again, wrote:

> The church is like Noah's ark; the stench inside would be unbearable if it weren't for the storm outside. This is the church we have. . . . The church of fact is always struggling to conform to the church of faith, and the Christian must live in the midst of this tension—a faithful part of the universal and the particular, of the visible and the invisible, of the faith and the fact. . . . The pettiness and failures, the division and discord can be disheartening at times. What a sorry mess we mortals often make in the name of the church! But our comfort comes from God's promise that He will build His church.[34]

Churches big and small are made of redeemed sinners, imperfectly making their way toward that city "whose builder and maker is God" (Hebrews 11:10, ASV). When we are a community committed to the truth, unashamed in our declaration of what is right and true, and living imperfect but authentic lives before the world, we can be a force for spiritual and social renewal.

3. Equip the Body of Christ

If churches are communities of saints, they are also equipping centers. I like pastor J. D. Greear's analogy of his church as an aircraft carrier. He wrote:

> Aircraft carriers equip planes to carry the battle elsewhere. . . .
>
> Churches that want to "prevail against the gates of hell" must learn to see themselves like aircraft carriers. . . . Members need to learn to share the gospel, without the help of the pastor, *in the community*, and start ministries and Bible studies—even churches—in places without them. Churches must become discipleship factories, "sending" agencies that equip their members to take the battle to the enemy.[35]

We read in Ephesians that the role of pastors and churches is to "equip the saints for the work of ministry" (Ephesians 4:12–16). Most churches do very well in helping their people know the Scriptures, apply them to their everyday lives, and share the good news of the Gospel with their neighbors. This is the primary role of the local body of Christ. But I think that there is more we can do to prepare people to live their faith amid the political and cultural realities of twenty-first-century America. Contrary to the left-wing narrative that Sundays in evangelical churches are Republican pep rallies, in my experience, church leaders often struggle to teach people how to think about politics and culture.

I'm not implying that pastors should become partisan and endorse candidates for political office. However, there is much more we can do to equip our people to go into their communities and engage with the important issues and policies that affect their neighbors. This is not "playing politics" but equipping our people to live out their faith in the world.

This involves, I believe, clarity from Scripture on what can be clearly deduced from it, such as the sanctity of human life from conception to natural death, the creational reality of gender, marriage, sexuality, and the importance of religious liberty. Other areas, such as specific economic ideas and foreign policy, have more nuance. Still, even in these gray areas where good Christians might disagree, it would be helpful if churches could at least point their people to useful resources or ongoing debates that can shape their public witness.

Furthermore, churches must not only equip their members with a robust Christian worldview but teach them how to communicate effectively and make good arguments in the public square. Christianity not only posits certain fixed truths about the world but provides a distinctly Christian way for us to speak with both boldness and compassion. How we declare what is true is just as important as the declaration itself.[36]

The truth is that many Christians wonder what it looks like to be faithful in their schools, businesses, and neighborhoods. One of the reasons our politics is so poisoned is that often believers' theology is shaped by pundits and politicians throughout the week. In many places, there is a huge vacuum of teaching on how to think about key cultural and social issues.

Imagine, too, if pastors and local church leaders were to help raise up and equip future civil servants who are Christians and who feel a calling to run for and hold office. Pastors could hold such future leaders accountable. It's a significant sacrifice to put together a campaign and to govern, especially in this political environment. Political work and work in a government, whether city, state, or federal, is often lonely work for a Christian. The difficulty won't be improved by pastors' discouraging them from even trying, and our political sphere won't be improved by Christians' refusing to enter it. It's easy to complain about the state of our politics, our towns, or our neighborhoods. It's hard to do anything about it, especially when any action is portrayed as compromise.

I'm often in Washington, DC, and know many committed believers who work in the federal government or on a congressional staff. They do this work because they feel a calling to serve their neighbors and their country. Yet among Christians, those who work in government often feel like outcasts or pariahs, either by those who cynically think anything associated with the government is corrupt or by pious fellow Christians who think that the political domain is always dirty.

I've spoken to Christians who work on political campaigns—which are grueling and difficult enterprises. They, too, attend church and wonder if their fellow believers think they are idolaters and bad people because they work in this arena.

Imagine if pastors were to help disciple, guide, and keep accountable those who want to serve God by serving their city, county, or country this way. By washing our hands completely of politics, we often miss opportunities to shape the public square by encouraging, coaching, and mentoring the next generation of civic leaders. If we are dissatisfied with the politicians who are currently in office, what are we doing to replace them?

The Church has a unique opportunity to direct the next generation of leaders toward virtue and humble service. If what is often missing in our politics is a sense of spiritual formation, the Church is the one place where we can find community, spiritual transformation, and accountability. "The church is the only human institution Jesus started," Tim Keller said, "and the only one inhabited by the Spirit and glory of God."[37]

4. Strengthen Families

American families are in deep crisis, bearing the bitter fruits of the sexual revolution. I'll explore this in depth in the next chapter, but it's important to note that the Church can provide a bulwark against a decaying culture and be a force for renewal by strengthening families.

According to Brad Wilcox, a professor of sociology at the University of Virginia, "Faith is the strongest predictor of marital quality—when compared to other factors like ideology, education, race, and income."[38] It's empirically true that families that attend church suffer fewer divorces, have more stable marriages, use pornography less, and develop important social skills.[39]

In recent years there has been a renewed effort by some elites, even some evangelical leaders, to encourage church leaders to soften their message on the family, not to talk about marriage so much, as it might offend those who are single or widowed or married couples who struggle with infertility. Pastors should be sensitive to those in their churches who fit into these categories and emphasize their honored place in the body of Christ. Still, this shouldn't make them sheepish about helping the married couples in their church find spiritual hope and help. The data show that the countercultural message of covenant marriage is exactly what Americans need. I'll dive into this a bit more in the next chapter, but church leaders should view marriage not in a defensive way but as something they can offer to their communities.

Churches can not only help equip their own families to endure and thrive in the twenty-first century but be a beacon of hope for struggling and broke families in their communities. As Pope John Paul II wrote, "As the family goes, so goes the nation, and so goes the whole world in which we live."[40]

5. *Work Toward Unity*

Francis Schaeffer, one of the most eloquent apologists for both Christianity and the Christian worldview, especially regarding the sanctity of human life, was also very concerned about the unity of Christ's Church. Unity, of course, must be based on the truth and not be a touchy-feely "Kumbaya" state with no conflicts or differences among Christians. Nor should it involve a refusal to confront the false ideologies of the age.

Christians must push back boldly against the un-Christian ideas that are permeating through our society and our institutions. We must be unafraid to stand up for the truth. Yet we must also prioritize Christian unity, the visible love of Christian brothers and sisters for one another. We really need to slow down, assume the best meaning of our fellow congregants' words, and recollect that none of us is right about everything.

Schaeffer, in an important book entitled *The Mark of the Christian*, wrote that Jesus' words in John 13 should remind us that Christian unity is an apologetic for the Christian faith:

> Upon his authority [Jesus] gives the world the right to judge whether you and I are born-again Christians, on the basis of our observable love toward all Christians. . . .
>
> The world may not understand what the Christians are disagreeing about, but they will very quickly understand the difference of our differences from the world's differences if they see us having our differences in an open and observable love on a practical level.[41]

This is especially important when we engage in politics. At times, I think we fail to understand that the Christianity we proclaim and defend also applies in the way we treat one another in the public square. Here is a dirty little secret that I've learned after a career in advocacy: Most of the nastiest underhanded opposition doesn't come from the Left, though the Left opposes much of what conservative Christians believe on every level; most of it comes from people who agree with you but are fighting for attention, for turf, for funds, for tribal affirmation. Many of them have a Bible verse in their social media profile and profess to be Christian. The narcissism of small differences flares up easily. A perceived traitor is far worse than a true enemy, our gut tells us. We should be careful of this instinct.

Politics, as we know, is a rough-and-tumble sport. It always has been. I'm not naive. Yet while we can strongly disagree, even in public, with other Christians when it comes to the application of our faith to public policy, we should treat one another with love and respect instead of trying to "own," destroy, and defame people with whom we will share eternity.

Churches can and should be places where we are both equipped to live our faith in the world and can put down our rhetorical swords and come together as the people of God, gathered from every nation, tribe, and tongue. We don't prioritize Christian unity enough when it comes to politics, and we should. This is something the Church can offer a polarized, angry, divisive nation.

6. Provide Community

Almost two decades ago, I had the opportunity to help a friend run for Congress. As someone who has followed politics my entire life, it was the opportunity of a lifetime. I was a senior strategist, though unpaid, for that campaign in my home district in the suburbs of Chicago.

I enjoyed much of that work, which involved introducing my

friend to the various evangelical and Catholic leaders and helping shape a message to reach socially conservative voters who care about their country.

But toward the end of the campaign, I began to experience a renewed sense of calling back to the local church. I enjoyed, of course, the thrill of the up-and-down nature of the campaign, the opportunity to meet prominent public officials and celebrities (Mike Ditka!), and the development of friendships with campaign staff and Christian leaders in the district.

Yet there is an existential nature to political campaigns, a kind of naive hope that turns to cynicism, and at times an end-justifies-the-means mentality that is often essential to helping put a candidate over the top. I'm not saying that a Christian cannot run, advise, and participate in campaigns. I think that Christians should be in those spaces. However, I recognized then that the most enduring institutions in the communities we visited were . . . its churches.

Campaigns come and go, but congregations large and small are preaching the love of Christ, resisting the darkness, and selflessly helping the most vulnerable in their communities, year after year.

I think of the yellow-shirted volunteers in my own denomination who come from churches around the country to help those in need every time there is a natural disaster. The Southern Baptist Convention is the country's third-largest disaster relief operation.[42] And it is not alone. Christian agencies provide trillions of dollars' worth of crucial social services around the nation. That was why President George W. Bush rightly saw religious institutions as "the armies of compassion."[43] This is one reason it is mystifying that every year some far-left group attempts to penalize these institutions by removing their tax-exempt status.

A local church, working with other local churches, has opportunities to do what government cannot do and help renew what politics cannot renew. I think of the community in suburban Nashville where we lived for almost a decade. In our town of Mt. Juliet, churches across the religious and political divide united to alleviate human needs. This nonprofit, founded by my former pastor Daryl Crouch, has four priorities: to see everyone fed, to see everyone free of addiction, to see everyone safe, and to see every student ready for life.[44] What excites me is that this kind of effort is being duplicated in communities across the country. Everywhere you see human need, you don't have to squint to see Christians rolling up their sleeves.

But imagine if every local church had the vision to see itself as a beacon of both spiritual and physical hope, uniting with other Christians where they can, to renew their cities. This is also part of what Jeremiah intended with his admonition to the people of God to "seek the welfare of the city" (Jeremiah 29:7, ESV). Both participating in local church ministry and engaging in politics and policy making are forms of loving our neighbors. They are not mutually exclusive.

Ultimately, however, regardless of how the next election goes or whether our favorite politician lives up to his or her promises, the Church's mission remains the same.

CHAPTER 7

The War on the Family

> The family is the cornerstone of our society. More than any other force it shapes the attitude, the hopes, the ambitions, and the values of the child. And when the family collapses it is the children that are usually damaged. When it happens on a massive scale the community itself is crippled.
>
> So, unless we work to strengthen the family, to create conditions under which most parents will stay together—all the rest: schools, and playgrounds, and public assistance, and private concern, will never be enough to cut completely the circle of despair and deprivation.[1]
>
> —*Lyndon B. Johnson*

IN THE SPRING OF 1965, A LITTLE-KNOWN ASSISTANT SECRETARY OF labor, policy, planning, and research in the administration of Lyndon B. Johnson issued an explosive report that would prove to be both controversial in the moment and unquestionably right half a century later. Congress had just passed and Johnson had just signed the Civil Rights Act of 1964, a necessary response to the ugly racial discrimination and segregation in the United States. Daniel Patrick Moynihan's report was meant to be a follow-up to that important step in closing the gap between America's promise and America's reality. In his view, an important step in continuing America's progress was to address the family, not only in Black communities but across racial and economic lines. The report, which can be accessed on the Department of Labor website,[2] became a lightning rod. The Left, led by radical feminists and others, decried his emphasis on the two-parent family. Moynihan, who later became a US senator, was hung out to dry by the White House, with Johnson quietly abandoning the ideas in the report after delivering a speech in favor of it when it was first released.[3]

Six decades later, Moynihan's conclusion that the family is the central building block of a flourishing society has, sadly, been proven right. At the time, 24 percent of Black children were born to single mothers compared to 3 percent of white children, a stunning disparity owed to, at the time, the bitter fruit of slavery and Jim Crow, which had broken up Black families. Moynihan was fully supportive of civil rights and the social safety net but warned of dire consequences if those measures did not incentivize marriage and family formation. He was ignored, and all these years later, after much social engineering, the sexual revolution, and the government's economic disincentive of stable families, the numbers are far worse: 62 percent of Black children and 23 percent of white children live with only one parent.[4]

Today, conversations about the shape of marriage and the priority of the family are often lumped together under a convenient label of "culture wars" by critics urging compromise, and conservatives who have something to say about these things—or worse, something to do about them—are labeled "culture warriors." Often it is Christians trying to arrest change who are labeled as the aggressors, backward and weird and retrograde, while the Left, which made the change in the first place, is the enlightened, fair-minded, justice-oriented cohort. Even some evangelical leaders dismiss fighting for families as mere "culture wars."[5]

The truth is that we are engaged in a fight for what is true and good and beautiful, whether we realize it or not. Some political skirmishes are stupid, but championing the family is not one of them. It's serious, and it matters.

Kevin DeYoung, a pastor, scholar, and author, reminded us of the necessity of the fight:

> I understand the aversion to the language of culture war. It has only negative connotations to most people. And yet, the reality of the thing itself cannot be avoided. The Lord is a warrior, right? (Exodus 15:3). The opposite of culture war is not culture peace but culture capitulation. There is a conflagration of competing visions in this country, and, with apologies to Billy Joel, we didn't start the fire. The cultural upheaval of the last 50 years has not been led by conservative Christians intent on reshaping America. So why is "culture warrior" an epithet only dished out to the right?[6]

He's exactly right. It is the Left that has waged the long and sustained war against the family, the consequences of which continue to be devastating for the flourishing of our communities and the health of the nation. If we don't catechize our kids, an episode of *Modern Family* will. It's notable that our efforts to preserve truths that have been held for much of human history is seen as being a "culture war" but radical ideas that show up in TV shows like that are seen as normal. The reality is that we should stand up for things not because they've lasted but because they're right. New ideas are good only if they're good. This is where Christianity's insistence on truth comes in; we have to insist, in our modern, nihilistic era, that we can find the truth together. God made a creation full of meaning, ready to be discerned by his creations. The value of family is one of the things that can be discerned.

In a perceptive three-part essay entitled "The Long War Against the Family," the Catholic theologian Ryan N. S. Topping outlined three areas in which progressive cultural elites have waged war on the family in the past century and a half:

> (1) the assertion that marriage makes men and women less free; (2) the assumption that children are a burden; and (3) the insistence

> that sexual differentiation is a fiction. . . . The first is the Marxist contribution; the second is the eugenicist; the third is the fruit of recent gender theorists.[7]

According to Topping, socialism's architects, Karl Marx and Friedrich Engels, viewed marriage not as the creational good designed by God for human flourishing but as a consequence of the human desire to conquer, dominate, and pass on property and wealth.[8]

Why Family Matters to Society

> **This mission—to be the first and vital cell of society—the family has received from God.**
>
> —*Pope Paul VI*[9]

Topping continued, "Whatever the defects of his theory, Engels was prescient at least about its ramifications: as socialism advances, family recedes. As the tasks of raising children, caring for the old, and making money are absorbed by the state, fewer and fewer reasons will remain for a man and woman to form a lasting bond." According to Engels, in such a world, "the single family ceases to be the economic unit of society," replaced by thin quasi-relationships and "the gradual growth of unconstrained sexual intercourse."

Thankfully, Marx and Engels's socialist hellscape never took hold in America, though conservatives would argue that the growth of government leans that way. Capitalism and free markets are alive and well here. However, Marx and Engels's vision of a kind of socializing family order has, we must acknowledge, become the elite consensus and growing norm in American society.

Topping is also right that progressives have targeted children as obstacles to human flourishing. This, of course, is essential for the dream of "unfettered sexual access" required by socialism's aims. Since the advent of birth control, when sexual intimacy became detached from procreation, children have been increasingly viewed in the West as a burden. Faithful Christians disagree on the prudence of birth control usage, and there is not room in these pages to engage in that ethical debate. The more insidious regime of abortion on demand, pioneered with wicked efficiency in the United States by the eugenicist Margaret Sanger, has even further stigmatized children while simultaneously glamorizing sexual expression. Not only has this resulted in the wanton killing of over 63 million unborn children in the United States,[10] it has also given men a convenient escape from the social responsibility of their sexual exploits. Pete Buttigieg, a former mayor of South Bend, Indiana, and Biden administration official, essentially said in a 2024 fundraising call for the Kamala Harris campaign that access to abortion makes men more free.[11]

Freedom, of course, is defined as the opportunity not to serve one's offspring but to serve oneself, to view women not as equal partners in the joy of raising a child but as temporary vessels for sexual self-gratification. This is not progress but regress. Even after the Supreme Court rightfully overturned *Roe v. Wade* and allowed the states to regulate abortion, there is still a significant majority of Americans who support the practice. Topping lamented that this reality "has been so overwhelmingly successful that great effort will be required to awaken the imaginations of the young to a world where children are not viewed as a social and economic burden. What atonement will be required for the holocaust of our little ones is difficult to imagine."[12]

Last, but perhaps most relevant to the current moment, the progressive war on the family has sought to blur the lines between men and women. Not only have progressives argued that there is nothing that distinguishes a man from a woman; now they argue that gender itself is a social construct and fluid and can be easily changed. This, too, is a war on the family. "If the ideology of gender is accepted, not only locker rooms will be undone; so will the family,"[13] Topping asserted. This has a devastating impact on the family. Consider Pope Benedict XVI's warning: "But if there is no pre-ordained duality of man and woman in creation, then neither is the family any longer a reality established by creation. Likewise, the child has lost the place he had occupied hitherto and the dignity pertaining to him."[14] Today we are seeing the impact of this philosophy on children, as they have become pawns in an Orwellian rejection of reality, subject to permanent disfigurement, sanctioned and often encouraged by the state.[15] What's more, we are told to accept ideas that ten years ago would have seemed absurd, such as the notion that men can get pregnant. In her confirmation hearings, Supreme Court Justice Ketanji Brown Jackson could not answer the simple question "What is a woman?" without upsetting the progressive elites who have decreed that what we know from creation and what we understand from science is simply not true.[16]

What's more, the slippery-slope arguments social conservatives made decades ago, often mocked by late-night hosts as ridiculous, have mostly come true. Consider this warning against redefining marriage in the legal system made by former Pennsylvania senator and presidential candidate Rick Santorum in 2008:

> Once you get away from the model of "what we know is best" and you get into the other options, from my perspective, there's no stopping it . . . you devalue what you want to value, which is a man and woman in marriage with a child or children. And when you devalue that, you get less of it. When you get less of it, society as a whole suffers.[17]

Or this prediction by the Southern Baptist ethicists Richard Land and Barrett Duke in 2001:

> If marriage is thus redefined, that already damaged institution will be further weakened, perhaps fatally. . . . As the meaning and value of marriage deteriorates, people see less need for marriage. After all, if marriage means anything, then it means nothing. In Norway, for example, where marriage is increasingly rare, couples are choosing simply to cohabitate rather than marry, even persisting in this attitude when children enter the relationship. Thus illegitimacy, with all its concomitant demonstrated disadvantages to children, is soaring.
>
> In addition, if our nation were to allow homosexual marriage, the nation's children would be overwhelmed with messages attempting to indoctrinate them about the legitimacy of same-sex marriage and affirming the normality of homosexuality. Their textbooks would be changed to show homosexual couples living "normal" lifestyles in the same way that heterosexual couples do. The very language used to refer to marriage would be changed. One could no longer refer to husbands and wives; children would be taught to think in sexless terms, like "significant other" or "life partner."[18]

These predictions have almost all come true. Redefining marriage, not merely through *Obergefell v. Hodges*, which legalized same-sex marriage, but also through no-fault divorce, perverse incentives in the tax code, the ubiquitous availability of pornography, and the increasing sexualizing of our culture, has resulted in plummeting marriage rates. Consider that a record 25 percent of American adults forty years of age and older have never married, up 5 percent from 2010, five years after the decision in *Obergefell v. Hodges* and up 19 percent from 1980.[19] Two-thirds of Americans report feeling no pressure to get married.[20] Over the last fifty years, the marriage rate has dropped by 60 percent.[21] This has led to a historic drop in fertility; Americans are having way fewer children than ever before.[22] *New York Times* columnist Ross Douthat, on the eve of *Obergefell*, wrote presciently:

> But with all that being said, there *is* something strange, even deeply strange, about a discussion of social and legal change in which it's never acknowledged that for all the hard-to-quantify elements in their vision, social conservatives do have a pretty decent predictive track record, including in many cases where their fears were dismissed as wild and apocalyptic, their projections as sky-is-falling nonsense, their theories of how society and human nature works as evidence-free fantasies.[23]

Sadly, the sky-is-falling predictions not only came true but were, in hindsight, understated. Consider that "If you don't want a gay marriage, don't get one" has grown into the silly notions that "trans women are women," "men can get pregnant," and the promotion of polyamory by cultural voices.[24] What's more, rather than a libertarian push for freedom, the movement against the family has become militantly aggressive, demanding allegiance in annual religious-like rituals such as Pride Month, and has aggressively demanded, under threat of government fiat, the acceptance of these new norms among those that the centuries-old religious institutions most deeply oppose.[25]

Thankfully, the Supreme Court has enshrined significant religious liberty safeguards into law, protecting religious institutions' right to believe, hire, and conduct their business according to their deeply held beliefs. But the damage to the country has already been done.

Why Should Christians Care What the Nation Thinks About the Family?

So what? many people ask about the evolving definitions of marriage and family in the wider American culture. Shouldn't Christians expect an increasingly pluralistic culture to have divergent views? Shouldn't believers expect the unbelieving world to have views that are counter to Christian faith and practice?

These questions might best be answered with a little history lesson. In 1992, Vice President Dan Quayle offended elite sensibilities when he offered this commentary on the tendency for pop culture to promote alternate family lifestyles:

> Failing to support children one has fathered is wrong. We must be unequivocal about this.
>
> It doesn't help matters when prime-time TV has Murphy Brown, a character who supposedly epitomizes today's intelligent, highly paid professional woman, mocking the importance of fathers by bearing a child alone and calling it just another lifestyle choice.[26]

Quayle's remarks were widely condemned at the time: by the media, by Hollywood, and by many politicians. But an interesting thing happened after the uproar. A year later, *The Atlantic*, not exactly a bastion of social conservative ideas, admitted that, well, maybe Quayle had been right; perhaps it's not ideal for children to grow up without a mother or a father. As Barbara Dafoe Whitehead noted:

> Children in single-parent families are six times as likely to be poor. They are also likely to stay poor longer. Twenty-two percent of children in one-parent families will experience poverty during childhood for seven years or more, as compared with only two percent of children in two parent families.[27]

Twenty years later, *The Washington Post*, again not a forum for the promotion of socially conservative thought, also admitted, that, welp, maybe that former vice president of the United States wasn't such a retrograde loser after all. Lamenting the decline of two-parent households, the columnist wrote:

> Those who live with their biological parents do better in school and are less likely to get pregnant or arrested. They have lower rates of suicide, achieve higher levels of education and earn more as adults. Meanwhile, children who spend time in single-parent families are more likely to misbehave, get sick, drop out of high school and be unemployed.[28]

Three and a half decades later, Quayle's concerns seem almost prophetic. In her book *The Two-Parent Privilege: How Americans Stopped Getting Married and Started Falling Behind*, the Brookings Institution scholar Melissa S. Kearney wrote soberly about the breakdown of the family in America:

> More than one in five children living in the U.S. today live in a home with an unpartnered mother, meaning a mother who is neither married nor cohabitating. A majority of these households do not include another adult, such as a grandparent or other relative. . . . U.S. children are more likely to live with only their mother than children around the world are.[29]

She continued:

> Over the past 40-plus years, American society has engaged in a vast experiment of reshaping the most fundamental of social institutions—the family—and the resulting generations of data tell us in no uncertain terms how that has played out for children. The data present some uncomfortable realities: . . . Two parent

> families are beneficial for children. . . . Places that have two parent families have higher rates of upward mobility.[30]

In a similar book entitled *Get Married: Why Americans Must Defy the Elites, Forge Strong Families, and Save Civilization*, University of Virginia sociologist Brad Wilcox concurred. According to his work, which synthesized the best research, "the best community predictor of poor children remaining stuck in poverty as adults was the share of kids in their communities living in a single-parent family. Not income inequality. Not race. Not school quality. Family structure was the biggest factor in predicting poor kids' odds of realizing the American Dream in communities across the country."[31] Kearney asserted that "marriage is the most reliable institution for delivering in high level of resources and long-term stability to children. There is not currently a robust, widespread alternative to marriage in U.S. society."[32]

There's no disputing the data; children flourish best in families with a mother and a father who have committed to each other for life. They are less likely to end up in prison, less likely to end up in poverty, more likely to attend college. Studies even show that neighborhoods that have a majority of two-parent families are safer and freer from crime.[33] And contrary to the narrative often portrayed on the screen, men and women who are married earn more money and are much happier than those who are not.[34] Writer Chris Bullivant and Brad Wilcox wrote, "The happiest, healthiest, and most financially secure Americans are married."[35]

This is why fighting the Left's attempts to redefine the family, to redefine gender, can't be dismissed as "culture wars"; it's a fight for the soul of the nation, it's a fight for what makes communities and civilizations thrive. It's a fight for justice. It's simple: To renew America's promise, we must renew American families. If you care at all about freedom and flourishing, you can't ignore the family. Yes, this culture war is a deeply patriotic one.

What Can Christians Do?

The good news is that Christians are in a position to help renew American families and thus help restore American society. To begin with, Christians hold the truth about the way God has ordered the world to flourish best. The Anglican scholar N. T. Wright reminded us that marriage between a man and a woman for life is at the heart of the biblical story: "The biblical picture of man and woman together in marriage is not something about which we can say, 'Oh well, they had some funny ideas back then. We know better now.' The biblical view of marriage is part of the larger whole of new creation."[36]

In a world of confusion and sexual anarchy, Christianity must not shrink back from declaring what is good, even if it costs us social capital. We should do this not out of self-righteousness but because we believe—and we can see with our own eyes—that the way God has ordered the world works best for human flourishing.

Of course, we must do this with compassion and grace toward those who disagree. As 1 Peter 3:15–16 reminds us, we are to "give a defense to anyone who asks" yet respond with "gentleness and reverence." Some people who bear witness to the goodness and beauty of marriage do it out of contention or spite, hatred and malice. Some do it to score cheap political points in an election year. Some who do it are hypocritical, not caring for their own families nor tending to their own virtue while lambasting that of others.

It's unhelpful, for instance, when the party of virtue—my preferred party, the GOP—champions as heroes men and women with questionable virtue who have little concern for their own family formation, much less that of the nation's families. There is a kind of raw "bar stool conservatism" that celebrates hypermasculine sexual prowess. We won't solve the family crisis by replacing Murphy Brown with Andrew Tate.

Still, we should not let poor messengers and social pressures deter us from pointing our friends and neighbors toward that which is good and from championing social policies that will have an impact on our communities and our country.

In recent years, many evangelical churches and pastors have been cowed into silence regarding marriage and family issues by contrarian voices who urge the Church to "stop idolizing marriage,"[37] as if the average church leader talks about it too much. The narrative is that evangelical churches put too much emphasis on marriage and family life at the exclusion of the pursuit of an authentic relationship with God—as if this is a binary choice. Or, the charge goes, churches are hurting singles by tending to the health of married couples.

While we shouldn't shame singles or make them feel unwanted, we should recognize that the body of Christ benefits from healthy marriages and healthy families. And can we actually look out at the wreckage in the world, the significant decline in stable marriages, and say we are talking about this topic too much? On the contrary, there are crumbling families in our communities who desperately need the hope and help that only Christianity can provide. Membership in a church community is not a magic elixir for marriage. Christians get divorced, too. But studies consistently show that couples who regularly attend church are 30 to 50 percent less likely to be divorced.[38]

The best churches are proactive in nurturing healthy family life, with marriage seminars and retreats, parenting classes, and free or low-cost counseling. One large church in Tallahassee, Florida, pairs older married couples in the church with younger ones for coaching, support, and friendship. Another church I know pays for babysitting for date nights for busy couples. There are still others that offer robust marriage and family intervention classes, helping those in their congregations who are on the brink of collapse.

The truth is that for families to thrive, it takes a community, and there is not a better community than the family of God. We cannot live out this mission alone, in isolation. We need the encouragement, help, and strength of our brothers and sisters in Christ.

But Christians can help marriage even outside their own communities. If healthy marriages are a leading indicator of community health, if social ills are downstream from broken families, is not helping to bring relief to the struggling households in our community a social justice issue? Imagine if every church were to adopt the hurting families in its community by offering marriage counseling or retreats. Imagine if struggling moms and dads could find help in building their parenting skills. What if single parents could find surrogate fathers and mothers?

Christians have two messages that seem to be competing but really are not: There is a way in which God has ordered the world that is best for human flourishing, and hope, forgiveness, and grace are found in the Gospel of Jesus Christ. The Church must not flinch from both declaring what is true and good and beautiful and offering to broken families, broken communities, and a broken world Christianity's unique message of renewal and redemption.

One ministry is working hard to do just that by pairing churches with struggling families in its zip code. Communio began with a pilot program in the city of Jacksonville, Florida. It paired churches with struggling families, and as a result the divorce rate in that city fell by 24 percent.[39] Now it is doing the same thing nationwide.

God's people can be the family many lonely people in our communities are missing, a way station for those who've suffered from divorce, for single moms struggling to raise their children, for young children who need love and care and direction. The church doors must swing wide open for those whom theologian Russell Moore calls refugees of the sexual revolution.[40] There are many, many families who stumble into church bearing the scars of failed marriages who will hear the Gospel's promise of a renewed life and a rebuilding of "the years that the swarming locust has eaten" (Joel 2:25, ESV). Pastors and church staff, let's be as bold when proclaiming this grace as we are when declaring the beauty of God's original design for marriage and family.

Beyond our communities, we might also begin to advocate for policies that will encourage, rather than discourage, healthy family formation. In his book *Family Unfriendly: How Our Culture Made Raising Kids Much Harder than It Needs to Be*, Timothy P. Carney lamented the way tax policies, economic realities, zoning laws, the education system, and a host of other factors have made it harder to raise children. Faithful Christians will disagree on the best public policy, but we should be open to ideas that nurture this essential building block, including but not limited to economic relief. I'm a committed free-market capitalist, but I am open to changes in the tax code that will sustain family life. For instance, I see no reason why a significantly expanded child tax credit should not be considered, even if it meant that mothers would have to work one less side job, fathers could eschew their side hustle, or blue-collar parents could take off a weekend shift. Other people have suggested making childbirth free. Some states have even started to begin Medicaid benefits at the time of conception. State and federal governments should also remove so-called marriage penalties that penalize low-income recipients of government aid for getting married.

In the long run, the short-term economic impact of family-building policies will be offset by the reduction in social costs. Of course, the government can do only so much to nurture healthy family life, but it can incentivize what we know to be good and true and beautiful. Most renewal of the American family will come not in courtrooms and boardrooms but in living rooms and lunch rooms.

Signs of Hope

We are seeing signs of hope. In recent years, the divorce rate has plummeted, reaching an almost fifty-year low.[41] Fewer people are getting married and they are getting married later in life, but their marriages are enduring longer than in previous generations. Wendy Wang of the Institute for Family Studies wrote that "this is great news for Americans who are married. It means that their marriages will likely be more stable, and their children will be more likely to grow up with two married parents, which provides them the best chance for success later in life."[42]

We are also seeing a bit of a vibe shift in the broader culture when it comes to the family. Support for same-sex marriage has dropped somewhat,[43] while many people are resisting radical gender ideology. What's more, the #MeToo movement has spurred a questioning of the orthodoxy of the sexual revolution. Louise Perry, a British journalist who describes herself as a "nonreligious feminist," published a widely read book, *The Case Against the Sexual Revolution*, in which she essentially wondered if consent is the best sexual ethic for human flourishing. Christine Emba, in a *Washington Post* column entitled "Let's Rethink Sex," wondered if "we might pursue the theory that sex possibly has a deeper significance than just recreation."[44] Even a book quoted earlier in this chapter, *The Two-Parent Privilege*, was written by an author with the left-leaning Brookings Institution.

This should give faithful Christians hope that many people are confronting the reality of God's natural law: the order and purpose he has built into the universe and the human experience. This is why we shouldn't be cowed into silence by the Left or embarrassed to speak about marriage and family. This is a real felt need in our nation and our communities. We must make winsome and compassionate arguments for the goodness of marriage and child bearing, step into the breach where families are broken, and advocate for policies that will help buoy households. And we should courageously model family life in our own homes.

Family by family, we can help heal the country by advocating for family-friendly policies, by rebuilding families through our churches, and by resisting the culture of intentional childlessness by having children of our own.

America is currently enduring a significant fertility crisis. According to the Centers for Disease Control and Prevention, Americans had 3 percent fewer children in 2022 than the year prior. It was the second consecutive year of decline. The birth rate of 1.6 children per woman is about half of what the country needs to sustain itself long term. This is a worldwide crisis, and America is doing better than many nations. Still, this demographic decline spells trouble for the country. Soaring entitlement programs, such as Social Security and Medicare, already on an unsustainable financial path, will become nearly impossible to fund. The fertility crisis will wreak havoc on our institutions. One executive of a baby formula manufacturer said he was shifting its focus to providing nourishment for those over fifty.

This crisis has been brought on by a confluence of factors: the fact that it is becoming more difficult and expensive to raise a family in the West, aggressive left-wing fearmongering about and mockery of the traditional family, and expressive individualism, which often sees children as a burden. The columnist and author Ericka Andersen wrote:

> Raising large families is harder in the West today because parents increasingly have to do it alone. The breakdown of supportive communities, the loss of cultural institutions, and the disappearance of nearby extended family deter people from having more children. Parents are lonelier than ever, which makes everything harder, and there's no immediate antidote to this problem.[45]

Yet I think the Church is uniquely equipped to counter this problem because in a healthy congregation, there are resources to help struggling families thrive. I like what pastor Kevin DeYoung wrote:

> Here's a culture war strategy conservative Christians should get behind: have more children and disciple them like crazy. Strongly consider having more children than you think you can handle. . . .
>
> In the not-too-distant future, the only couples replacing themselves in America will be religious couples. . . .
>
> Do you want to rebel against the status quo? Do you want people to ask you for a reason for the hope that is in you (1 Peter 3:15)? Tote your brood of children through Target. There is almost nothing more countercultural than having more children. And once we have those children, there is almost nothing more important than catechizing them in the faith, developing their moral framework, and preparing them to be deeply compassionate lovers of God and lovers of people and relentlessly biblical lovers of truth.[46]

It may not seem like it at first, but having children is a deeply patriotic thing to do. If we love America, we'll work as hard as we can to rebuild her most basic element: the family.

CHAPTER 8

Christians Can't Abandon Schools

Education, in a great measure, forms the moral characters of men, and morals are the basis of government.[1]

—Noah Webster

LONG BEFORE THE MEDIA SPECTACLE AND PAGEANTRY OF THE MODERN State of the Union address, America's first chief executive fulfilled the duties to update Congress annually by sending it a modest letter eight months after reluctantly accepting the role as the leader of his beloved fledgling nation. George Washington, who nine years earlier had seen the greatest fighting force in the history of the world—the British Royal Navy—retreat in defeat from Yorktown, put pen to paper and shared his hopes and concerns for the United States in 1790.

In his handwritten State of the Union address, he shared his hope that the new experiment in human government would endure and outlined some of his concerns. His was a small yet consequential list of items, unlike the mostly forgettable laundry list that presidents today drone on about in their State of the Union speeches. He urged Congress to deal with immigration, to develop a standing army and fund diplomatic efforts with foreign nations, to establish a national currency and post office and a unified measuring system. But an urgent priority was education. "There is nothing which can better deserve your patronage than the promotion of science and literature," he urged. "Knowledge is in every country the surest basis of public happiness. . . . To the security of a free constitution it contributes in various ways: By convincing those who are entrusted with the public administration that every valuable end of government is best answered by the enlightened confidence of the people."[2] He mused about whether existing institutions would suffice or if perhaps Congress should fund a national university.

His passion for education did not wane during his eight years in office. His last report to Congress contained a similar concern, this time with a more forceful call for a national university, whose goal should be "the education of our youth in the science of government. In a republic what species of knowledge can be equally important and what duty more pressing on its legislature than to patronize a plan for communicating it to those who are to be the future guardians of the liberties of the country?"[3]

Washington wouldn't see his dream of a national university fulfilled, but he shared with his fellow Founders a concern about the quality of American citizens' education. This is why several of the Founders were integral in founding America's key educational institutions.[4] It was why Abraham Lincoln issued land grants for state universities. Men such as Washington and Lincoln believed that a well-informed, well-educated citizenry would be a responsible citizenry.

Today, we might ask ourselves: What has become of that dream? More deeply, it's easy to slide into cynicism and ask: What is the use of education, given the behavior of supposed educators and the supposedly well educated?

Today, there is a lot of frustration across the political divide about the plight of modern American education.

But this concern about efficacy is increasingly accompanied by parents' concern about radicalism and niche ideologies capturing the academy. In recent years, Ivy League schools, supposedly the crème de la crème of imparting wisdom, have presented stunning scenes of their students protesting conservative speakers, harassing and attacking Jewish students, and calling for increasingly illiberal and extreme "anti-racist" policies. In the aftermath of the October 7, 2023, terrorist attacks on Israel, it was jarring to see, on American campuses, protests and encampments in favor of Hamas and Hezbollah, featuring their flags and the shouting of genocidal slogans. What's more, a left-wing ideological bubble enclosing the leadership of too many taxpayer-funded institutions has led to a significant cohort of America's young people being introduced to ideas such as Marxism, Critical Race Theory (CRT), and other anti-American, anti-Christian ideologies without any significant pushback. In perhaps the most embarrassing example, in May 2024, several college presidents were summoned before Congress and failed to condemn the egregious acts of antisemitism taking place on their campuses.[5]

One professor at the University of California at Santa Barbara wrote, "On one-party campuses, radical-left faculty have established a political orthodoxy that student mobs enforce, and the political culture of the nation is poisoned as those students take home with them their professors' habit of seeing opinions that differ from theirs as an evil not to be tolerated." He asserted that that regression has led to a diminishing of the population's understanding of American civics and values, what he calls "a nationwide reversion to civic illiteracy."[6]

The situation of K–12 education has also generated concern. The frustration of many parents had been brewing for a while, but covid shutdowns exacerbated and highlighted the decline of some of America's public schools. Not only were many shut down for an irrationally long time against the best scientific wisdom around the world, but parents got an up-close look at the ideologies some of the schools were teaching. Marxism, CRT, and LGBT propaganda have often been prioritized while reading and math scores and basic civics have plummeted.

Former Attorney General William Barr, in a 2021 speech, warned that this is a growing threat to American liberty and prosperity:

> We are rapidly approaching the point—if we have not already reached the point—at which the heavy-handed enforcement of secular-progressive orthodoxy through government-run schools is totally incompatible with traditional Christianity and other major religious traditions in our country. In light of this development, we must confront the reality that it may no longer be fair, practical, or even constitutional to provide publicly funded education solely through the vehicle of state-operated schools.
>
> In many places in the country, the state of our public schools is becoming an absurdity that can scarcely be believed. While an astonishing number of public schools fail to produce students proficient in basic reading and math, they spare no effort or expense in their drive to instill a radical secular belief system that would have been unimaginable to Americans even 20 years ago.[7]

In many school districts, LGBT curriculum is mandated, and in many others, teachers are forbidden to inform parents when their children are transitioning genders. Some more left-leaning states even offer themselves as "sanctuary states" where children, unbeknown to their parents, can get state-sponsored gender transition surgery. Some conservative states have started to push back, banning these surgeries, regulating the sex education curriculum for appropriate ages, and requiring teachers to inform parents when their children are considering a gender transition.

Beyond the cultural flash points, there is a growing concern that America is not fulfilling the Founders' desire to provide children with a quality education in the metrics that matter: math, science, reading, civics, and other important subjects.

I want to make clear that these issues are not a problem in every school district across America, and in the ones where they do exist, Christians should determine just how significant the problem is. I don't want to impugn every public school in this country nor to overlook the many thousands of faithful, hardworking teachers and school administrators who wake up every day and see it as their calling to serve children well. This includes thousands of Christians who serve their students selflessly.

It's also important to note that there are many fine colleges, both public and private, that prioritize learning, scholarship, and academic freedom. Yet we cannot ignore the obvious fact that renewing the American experiment will involve renewing American education. It's time for American patriots to roll up their sleeves and do the hard work of reforming existing institutions and creating new, vibrant ones that can fulfill the original mission of education. While we should applaud the growing school choice movement and new and refreshing educational alternatives, as a big-picture matter we do have to aspire to renewing America's entire school system.

You're Not Crazy: Schools Really Have Changed

What's at stake in education is a battle of ideas. Normal Christian ideas that describe our political history have become anathema in our secular culture. One journalist hinted darkly at the promised takeover of Christian nationalists in education. What example did he cite? A curriculum for Florida teachers that allows them to teach students that the American Founders were "steeped in the Judeo-Christian tradition" and explain that, in ancient history, "Christianity challenged the notion that religion should be subservient to the goals of the state," an understanding that was eventually reflected in America's founding. Horror of horrors! The journalist continued, "Other slides in the teacher training claim, without any citations, that the basis of law in the United States is the Ten Commandments ('Decalogue') and that the phrase 'all men are created equal' is derived from the biblical concept that 'man is made in the image of God.'"[8]

Without any citations! Will the Christian fascism never stop?

Meanwhile, many Marxist assumptions have been baked into America's school curricula without challenge. Marxism's long, slow march through our institutions didn't begin with Hamas signs on campuses and rainbow flags in public schools but with a set of ideas: LGBT, Marxism, and CRT. I discussed the war on the family in the previous chapter, so I won't belabor that point. Marxism, the political theory of Karl Marx that eventually consigned over 40 million people to death in Communist countries around the world, is fundamentally at odds with the American experiment.

We shouldn't be naive. Marxism isn't about getting better health care, though its advocates may disguise their aims under the least objectionable aspects of their theory. Marxist true believers advocate violent revolution by the lower classes against the ruling classes and empower the state to create a utopia, eliminating individual liberty, private property, and religion. They seek equality of outcome versus equality of opportunity, trampling on the creational reality of the uniqueness of the individual. Some of these ideas sound good on paper, but when put into practice, they result in human misery. Ben Shapiro was right when he described Marx's vision:

> Marx offered a transformative vision of humanity, a system of meaning and purpose. He acknowledged that suffering would follow from his recommended policies but suggested that such suffering would in the end result in a Messianic age of man, in which collective reason would unify with individual meaning.

> Marx's specter would indeed come to dominate the world, looming astride civilization like a vengeful anti-deity. His philosophy would damn millions to slavery—and haunt the openness and freedom of the post Enlightenment world with the specter of glorious utopianism.[9]

The twentieth century showed us the failure of Marxism. In countries where it was put into place, those who resist—as we saw in the former Soviet Union and see in today's Communist China—are consigned to the margins; they risk being sent to prison or a labor camp or even being executed by the state. Marxism, while thankfully not taking hold in America in a meaningful way, still has naive adherents on the far left who wish to see the death of American freedom, capitalism, and Christianity.

Marxism is more than just an economic proposal; it's a worldview with deep implications about the purpose of man. Writing as the Soviet Union's dominance in Europe was collapsing, Chuck Colson contrasted Marxism to Christianity:

> Philosophically, Marxism is certainly a religion. It offers a comprehensive explanation of reality and claims to put adherents in touch with higher powers—namely, the inexorable laws of history. Its eschatology is millennial. At the end of the class struggle against capitalism lies the classless society where exploiters are banished, the state withers away, and man's natural goodness flows forth unobstructed. The laws of history will bring justice to the oppressed and wipe away every tear. It's a system that an atheist can put his faith in.[10]

Today, it is Marxism's cultural cousin, critical theory, that is more in vogue. A complex system that has been floating around academia for decades, this idea is similarly destructive. I highly recommend

Critical Dilemma: The Rise of Critical Theories and Social Justice Ideology—Implications for the Church and Society by Neil Shenvi and Pat Sawyer, which carefully analyzes critical theory and its incompatibility with both Christianity and the American experiment. They summarize the four basic teachings of contemporary critical theory like this:

1. THE SOCIAL BINARY: A society is divided into categories of oppressed and oppressor based on race, class, gender, sexuality, physical ability, age, and other characteristics.

2. HEGEMONIC POWER: The dominant group maintains power by imposing its ideology on everyone else.

3. LIVED EXPERIENCE: Lived experience by the oppressor class becomes a form of truth that is irrefutable.

4. SOCIAL JUSTICE: A perverted sense of justice is created in which the goal should be the never-ending struggle to liberate the oppressor class.[11]

While we can see some connections to Christian cosmology here, it's also obvious that these categories sidestep transcendent ingredients of a worldview, such as "objective truth" and "good and evil." To have power is to be inherently corrupt, inherently part of the "oppressor class." The more "oppressed class" identity markers a person has, as determined by the social binary scale of intersectionality, the more righteous that person is deemed to be. What this logic does is transform a noble instinct to defend the weak into a valorization of anything "weak" people do. Their sins are clearly just the result of oppression. If you're in an oppressed class, you have no moral agency, and no one should blame you for rebelling against an unjust system, no matter your chosen manner of resistance.

Meanwhile, "lived experience" as a category replaces objective truth. Everyone has their own truth, which should not be challenged by others. When a teacher, for instance, explains something true, she is really just transferring her hegemonic ideas onto the uncolonized minds of the young. As you can see, this idea, within reason, could create in a teacher humility about their cultural blind spots, but taken to its logical conclusion, it undermines the idea of leadership and teaching entirely.

Variations of this kind of teaching on college campuses and in high school classrooms have helped foment the kind of thinking that led to the sanctioning and even glorification of violence and property destruction in the riots of 2020 and acts of violence and anti-Semitism in response to the Hamas slaughter of Israelis on October 7, 2023. Jewish people, who have actually faced oppression throughout human history, are seen by many young people as belonging to the white oppressor class.

This ideology, a perversion of actual work for justice and equality, is at odds with genuine civil rights work. It is regress, a retreat from Martin Luther King Jr.'s vision of judging fellow Americans, "not . . . by the color of their skin but by the content of their character."[12]

Two scholars wrote, "The Marxist narrative that all of society for all of history has been divided into categories of the oppressed and their oppressors is played over and over. The government, and all society, the purveyors of CRT say, must thus treat people not as individuals with liberties, but as categories that deserve special treatment and benefits as members of these categories."[13] It renders minority groups helpless and without agency and assigns fixed character traits based on immutable characteristics such as skin color.

As mentioned in an earlier chapter, American Christians shouldn't be intentionally blind to the egregious injustices in American history and the ways in which sin can insert itself into laws and systems and prey on the vulnerable. Chattel slavery and Jim Crow were both individual acts of evil and systems that commodified and hurt Black people. Though the United States has made tremendous progress, it is not a country free of injustice.

However, it is unhealthy to see everything through the distorted lens of Critical Race Theory and to divide the world into the categories of oppressors and the oppressed. We should resist the temptation to create more categories of human beings who are to be given special exemptions and more categories of human beings whom we deem irredeemable based on their ethnicity or social location. Instead, we should see all humans the way God sees them, as bearers of his image who are deserving of respect and dignity,[14] and we should continue to work for an America that lives up to its founding values.

A small but vocal group of folks on the right who consider themselves the "dissident right" against "the regime" feel that the only effective response to left-wing Marxism and CRT is to develop a version of their own. If these are the new rules, some wonder, why not play by them? I agree with the conservative commentator Erick-Wood's Erickson, who rejected this approach:

> Just as the left interprets that Marxist power dynamic through an intersectional lens, [the Marxist Right] is doing the same thing in reverse. The left sees the non-white, non-heterosexual, non-Christian class as the one with the moral authority because it is the chief victim of the oppressor class of conservatives. [The Marxist Right] sees the white, heterosexual, Christian class as the one with moral authority because it is the chief victim of the oppressor class of progressives. In both, the oppressed must rise to power and suppress their oppressor for peace in our time.[15]

I have a better idea: Instead of embracing the logic of Marxism and fighting the victimhood mindset by saying that we are the *true* victims, why not combat bad ideas with better ideas and work to reinvigorate our institutions by turning them back toward their original mission?

Renewing K–12 Education

Fortunately, many of our fellow citizens are freshly awakening to the need for reform and renewal. And it's not just conservatives who see this need. In the last few years, even many independents and democrats have come to want education reform.

What a great opportunity to both secure a better future for our own children and to obey the Great Commandment to love our neighbors as ourselves (Matthew 22:39) and "seek the welfare of the city" (Jeremiah 29:7, ESV).

Consider these startling numbers:

- Two-thirds of students who cannot read proficiently by the end of fourth grade will end up in jail or on public assistance.
- 75 percent of state prison inmates did not graduate from high school.
- 50 percent of adults with low literacy do not have a job.[16]

Education matters, both for our own children and for the children in our communities. And the solutions are not one size fits all. Faithful Christians often disagree on the best educational options for their children. In our season of life, we've prayerfully and sacrificially decided to enroll our children in a private Christian school. In the past, we've homeschooled, we've had our kids in public school, and we've utilized charter schools.

I don't believe in a one-size-fits-all option for kids. At times, even within a family, there are options that will work for some kids that won't for other kids. But let's face it, for many, perhaps most, Americans, there are not many choices beyond their local public school, and we should, as a rule of thumb, try to engage in our communities, not withdraw from them.

Still, Christians should be active, not passive, in their communities and should work to renew education. Even those who do not enroll their children in the local public school should care about what is being taught there. Those kids are our neighbors and future husbands and fathers, wives and mothers, business and community leaders. Every community needs convictional, compassionate Christians helping to shape their schools' policies and curricula. We cannot simply close our shutters and ignore what is going on. And we shouldn't be cowed by critics who say that any effort on this front is "culture war."

There are real opportunities for local churches to shape their local public schools with outreach and care. I'm encouraged by the way many churches help equip students with materials, food, and even mentoring. I've been surprised by how welcoming public school principals are to Christian ministry, whether it's student-led Bible clubs, fellowships of Christian athletes, or even volunteer reading and tutoring programs.

In Memphis, one church has pioneered a very successful reading program in underserved communities. Bellevue Baptist is a megachurch pastored by Steve Gaines, a former president of the Southern Baptist Convention. His wife, Donna Gaines, started ARISE2Read, a ministry that enlists church volunteers to help elementary students in Memphis learn to read.[17] Now the denomination has taken the program nationwide as a model for community engagement. Many other such nonprofit volunteer efforts are taking place across the country, often led by people of faith.

Christians Can't Abandon Schools

The sober reality is that the United States essentially has an educational caste system. Education quality is too often determined by the size of one's pocketbook. Some parents have the resources to move to a good school district, enroll their kids in a charter school, homeschool them, or pay for private school. But there are many families who, due to their lack of resources, have no such opportunity. A 2016 Stanford University study revealed that:

- "The most and least socioeconomically advantaged districts have average performance levels more than four grade levels apart."
- "Average test scores of black students are, on average, roughly two grade levels lower than those of white students in the same district; the Hispanic-white difference is roughly one-and-a-half grade levels."
- "Achievement gaps are larger in districts where black and Hispanic students attend higher poverty schools than their white peers; where parents on average have high levels of educational attainment; and where large racial/ethnic gaps exist in parents' educational attainment."[18]

Every child who lives in our community is a bearer of the image of the Almighty, regardless of their socioeconomic status. Not far from where many of us live, there are kids who are trapped in bad schools. I once spoke to a middle school principal who confided to me what she saw daily: "Many of my kids will experience more trauma before they walk in the door than you could even see in a movie or read about in a book."

This is why opening educational choices to more people makes so much sense. One encouraging development is the growth of the Christian, classical, and homeschooling movements around the country. Our children attend a traditional Christian school and really flourish in that institution, which is not merely a defensive measure against anti-Christian ideologies but a return to the formational and spiritual mission of education. It's a tremendous financial sacrifice that many Christian parents are making but it is worth it.

Sadly, however, not all parents can afford to make that investment. Many live from paycheck to paycheck. This is where policies such as school choice, specifically vouchers, can level the playing field. Voucher programs give all parents the option of where to have their kids attend school. It also keeps the state one degree away from restricting the deeply held beliefs of private religious schools while avoiding the mistake of favoring one religion over another. Teachers' unions and other left-leaning interest groups oppose vouchers because they say that they come at the expense of public schools, but that's not true. States that invest in school vouchers still invest heavily in public schools, but they recognize that by allowing students, regardless of income, the option to attend better schools, they will help their population in the long run.

A majority of Americans seem to agree. Seventy-one percent of Americans support school vouchers, including 66 percent of Democrats and 80 percent of Republicans.[19] Former Secretary of State Condoleezza Rice was right when she said that school choice is a matter of fairness:

> If you're really wealthy, you will send your kids to private school. So who's stuck in failing neighborhood schools? Poor kids. A lot of them minority kids. . . .
>
> How can you say you're for civil rights, how can you say you're for the poor when you're condemning those children to not being able to read? By the time they're in third grade, they're never going to read.[20]

What's even more hypocritical is that many public officials who most vociferously oppose school choice send their kids to private schools.

Aside from helping their local public schools, I believe that more churches should consider starting private schools or financially supporting the Christian schools in their communities as part of their local mission outreach. The prestigious private schools with million-dollar endowments often get the most press, but many private schools operate on a shoestring budget with underpaid but highly qualified teachers.

Imagine, too, if wealthy conservative political donors, who don't flinch from writing massive million-dollar checks to losing candidates, were instead to invest in quality private schools. In the long run, this might be more effective than funding a fifth-place presidential candidate. What if wealthy conservative Christians were to dream up a Bill & Melinda Gates Foundation–type enterprise that would fund conservative Christian K–12 education?

School choice isn't a magic button that will fix every problem in K–12 education, but it could help ignite the renewal of American society and, most important, might give some of the least advantaged kids more of a fighting chance. Education isn't a neutral space; as we have seen, the tenets of critical theory end up undermining the entire institution. Schools need to be reformed with an eye toward restoring belief in truth, not just power.

Renewing Higher Education

What about higher education? What can faithful Christians do? In some of our most storied institutions, it seems as though left-wing ideology is so entrenched that there is little room for diversity of opinion. I spoke with a conservative professor at an elite state school who told me that as an evangelical, he is allowed to teach, but he will never be promoted or be in a position of influence. The truth is that the Left has had ideological control of many of our college campuses since William F. Buckley Jr. first published *God and Man at Yale: The Superstitions of Academic Freedom* in the 1950s.

Yet even here, there are glimmers of hope. Consider the work, for instance, that Governor Ron DeSantis has been able to do in diversifying the boards of state institutions in Florida.[21] This has borne fruit at institutions such as the University of Florida, where former Nebraska Senator Ben Sasse was able to institute real academic diversity and provide students with a more balanced education. *The Wall Street Journal* recently called UF "the Harvard of the unwoke."[22] Similar efforts are happening in Texas and Tennessee, where Governors Greg Abbott and Bill Lee have used their power of appointment to ensure ideological diversity in publicly funded state schools.[23] This is also starting to happen in other states.

Even Harvard University, embarrassed after its now-deposed president was unable to condemn anti-Semitism in an appearance before Congress, is now asking new applicants in its supplemental essay form, "Describe a time when you strongly disagreed with someone about an idea or issue. How did you communicate or engage with this person? What did you learn from this experience?"[24]

Some conservatives have begun to wonder if a college education is worth the effort. They point to blue-collar careers that often pay really well and avoid the trap of building thousands of dollars of debt for a degree some people consider to be out of step with today's job market. I don't think every kid has to go to college. There is plenty of meaningful work in vocations that don't require an undergraduate degree, provided there is the possibility of getting vocational training.

Yet it is clear that for many, perhaps most, people, a degree is not only the ticket to a well-paying career but has the possibility to be a formative influence in the life of a young person.

Consider the economic advantages of a college degree. One recent study shows that:

- "College graduates are half as likely to be unemployed as their peers whose highest degree is a high school diploma."
- "Typical earnings for bachelor's degree holders are . . . 86 percent higher than those whose highest degree is a high school diploma."
- "87% of bachelor's degree holders report financial wellbeing, 20 percentage points higher than groups with any other level of education."
- "Median lifetime earnings are $1.2 million higher for bachelor's degree holders."[25]

But beyond the economic advantages, I think that there are real opportunities, at college age, for moral and spiritual formation. Here are some facts that might surprise you. Did you know that one of the predictors of both a healthy marriage and faithful church attendance is . . . a college degree? It's true. In their book *The Great Dechurching: Who's Leaving, Why Are They Going, and What Will It Take to Bring Them Back?*, Jim Davis and Michael Graham noted that those with college degrees were more likely to attend church on a regular basis, while those who have stopped going to church are predominantly those with only a high school diploma.[26] Ryan Burge, a sociologist who studies religion, said, "The people who are the most likely to go to church this Sunday are people with a postgraduate degree. People who are least likely are those without a high school diploma."[27] It may also surprise you that the most likely cohort to get married and stay married is—you guessed it—college graduates, according to Pew Research Center.[28]

Why is this the case? Some of it, as Brad Wilcox pointed out in his work, is due to the fact that elites often "talk left but walk right."[29] Still, I think there is something to the potential of college to be a formative influence in a young person's life. This assumes, of course, enrollment in a school with a positive learning environment.

There is a lot of opportunity for Christians to engage the next generation during an important season of their lives. I'm encouraged by Christian groups that invest in college ministry. One church-planting network, the Salt Network, intentionally plants churches near some of the biggest college campuses. These churches have met the hunger for hope and meaning with the Christian Gospel, helping students not only avoid the temptations that can befall young students but also become influential leaders on their campuses and as they move into their careers. The churches that do this work, along with the many vibrant campus ministries such as Cru, Intervarsity, Reformed University Fellowship, and Baptist Student Ministry, are doing fruitful work of evangelism and discipleship. At many of these places, in the last few years, there have been amazing, revival-like experiences. It is exciting to consider that the young people who participate in them may be tomorrow's church, business, and political leaders.

Alongside these ministries to "secular" campuses, there are many vibrant Christian colleges that teach liberal arts and humanities and train students for ministry. While remaining faithful to the Christian tradition, they are helping to rejuvenate the classic mission of education by exposing students to the broad range of thought in the Western canon while equipping them to live their varied callings in the marketplace or the ministry.

Francis Schaeffer wrote of the important task of Christian higher education, that it gives students

> the framework of total truth, rooted in the Creator's existence and in the Bible's teaching, so that in each step of the formal learning process the student will understand what is true and what is false and why it is true or false. It is not isolating students from human knowledge. It is teaching them in a framework of the total Biblical teaching, beginning with the tremendous central thing, that in the beginning God created the heavens and the earth. It is teaching in this framework, so that on their own level, as they are introduced to all of human knowledge, they are not introduced in the midst of a vacuum, but they are taught each step along the way why what they are hearing is either true or false. That is true education.[30]

Approached the right way, a college degree can be more than mere information transfer or a credential; it can involve the formation of the whole person.[31] College students are not mere future work bots but future husbands and fathers, wives and mothers, business and community and church leaders. They are future citizens of our great country.

As a Christian educator, I'm not unaware of the challenges our institutions face, including demographic decline, economic uncertainty, and the constant legal threat of state and federal governments intent on forcing confessional institutions to yield to the orthodoxies of the sexual revolution. Our times demand both the ingenuity to create business models that will allow us to deliver quality education and the courage to remain steadfast to our mission in the face of cultural pressure. Still, I believe that what Christian institutions of higher education offer is an antidote, a recovery of the original educational mission.

In summary, those who love their country, should, as our first president did, see the importance and value of a well-educated citizenry. And faithful, patriotic followers of Christ have an opportunity to invest in America by investing in our most important academic institutions. The great eighteenth-century educator and political leader Noah Webster, a Christian, was right when he said, "In despotic governments, the people should have little or no education, except what tends to inspire them with a servile fear. Information is fatal to despotism."[32]

CHAPTER 9

Restoring "E Pluribus Unum"

> What concerns me most as a military man is not our external adversaries; it is our internal divisiveness. We are dividing into hostile tribes cheering against each other, fueled by emotion and a mutual disdain that jeopardizes our future, instead of rediscovering our common ground and finding solutions.
>
> All Americans need to recognize that our democracy is an experiment—and one that can be reversed. We all know that we're better than our current politics. Tribalism must not be allowed to destroy our experiment.[1]
>
> —*General James Mattis*

IN HIS FAREWELL ADDRESS, PRESIDENT GEORGE WASHINGTON, AMERICA'S first and greatest statesman, warned about a danger he thought threatened the American experiment, something he called a "party spirit":

> The alternate domination of one faction over another, sharpened by the spirit of revenge natural to party dissension, which in different ages and countries has perpetrated the most horrid enormities, is itself a frightful despotism. But this leads at length to a more formal and permanent despotism. The disorders and miseries which result gradually incline the minds of men to seek security and repose in the absolute power of an individual, and sooner or later the chief of some prevailing faction, more able or more fortunate than his competitors, turns this disposition to the purposes of his own elevation on the ruins of public liberty.[2]

Washington's fear was that division and tribalism would lead to despotism. It might be in the form of a tyranny of anarchy and warring tribes, or it might lead to authoritarian strongmen taking advantage of social chaos and running roughshod over our freedoms.

Imagine if the first president could visit America today. He'd likely be impressed with our innovation, with the progress we've made toward living out "All men are created equal," and our strength in defeating fascism and communism in the twentieth century. But we have to be honest: his warnings about "the party spirit" are as prescient today as they were at the dawn of the country he helped create.

The twenty-first century has not been kind to the idea of "E pluribus unum." The aggressive sexual revolution, two wars in the Middle East, the Great Recession, and a worldwide pandemic have not brought Americans together but seem to have forced them further apart. What's more, many of our political leaders have resisted opportunities to use their positions of power to appeal to America's better angels. We just endured a divisive election in which one side claimed that a vote for it was the only way to ensure that our democracy would endure and the other darkly warned that without its victory, it might be the last election. Both sentiments, of course, are irresponsible hyperbole issued by political actors trying to motivate people to vote for them based on fear of the other.

Yet there is a lingering sentiment in the country that we do not just disagree but that two different countries, two different worlds, exist in America. I've not forgotten one study from several years ago that revealed that one in five Americans who identify with one of the major political parties believes that members of the opposing party "lack the traits to be considered fully human."[3] What's more, as divided as we are, we know we are divided. Eighty-one percent of Americans believe that we are more divided than united.[4]

The tricky thing about all this is that for most of this book, I've been advocating engagement that, by its nature, will cause division.

Taking a political stand for one thing means rejecting another thing. Choosing traditional marriage means rejecting other supposed families as illegitimate. Urging unity on matters of genuine disagreement is merely prioritizing the status quo over the truth. But it's easy to leap from "We shouldn't agree with lies" to "All agreement is a lie." We can see this spirit of divisiveness at work everywhere.

So we know we have a problem, but, like someone suffering from an addiction, we don't quite know how to quit it. What's worse, in this digital age, we are incentivized to create division. The big social media platforms work the algorithms to gin up the most inflammatory content. Media moguls on all sides of our debates stoke the fires of division in order to make money. Partisans understand that if they ratchet up their rhetoric, they'll be rewarded with more clicks, more followers, and more revenue. David Zahl was right when he wrote, "Whatever your conviction or interest, no matter how fringe or toxic, a community exists online that will reinforce it. A few clicks are all it takes to find allies who will confirm the righteousness of your opinions, as well as common enemies to fortify your tribe. It's intoxicating, radicalizing."[5]

So what can be done?

Whither Civil War?

A couple of years ago, I was speaking at an event at Gettysburg College, located just a couple of miles from the historic Civil War battlefield. Ironically, I was at an event designed to bring people together across partisan lines. I'd been to Gettysburg before; as an amateur historian, I'd even dragged my kids to that "hallowed ground" in Pennsylvania. But this time, I was overwhelmed by the sadness of the place.

I'll be honest with you. I'm glad the North won that battle, and I'm proud of the volunteer regiment from my home state of Illinois for firing the first shot. I shudder to think what would have happened if the Confederacy had prevailed there. That stunning blow would have set back the Union effort and might have cost Abraham Lincoln reelection. It's very likely that the United States might never have been reconciled, slavery might still exist in some form, and we'd be a balkanized series of small, warring countries.

Yet it's hard to walk the trails and see the monuments to young boys on both sides—all Americans—who fought each other to the death at Gettysburg. To see, for instance, the wheat field where, after fierce fighting, four thousand bodies were piled high and blood stained the rivers. Brother against brother for the soul of the nation.

This image burns in my brain as I hear partisans on both sides warn of a "coming civil war," some of them almost giddy at the prospect of a national cleavage and a bloody internal conflict. I even have friends, some of whom consume far too many fringe podcasts, who darkly predict civil war. What I wish they could understand is that civil war is not something you watch on the History Channel after driving through Starbucks. Civil war means that your town is ransacked, your family is dead, and you are struggling to survive. Civil war means unnecessary bloodshed, death, and carnage. It means families split apart and communities permanently ravaged.

Instead of fantasizing about unlikely conflicts like this, we should instead turn our attention to healing our national wounds and restoring civic virtue. And we should square with reality: though America is increasingly polarized, we are far from being as divided as we've ever been. Not only did we fight an actual civil war, consider other times in our history, such as the 1960s and 1970s, which witnessed three political assassinations, an unpopular war in Vietnam, race riots, the Watergate scandal, and domestic political terrorism. Consider the 1920s, often called the "Tribal '20s," beset by racial violence and the terror of the KKK.

That isn't to say we shouldn't heed the warnings of folks such as General Jim Mattis about the way increasing polarization is weakening us or others such as Francis Fukuyama, who wrote:

> Democratic societies are fracturing into segments based on ever-narrower identities, threatening the possibility of deliberation and collective action by society as a whole. This is a road that leads only to state breakdown and, ultimately, failure. Unless such liberal democracies can work their way back to more universal understandings of human dignity, they will doom themselves—and the world—to continuing conflict.[6]

But in addressing the tears in the fabric of American society, we shouldn't yield to cynicism and despair but instead should work to strengthen our civic virtue. We can first do this, I believe, by turning away from the temptation to demonize our political adversaries and working, with what little influence we have, toward common ground with our neighbors.

To some people, this sounds like compromise and capitulation on key policy issues. I assure you that it is not. Robust public debates about the future of our country are vital to our democracy. As a lifelong Reagan conservative, I will continue to articulate and champion ideas that I think are best for the country, and I'll oppose what I consider to be destructive policies from the Left. Yet even as I do this, I must remember that I live in a country where at least 50 percent of the country disagrees with me. And even as I try to persuade, even as I oppose bad policies, I must do it in a way that recognizes the humanity of those on the other side of the political aisle.

That was the approach Dr. Martin Luther King Jr. took even as he fought heroically for civil rights. In a 1965 sermon at Ebenezer Baptist Church, he appealed to the biblical teaching of the *imago Dei*:

> There are no gradations in the image of God. Every man from a treble white to a bass black is significant on God's keyboard, precisely because every man is made in the image of God. One day we will learn that. We will know one day that God made us to live together as brothers and to respect the dignity and worth of every man.[7]

As Christians, we are compelled to see our neighbors—even those who most vociferously disagree with us—not as garbage or trash or, as one right-wing commentator describes his opponents, as "unhuman." I could find similar dehumanizing rhetoric on the left. We should resist this kind of dehumanizing rhetoric because it tears at the fragile unity of our country. Arthur Brooks warned against this in his book *Love Your Enemies: How Decent People Can Save America from the Culture of Contempt*, urging us to "be on the lookout for dehumanization in everyday life. You will start to see it. For example, perhaps your favorite newspaper pundit refers to certain people as pigs. The point is to destroy your empathy for the object of his or her derision through dehumanization. Perhaps that seems like no big deal, but make no mistake: You are being manipulated to hate a fellow human being."[8]

Of course, hate-mongering is not how this temptation presents itself. Usually, it's sold as righteous anger or manly style on the right or, on the left, rejecting the civil tactics of the ruling class or "punching up." Maybe, sometimes, these things are true, but consider: Are you acting from concern for the truth or merely venting your spleen? Are you angry that God's reputation is being dishonored, or do you just want to win an argument to gain the admiration of strangers?

Incivility on my own side is often justified by pointing to a corresponding worse action on the other side—in this case, the Left—and using that outrage to justify our own incivility. Some people use a phrase such as "Know what time it is" to argue that we need to abandon love and dignity for our fellow Americans who vote differently. The stakes, many on the right might say, are too high to observe such niceties. I won't deny that the Left has been opposed to conservative Christianity for decades now. The anti-family and anti-Christian policies I outlined earlier have been devastating for human flourishing.

Even so, as a Christian, this is not an excuse to respond with similarly evil tactics. As we saw earlier, it's not merely important for Christians to engage in politics, it's also important to embody Christlikeness as we do it. The call of a Christian to "walk worthy of the calling" (Ephesians 4:1) and to "keep in step with the Spirit" (Galatians 5:25) to cultivate spiritual virtues is not negated just because we engage in politics. We should not resort to evil "that good may come" (Romans 3:8).

Even as we make strong arguments against false ideologies, we should model Christian behavior by seeing our fellow Americans, especially our ideological opponents, not as avatars to be crushed but as human beings, made in the image of God and worthy of respect and dignity (Genesis 1:26; James 3:9). This idea of exercising kindness while holding fast to our principles is not a temporary political tactic but something we are commanded to do, based on our relationship with God through Christ (2 Peter 2:17).

Consider Dietrich Bonhoeffer, who while awaiting execution for opposing Hitler's Nazi regime wrote this: "Because spiritual love does not desire, but rather serves, it loves an enemy as a brother. It originates neither in the brother nor in the enemy but in Christ and his Word. Human love can never understand spiritual love, for spiritual love is from above; it is something completely strange, new, and incomprehensible to all earthly love."[9]

Some people see this kind of love as a sign of moral weakness and the unwillingness to hurl invective at the other side all day long as being soft or, as the extremely online cohort says, "beta." But the Christian Gospel describes the world differently, empowering faithful Christians to have so much confidence in our positions that we don't have to resort to worldly means to accomplish our goals.

Public engagement today will require both boldness and the willingness to make arguments that persuade, rather than simply scoring cheap partisan points with folks who already agree with us. This kind of civility doesn't mean that we should stand down when it comes to bad policies and bad actors. Nor does it imply that we should stop fighting to elect good candidates and hold them accountable. What it does mean is that in order to preserve the country we love—to keep this republic—we will have to learn to live side by side with people who radically disagree with us. We have to share the country with them. Our liberty and freedom depend on it.

Wage Peace, Where Possible

Beyond civility, how can American Christians further restore civic virtue and help bind our country together? I talk to far too many Christians who are deeply cynical about America and see no bright future for the country. They wonder if it's worth the work to renew American democracy. I don't share this doomsday outlook, but even if it were remotely true, that doesn't negate our responsibilities as citizens.

If the exiles in Jeremiah's day were told by God to build and plant, to seek the welfare of their city, even in the midst of a pagan idolatry that would make San Francisco blush, should not Christians try to preserve the American experiment for future generations?

What's more, we are told in the New Testament that God's people should, "if possible, as far as it depends on you, live at peace with everyone" (Romans 12:18, CSB). This implies that we should not merely seek our own welfare but understand that we share this country with folks who see things from a far different perspective. How can we live at peace with them? It might begin with the acknowledgment that our ideological foes are not "bitter clingers," "deplorables," "garbage," or "animals" but humans made in the image of God.

Over the past few years, I've been part of a movement called Braver Angels. It began with an experiment in the wake of the 2016 election. A small group of people, half Hillary Clinton voters and half Donald Trump voters, met to see if they could . . . get along and listen to one another. The experiment not only worked but fostered the founding of the group Braver Angels by three men: David Blankenhorn, David Lapp, and Bill Doherty. The organization has since grown into chapters in cities around the country, an annual conference, and ongoing subgroups.

I've had the privilege of being invited both to speak at Braver Angels and to participate in the faith caucus. The annual event is one of the most unusual events I've ever attended. Every attendee wears a red, blue, or yellow lanyard, signifying where they stand politically. There are workshops, music, plenaries, and a variety of other events. I've been struck by the spirit of the folks who attend and those who organize. Each of us comes with our ideological positions, and there is zero pressure to change them, yet for several days we zoom out and think about how we can preserve this great democracy and how people who disagree can live side by side.

Through my involvement with Braver Angels, I've struck up a friendship with a retired Episcopal bishop from the Northeast with whom I have very little in common theologically and politically. Yet Mark and I have become great friends. I've learned from Mark, and he's learned from me. Events such as this, organized to help bring people together and work on the future of the country, make me more optimistic about what is ahead.

Conservative Christians can participate in these kinds of efforts without losing our ability to fight for the policies about which we care. This is not just a performative "Kumbaya" moment but real people with genuine political differences talking to one another, refusing to yield on their convictions but recognizing that we all have a stake in keeping this nation bound together. This is civic virtue at the most basic level. It's about understanding that before we are Republicans or Democrats or Independents, we are Americans.

Civic virtue is defined by *Encyclopaedia Britannica* as "personal qualities associated with the effective functioning of the civil and political order, or the preservation of its values and principles."[10] This is the kind of behavior noted by Alexis de Tocqueville during his tour of the United States. In *Democracy in America*, he observed the presence of many civic associations that nurtured neighborliness and citizenship. These are vital institutions situated between the state and the individual. Alexandra Hudson wrote about why this matters for America's long-term survival:

> Tocqueville noted a tension at the heart of American social life, a tension that is also at the heart of human communities in all times and places. This tension was between individualism and communalism or, put another way, between our self-love and sociability in our nature. Left unchecked, individualism—in both America and beyond—was a recipe for personal alienation and societal deterioration. It was also a threat to American democracy. Tocqueville noted that voluntary acts of kindness, including spontaneous efforts to "join" together and help one another in need, kept this individualistic impulse in check. Efforts to work together to solve a common problem became "schools of citizenship" where Americans developed the habits of democracy. Civility and civil

> society were the social glue that made the fragile project of American democracy work.[11]

Faithful Christians have the opportunity, in our churches and communities, to nurture these "schools of citizenship." This is basic neighborliness and civic involvement, where we resist and refuse to make politics an all-consuming passion. Citizenship is more than just showing up to vote every election cycle but helping strengthen and rebuild institutions that make America strong.

Civic virtue also requires civic education. Sadly, many Americans are indifferent to or apathetic about the basic functions of government. Timothy S. Goeglein, in his book *Toward a More Perfect Union: The Moral and Cultural Case for Teaching the Great American Story*, argued that civics and a balanced view of US history should be returned as a core feature of education. Thankfully, many private schools and some public schools are making them priorities once again.

But churches and families can do this as well. There are really three concrete ways we can develop and spread civic virtue. First, we should exhibit these qualities in ourselves. Benjamin Franklin, in his autobiography, listed thirteen precepts he urged others to live by:

1. Eat not to dullness. Drink not to elevation.
2. Speak not but what may benefit others or yourself; avoid trifling conversations.
3. Let all your things have their places.
4. Resolve to perform what you ought. Perform without fail what you resolve.
5. Make no expense but to do good to others or yourself, i.e. waste nothing.

6. Lose no time. Be always employ'd in something useful. Cut off all unnecessary actions.

7. Use no hurtful deceit. Think innocently and justly; and, if you speak, speak accordingly.

8. Wrong none by doing injuries or omitting the benefits that are your duty.

9. Avoid extremes. Forbear resenting injuries so much as you think they deserve.

10. Tolerate no uncleanness in body, clothes or habitation.

11. Be not disturbed at trifles or accidents, common or unavoidable.

12. Rarely use venery but for health or offspring.

13. Imitate Jesus and Socrates.[12]

You don't have to read closely to see that these virtues echo what the New Testament calls the "fruit of the Spirit." For Christians, a relationship with God through the power of the Spirit enables us to embody virtues such as love, joy, peace, gentleness, and other good qualities. Yet we might encourage these in others who are not believers and look for them in those we support for public office. No politician is perfect, yet as much as we can, we should choose leaders not only for their policy but for their high personal moral character. We should encourage leaders to, at times, put their country above their party. This is not always possible, given the choices that other voters make in political primaries. The system often gives us less-than-stellar choices for various offices. Still, we should not so easily dismiss virtue, even and perhaps especially when our preferred party seems to do so.

Civic virtue also demands that we constantly ask, in the midst of our political activism: Is what we are doing healing our social fabric or tearing it? This includes accepting the outcomes of elections when we lose and being gracious in victory when we win. It means we stop catastrophizing every election as if our candidate doesn't win, the country will cease to exist.

Last, Christians should not hesitate to embody and teach American patriotism and the nobility of public service. As I described in the opening pages of this book, patriotism, rightly ordered, is an important aspect of Christian discipleship. What does rightly ordered patriotism look like? At the very least, we should not hesitate to celebrate what is good about our country and roll up our sleeves, in whatever way God calls us, to help preserve the American experiment. But perhaps more important, we should be proactive in handing down a sense of love and duty to our children. We should have healthy conversations about current issues around the dinner table. We should mark important moments in American history. And if our time and budget allow, we should perhaps take our family to see the important landmarks in American history, which will help foster a sense of curiosity about and love of country in them. Take your family to Washington, DC, to see the memorials and museums and to Virginia to visit Mount Vernon. Take them to Colonial Williamsburg or the battlefields of Gettysburg, Vicksburg, or Antietam or the Lorraine Motel in Memphis. Take a trip to Boston and walk the freedom trail and visit Plymouth Rock or Braintree, where John Adams and John Quincy Adams lived. In short, Christians should own our country's future and encourage our children to be just as passionate about it.

If we take seriously the words of Jeremiah to the exiles to "seek the welfare" of our community, our cities, and our country, we'll root for and not against America. I'm amazed how many on the right genuinely feel like "If we don't win this election, we'll never have another one" and folks on the left who act as though the election of a Republican will mean the end of our democracy. Let's stop this doomerism! Yes, we've seen significant failure in our institutions, from failed wars to overzealous covid policies. Yet it's not too Pollyannaish to say that America, in the form of her good leaders, people, and institutions, is much better and more just than her bad leaders and their choices are. There is a perverse incentive not to look at the many good things that still exist in this country, but we should resist doing so and face reality. Consider that child poverty and teen pregnancy are at historic lows. Or that we have the strongest protections for free speech and religious liberty of anywhere in the world. You might argue that due to a more originalist Supreme Court in the twenty-first century, these rights are more protected than ever. The United States' GDP is significantly higher than those of our competitor nations. The GDP of the states of Texas and California alone outranks that of most Western nations.[13]

Yes, the United States has problems, but let's acknowledge that it is the greatest country in the world. People are literally dying every day to get in here, so much so that we are forced to put up walls to stop them. Maybe it's time to start believing what those who are desperate to get in here already know.

Christians should be grateful for this country, should love America, and should unabashedly root for her success. The nurturing of this civic virtue often happens away from cable TV studios, marble-clad government halls, and social media platforms in everyday interactions in our neighborhoods, towns, and cities. The civic associations Alexis de Tocqueville wrote about are vital to the health of our country. I earlier discussed the importance of the Church as one of these vital institutions, but there are many others that deserve reformation and renewal. It is these local "little platoons," as described by Edmund Burke, to which I turn my attention in the final chapter.

CHAPTER 10

Saving America from Your Backyard

> To be attached to the subdivision, to love the little platoon we belong to in society, is the first principle (the germ as it were) of public affections.[1]
>
> —*Edmund Burke*

BOB VANDER PLAATS IS ONE OF THE MOST INFLUENTIAL SOCIAL CONSERVATIVE leaders in the country. He ran for governor in Iowa three times and is a highly sought after voice every time there is a competitive Republican presidential primary. He hosts conferences, interviews candidates, and mobilizes Christians through his organization, the Family Leader.

In 2014, however, Bob and his team saw a critical need to connect local church pastors and government officials once the national candidates left Iowa, after the ballots were counted and the elections were over. They began connecting churches from a variety of denominations and traditions with the various branches of government in Iowa, not to lobby for particular legislation but for pastors to pray for public officials and for public officials to seek the help of the Church in meeting real human needs in their communities. The effort really took off, and soon other states began asking Vander Plaats and his team how to replicate this model in their states, both red and blue. Today, the Church Ambassador Network has chapters in several states.

Vander Plaats and the pastors around the country have not given up on politics, nor do they discourage Christians from voting and engaging in elections, but what they have done is to help build relationships between churches and government agencies and officials. The pastors commit to praying for specific officials, and the officials gain a greater awareness of the manifold ministries each church is doing. For instance, in many states, there is a mental health crisis. Through this network, the state agencies can work locally with churches that have robust counseling ministries. In many communities, there is a significant foster care backlog and a need for Christian families to step in and provide short- and long-term care for at-risk children. And there are still other human needs, such as hunger, addiction, and illiteracy, to counteract on which those in office can work in harmony with religious institutions to provide the best care and support for the vulnerable.

Perhaps because of the influence of social media and cable news networks, we often think of politics and patriotism solely in terms of speaking out on policies and stories of national interest. Every four years, of course, the presidential election captures our attention.

As you can see from this book, I'm not advocating that we ignore national news or skip out on election season; however, there is much more to loving your country than tweeting about the latest gaffe by a despised candidate. There's work to be done in our communities. The races for the presidency, Congress, and governorships are vitally important, but despite who wins, there are real human needs present in our communities and real opportunities for Christians both to meet these needs locally and to strengthen institutions that will keep our communities strong.

My friend Bryan English, who runs the Church Ambassador Network where I live in Texas, summed up its work:

> We genuinely care about the men and women serving in government. We want to help them to see themselves as shepherds serving in an institution God gave us "for our good" (Romans 13:1–4).

> We also want them to see the Church as an effective problem solver and a potential partner for meeting needs.
>
> Ultimately, the problems government is trying to solve are little more than the physical manifestation of spiritual problems. Government is not equipped, nor is it called, to address spiritual needs.
>
> Government needs the church.[2]

Christians need to embrace what is often called "localism." In our communities, the opportunities available to renew and restore society are right in front of us. This isn't about neglecting the national policies discussed in this book, nor is it a myopic Jonah mentality that we cannot love people from the other nations of the world, but it is about strengthening our country by refusing to let the sheer number of bad policies, tragic news stories, and crooked politicians cascading across our timelines keep us from rolling up our sleeves and doing something tangible in the places where we live.

We are tempted to think that going online and saying something about everything is the sum total of activism. But nursing constant, performative outrage over national issues can actually blind us to the needs in front of us and opportunities to love our country by loving our immediate communities. My friend Drew Dyck, the author of *Just Show Up: How Small Acts of Faithfulness Change Everything*, wrote, "When we are young, we're told, in a million ways, that doing something big will give our lives meaning. It's a message you hear in movies and magazines, at graduation speeches and even from pulpits. *Go out and do something huge! Change the world!*" Dyck says that this kind of inspiration can be helpful and that often God calls Christians to do big things and to steward a growing audience, but primarily, our best work might be right in front of us. "Trying to do something big can prevent us from showing up for the people right in front of us. Striving to be famous can prevent us from being faithful. We may influence the wider world, yet ultimately our greatest contribution will likely be to the lives of the people around us, to our family, our friends, and our communities."[3]

The messages we receive now are that we have two options: to do something big or to do nothing. These messages are paralyzing in the same way, the one because it feels impossible and the other because it says that nothing is possible. Christians must recognize that doing anything big has to start with doing small things. God, in his wisdom, insists that we start small, live in time, wait, and see through a glass darkly before we can see clearly.

Much public engagement in our time is about trying to find shortcuts around these rules of gaining wisdom. The temptation to "try to do something big" has become more seductive in the digital age. This is why so much of our politics is not actually politics at all but performance. Instead of trying to make changes to the body politic, influencers create online outrage to gain a bigger audience. God grants some of them a measure of influence and fame to be stewarded for his glory, but most of the work of renewing America and seeking the welfare of our country will be carried out in small places by people whose work will never be featured on cable news.

Small efforts snowball. Very few big things that last represent a zero-to-sixty moment of willpower and luck. Rather, they represent a million choices that culminate in greatness.

All Politics Is Local

How can you get started locally? You could connect with a chapter of the Church Ambassador Network or a similar organization in your city and begin building relationships with local public officials. Or you can do something like what my friend Daryl Crouch did. He was the pastor of the church we attended in a suburb of Nashville,

Tennessee. Daryl was increasingly burdened by the needs of his community, Mt. Juliet. So he began introducing himself to local leaders, such as the city manager, the mayor, and the public school officials. He began with a simple question: What needs does this city have that our church could reasonably meet?

Green Hill Church, where Daryl pastored, wasn't a megachurch, but it did have a willing congregation who loved their community. Soon Daryl was connected to genuine needs in the Mt. Juliet public schools: addictions, food insecurity, and illiteracy. He began mobilizing area churches and plugging Christians in to where their gifts and talents best matched. Soon he launched a nonprofit, Everyone's Wilson. Today it's a thriving nonprofit connecting the body of Christ to the needs in Wilson County and has become a model for similar work across the state of Tennessee. He regularly coaches pastors and church leaders on how to engage their communities well.

The church I attend with my family here in Fort Worth, Texas, tried to help meet a similar need. Rebekah Naylor, a retired missionary with the Southern Baptists' International Mission Board who had spent most of her life as a medical missionary in Bangalore, India, could not look away from the medical needs of the community around Travis Avenue Baptist Church. So in 2011, she helped launch Mercy Clinic in Fort Worth, which mobilized 140 volunteers to provide wellness checkups, well-woman visits, sick visits, dental extractions and fillings, and limited laboratory and prescription services to uninsured people in their zip code.

In West Virginia, a political fundraiser, Erin DeLullo, who has raised money for many successful political candidates, was troubled by the growing fentanyl problem in her own backyard. DeLullo, a wife and mother of two, started a newsletter and a podcast, *The Poisoning*, highlighting the problem, helping warn parents and teens about fentanyl's dangers, and calling the local government to account over the use of funds earmarked for the crisis.

These are just three of hundreds of stories happening around the country as people of faith roll up their sleeves and use their gifts and talents to love their country by renewing their local communities. Notice that in each example I've offered, these Christians didn't let the overwhelming national crises in the country prevent them from doing something meaningful and tangible where they live.

True patriotism is both national and local: pride in our country but also pride in our communities. It's the local, the "little platoons" of Edmund Burke, or the manifold civic associations that hold the national together. This is why we should care about the health of these institutions. Some need to be revived, but there might also be the need to start new ones. Seth Kaplan, the author of *Fragile Neighborhoods: Repairing American Society, One Zip Code at a Time*, wrote that "adopting a more localist view of where our responsibilities lie requires a major shift in our understanding of patriotism and political engagement. Instead of defining patriotism as merely pride in the abstract idea of our country, we can revive an older idea of American patriotism as a commitment to the places we know intimately."[4]

In my twenties, I helped a friend of mine (unsuccessfully) run for Congress, and as part of my duties, I attended nearly every parade on the calendar in every town in the district. The job is to accompany the candidate, smile and wave, and hand out candy to eager children along the parade route.

Though I have no desire to repeat that marathon parade attendance, I do still believe that there is something special about local town parades that both celebrate the national pride of being American and find joy in the local expressions, symbols, and heroes of the town. Events like these can galvanize a community and bring Americans together across ethnic and political lines. If you can, attending your town's Fourth of July parade, however pedestrian it might seem, is a way to express your patriotism in a local way.

You might also consider exploring, with your family, the American history in your community. When we lived in Illinois, we took trips to Springfield to see the Abraham Lincoln Presidential Library and Museum and often toured the places where Lincoln had lived and practiced law in Illinois's capitol. During our time in Nashville, we explored the history of the Hermitage, the home of Andrew Jackson, a complicated American leader, and toured some of the Civil War sites in Tennessee. And though we've lived in Fort Worth only a short time, we've explored American history in Texas.

Even if you aren't a history nerd like me, your family can appreciate some of the local history in your own town. Most towns have a museum where military veterans are honored. Some have memorials and shrines to those who fought for our freedoms. You might even ask veterans in your church to tell their story and use the opportunity to thank them for their service. It's good to understand how our local communities fit, historically, into the mosaic of communities that make up the United States of America.

Stewarding our citizenship locally might also mean getting involved in the local governments where we live. Kaplan wrote:

> Our political citizenship requires more of us than voting in presidential elections; it means participating in our local governments, communities, and associations. Instead of showing up only to cast a ballot every four years, we can show up for local elections, school board meetings, town council sessions, etc. We can shift our energy and attention to the battles that truly matter in our communities; improving our schools, keeping our streets clean, and organizing others to lobby for change at the local level.[5]

That isn't to say that getting involved in local politics is easy. Budget fights, zoning questions, school referenda, and other matters can be just as divisive and conflict laden. Sometimes national entities and ideas come in and crowd and even hurt the local government.

Still, if we wish to love our neighbors well and seek the welfare of our communities, the place where we live is an important place in which to start. And often, it is in cities and towns that people are forced, by proximity, to work together for the common good. Every town needs faithful Christians to step up and run for town council, mayor, the legislature, and other important offices.

Last, we can love our country by doing good work for an honest day's wage in ways that help our fellow Americans. We don't often think about the way our work serves our neighbors, but to produce good products, to serve people with a smile, to build businesses and lead institutions is a way we stitch together the fabric that helps our cities and towns flourish. Hard work is a form of patriotism.

Most Christians' love of country will be lived out in small things, in the everyday rituals of their lives as they attend church, raise their families, go to work, and use their voices and votes to make their opinions known about issues that matter. This "peaceful and quiet life" (1 Timothy 2:2, ESV), lived with love before God and man, multiplied by millions of lives across our great country, is the essence of what can be good about America.

I want to end this book where I began, by repeating these helpful words of the British writer G. K. Chesterton:

> The fundamental spiritual advantage of patriotism and such sentiments is this: that by means of it all things are loved adequately, because all things are loved individually. . . . Patriotism begins the praise of the world at the nearest thing, instead of beginning it at the most distant, and thus it insures what is, perhaps, the most essential of all earthly considerations, that nothing upon earth shall go without its due appreciation.[6]

Patriotism, then, is not to be parochial or to prefer one's race, as it is often claimed to be by those on the left. Patriotism is about loving one's home, about having gratitude and affection for the places—both local and national—where God has placed us. For some people it might mean engaging on big, hairy national issues. It might mean working in Washington, DC, or a state capital. For others it's doing quiet work in their communities.

The truth is, we all have a stake in ensuring that our republic endures. Benjamin Franklin's timeless words celebrating "a republic, if you can keep it" should be etched on our minds. America will not merely endure on autopilot; it will require investment by every generation to secure freedom and liberty.

The American experiment is rare in human history. The words of Ronald Reagan almost six decades ago ring true today: "Freedom is a fragile thing and it's never more than one generation away from extinction. It is not ours by way of inheritance; it must be fought for and defended constantly by each generation, for it comes only once to a people. And those in world history who have known freedom and then lost it have never known it again."[7]

Christians are invested in America's flourishing, not because we believe this beautiful land is the new Jerusalem but because we love our neighbors as Jesus commands (Mark 12:30–31) and seek the shalom of our communities, cities, and nation (Jeremiah 29). Our patriotism is guided by our ultimate allegiance to Christ and his kingdom.

For our children, for our neighbors, for the glory of God, let's love this country.

ACKNOWLEDGMENTS

THIS BOOK IS THE PRODUCT OF MANY HANDS. IT'S A PROJECT THAT HAS been rattling around in my head and heart for years. Now, thanks to some dear people, it is here at last in print. First, I want to thank my agent, Erik Wolgemuth, who is always ready to hear yet another idea and help me discern whether said idea is a passing fancy or worthy of a book.

This is my first time working with my editor at Broadside, Hannah Long, who put me through the paces to extract the very best of what I was trying to say. We worked it over via Zoom and Twitter messages and emails and phone calls. There is an art to book editing, and Hannah is an artist. I'm so grateful for her incisive mind and careful pen. To be edited deeply and fully is a gift. I admit that in the middle of the process I didn't always see it that way, but I love the pearls that have emerged from the oyster. Thank you, Hannah and Broadside, for believing in this idea from the start.

I'm thankful for Southwestern Seminary, where I lead the Land Center, and for the mentorship and brilliant mind of Richard Land himself. It's great to serve at a place that encourages me to study and to publish, to apply Christianity to the common good. It's a joy to serve under the leadership of David Dockery, our president, and

Madison Grace, our provost. I can't forget interns Evan Anderson and Dakota Wallace, who helped with some research. I'm grateful for scholars and friends near and far, including Nathan Finn, Hunter Baker, Joseph Williams, Andrew Walker, John Wilsey, Thomas Kidd, Jonathan Leeman, Kevin DeYoung, Eric Patterson, Collin Hansen, Tim Goeglein, Justin Taylor, Michael Graham, Trevin Wax, Mark David Hall, and so many others whose wisdom and words catalyzed my thinking. Great Americans all.

I must thank my family, who endured, yet again, the light on in my study late at night as I leaned over my MacBook, fingers flying. My wife, Angela, is a joy and a treasure, walking together with me on this strange and wonderful path of life. My children, Grace, Daniel, Emma, and Lily, growing in age and maturity and love of God, make me so proud. I pray that the America we bequeath to them and their children evokes the same sense of awe and wonder in them that it evoked in me from the start.

Finally, all glory goes to God, in whom we live and breathe and have our being (Acts 17:28) and his Son, Jesus, who upholds "all things by the word of his power" (Hebrews 1:3, ASV).

Introduction: Reject Embarrassment; Choose Gratitude

1. Bill McInturff, "Key Data by Generation," Public Opinion Strategies, accessed June 18, 2024, https://pos.org/wp-content/uploads/2024/04/Generations-deck-2024-d1g.pdf.

2. Kenneth A. Briggs, "Carter's Evangelism Putting Religion into Politics for First Time Since '60," *New York Times*, April 11, 1976, https://www.nytimes.com/1976/04/11/archives/carters-evangelism-putting-religion-into-politics-for-first-time.html.

3. Thomas S. Kidd, "Jimmy Carter's Most Perplexing Legacy," *The Dispatch*, December 31, 2024, https://thedispatch.com/article/jimmy-carters-most-perplexing-legacy.

4. Thomas S. Kidd, *America's Religious History: Faith, Politics, and the Shaping of a Nation*, enhanced ed. (Zondervan, 2029); Thomas S. Kidd, *God of Liberty: A Religious History of the American Revolution* (Basic Books, 2012).

5. CRC Staff, "Apathy Among Christian Voters Could Be 'Gamechanger' in 2024 Election," Arizona Christian University, October 8, 2024, https://www.arizonachristian.edu/2024/10/08/apathy_among_christian_voters_could_be_gamechanger_in_2024_election.

6. Ryan Burge, "Are Liberal Christians More Politically Engaged than Conservative Ones?," Religion Unplugged, March 13, 2024, https://religionunplugged.com/news/2024/3/11/are-liberal-christians-more-politically-engaged-than-conservative-one.

7. "The Epistle of Mathetes to Diognetus," New Advent, accessed May 2, 2024, https://www.newadvent.org/fathers/0101.htm.

Chapter 1: Since When Is Faith in Politics Scary?

1. John Adams, "From John Adams to Massachusetts Militia, 11 October 1798," National Archives, accessed May 9, 2024, http://founders.archives.gov/documents/Adams/99-02-02-3102.

2. "Ronald Reagan: Remarks at an Ecumenical Prayer Breakfast in Dallas," American Rhetoric, August 23, 1984, https://www.americanrhetoric.com/speeches/ronaldreaganecumenicalprayer.htm.

3. Face the Nation, *Rep. Mike Johnson Gives First Speech as House Speaker*, YouTube, October 25, 2023, https://www.youtube.com/watch?v=dbJfDMOfjiI.

4. Katelyn Fossett, "'He Seems to Be Saying His Commitment Is to Minority Rule,'" *Politico*, October 27, 2023, https://www.politico.com/news/magazine/2023/10/27/mike-johnson-christian-nationalist-ideas-qa-00123882.

5. Andrew Whitehead and Samuel L. Perry, "The Christian Nationalism of Speaker Mike Johnson," *Time*, October 27, 2023, https://time.com/6329207/speaker-mike-johnson-christian-nationalism.

6. Thomas B. Edsall, "'The Embodiment of White Christian Nationalism in a Tailored Suit,'" *New York Times*, November 1, 2023, https://www.nytimes.com/2023/11/01/opinion/mike-johnson-christian-nationalism-speaker.html.

7. Russell Cobb, "Cracks in the Christian Ascendancy," *Slate*, June 26, 2006, https://slate.com/culture/2006/06/michelle-goldberg-s-kingdom-coming.html.

8. Howard Fineman, "Bush's Next Challenge: Dodging No. 41's Fate," *Newsweek*, December 30, 2001, https://www.newsweek.com/bushs-next-challenge-dodging-no-41s-fate-148243.

9. Paul Kengor, "Undivine Double Standard," *National Review*, September 7, 2004, https://www.nationalreview.com/2004/09/undivine-double-standard-paul-kengor.

10. "What a Friend We Have in Jesus," *Wall Street Journal*, January 2, 2004, https://www.wsj.com/articles/SB107300222088998200.

11. Eamon Javers, "Obama Invokes Jesus More than Bush," *Politico*, June 9, 2009, https://www.politico.com/story/2009/06/obama-invokes-jesus-more-than-bush-023510.

12. Napp Nazworth, "We're Commanded to Pray for Presidents but Not to Give Them Photo-Ops," *Christian Post*, June 6, 2019, https://www.christianpost.com/news/were-commanded-to-pray-for-presidents-but-not-to-give-them-photo-ops.html.

13. Alan Rudnick, "There's Nothing Wrong with Praying for the President, Except When It's Not Really about Prayer," Baptist News Global, June 12, 2019, https://baptistnews.com/article/theres-nothing-wrong-with-praying-for-the-president-except-when-its-not-really-about-prayer.

14. Emma Green, "On Praying for the President," *Atlantic*, June 3, 2019, https://www.theatlantic.com/politics/archive/2019/06/trump-prayer-mass-shooting/590920.

15. Daniel Darling, "Theocracy for Me, but Not for Thee," *World*, April 22, 2022, https://wng.org/opinions/theocracy-for-me-but-not-for-thee-1650626337.

16. Lauren Gambino, "'Righteous Fight': Warren and Booker Call on Religious Voters to Resist Trump," *Guardian*, May 23, 2018, https://www.theguardian.com/us-news/2018/may/23/elizabeth-warren-religious-voters-fight-trump-cory-booker.

17. TheGrio Staff, "Chicago Pastor Retires from City's Largest Black Church After Almost 40 Years," Yahoo! News, January 10, 2023, https://www.yahoo.com/news/chicago-pastor-retires-city-largest-142227497.html.

18. Kenneth L. Woodward, "The Myth of White Christian Nationalism," *First Things*, May 1, 2024, https://www.firstthings.com/article/2024/05/the-myth-of-white-christian-nationalism.

19. Bradley Onishi, *Preparing for War: The Extremist History of White Christian Nationalism—and What Comes Next* (Broadleaf Books, 2023), 221.

20. Mark David Hall, *Who's Afraid of Christian Nationalism?: Why Christian Nationalism Is Not an Existential Threat to America or the Church* (Fidelis Books, 2024), 28.

21. John Fea, *Was America Founded as a Christian Nation?: A Historical Introduction*, illustrated ed. (Westminster John Knox Press, 2011); Kidd, *God of Liberty*; John D. Wilsey, *One Nation Under God?: An Evangelical Critique of Christian America* (Pickwick Publications, 2011); Mark David Hall, *Did America Have a Christian Founding?: Separating Modern Myth from Historical Truth* (Thomas Nelson, 2019).

22. John D. Wilsey, "Was America Founded as a Christian Nation? A Historical Introduction" (review), *Themelios* 37, no. 2, accessed May 14, 2024, https://www.thegospelcoalition.org/themelios/review/was-america-founded-as-a-christian-nation-a-historical-introduction.

23. Adams, "From John Adams to Massachusetts Militia, 11 October 1798."

24. George Washington, "Washington's Farewell Address 1796," Avalon Project, accessed May 14, 2024, https://avalon.law.yale.edu/18th_century/washing.asp.

25. Benjamin Franklin, "Constitutional Convention Address on Prayer," June 28, 1787, American Rhetoric, accessed May 14, 2024, https://www.americanrhetoric.com/speeches/benfranklin.htm.

26. Gary Scott Smith, *Religion in the Oval Office: The Religious Lives of American Presidents* (Oxford University Press, 2015), 98.

27. Fea, *Was America Founded as a Christian Nation?*, 21.

28. Mark A. Noll, *The Civil War as a Theological Crisis* (University of North Carolina Press, 2015).

29. Abraham Lincoln, "Abraham Lincoln's Second Inaugural Address," March 4, 1865, American Battlefield Trust, accessed May 14, 2024, https://www.battlefields.org/learn/primary-sources/abraham-lincolns-second-inaugural-address.

30. Allen C. Guelzo, *Our Ancient Faith: Lincoln, Democracy, and the American Experiment* (Alfred A. Knopf, 2024), 21–22.

31. Smith, *Religion in the Oval Office*, 159–95.

32. Fea, *Was America Founded as a Christian Nation?*, 67.

33. Smith, *Religion in the Oval Office*, 200.

34. Franklin D. Roosevelt, "D-Day Prayer," June 6, 1944, History Place, accessed May 9, 2024, https://www.historyplace.com/speeches/fdr-prayer.htm.

35. Harry S. Truman, "Address at the Cornerstone Laying of the New York Avenue Presbyterian Church," April 3, 1951, Harry S. Truman Library & Museum, accessed May 14, 2024, https://www.trumanlibrary.gov/library/public-papers/68/address-cornerstone-laying-new-york-avenue-presbyterian-church.

36. Dwight D. Eisenhower, "Inaugural Address of Dwight D. Eisenhower," January 20, 1953, US Government Printing Office, accessed May 9, 2024, https://www.eisenhowerlibrary.gov/sites/default/files/research/online-documents/inauguration-1953/1953-01-20-inaugural-address.pdf.

37. Gilbert K. Chesterton, *What I Saw in America* (Hodder and Stoughton, 1922), 5.

38. Heidi Przybyla, "The Right Way to Cover the Intersection of Religion and Politics," *Politico*, February 29, 2024, https://www.politico.com/news/magazine/2024/02/29/the-right-way-to-cover-the-intersection-of-religion-and-politics-00144261.

39. Richard John Neuhaus, *The Naked Public Square: Religion and Democracy in America* (W. B. Eerdmans, 1984), 86.

40. Peter Berkowitz, *Virtue and the Making of Modern Liberalism* (Princeton University Press, 2000), 104.

41. John Locke, *An Essay Concerning Human Understanding* (Clarendon Press, 1975), 69.

42. *Abington School District v. Schempp*, 374 U.S. 203 (1963), Justia, https://supreme.justia.com/cases/federal/us/374/203.

43. Thomas Jefferson, *Notes on the State of Virginia* (Stockdale, 1787), Jefferson Monticello, accessed January 27, 2025, https://www.monticello.org/research-education/thomas-jefferson-encyclopedia/quotations-jefferson-memorial.

44. Richard John Neuhaus, "The Naked Public Square: Without Religious Ideals, Democracy Becomes Dangerous," *Christianity Today*, October 5, 1984, https://www.christianitytoday.com/1984/10/naked-public-square-without-religious-ideals-democracy.

45. Kurt Vonnegut, *If This Isn't Nice, What Is?: The Graduation Speeches and Other Words to Live By* (Seven Stories Press, 2024).

46. Russell Contreras, "Axios Explains: Christian Nationalism on the March," Axios, June 24, 2024, https://www.axios.com/2024/06/24/christian-nationalism-america-trump-republicans.

47. "Faith Among Black Americans," Pew Research Center, February 16, 2021, https://www.pewresearch.org/religion/2021/02/16/faith-among-black-americans.

48. Gary Alan Taylor, "Why Evangelicals Love the Ten Commandments," Sophia Society, July 2, 2024, https://www.sophiasociety.org/blog/louisiana-ten-commandments-law.

49. Karl Zinsmeister, "Less God, Less Giving?," Philanthropy Roundtable, Winter 2019, https://www.philanthropyroundtable.org/magazine/less-god-less-giving.

50. Brian J. Grim, "$1.2 Trillion Religious Economy in U.S.," Religious Freedom & Business Foundation, May 10, 2018, https://religiousfreedomandbusiness.org/1-2-trillion-religious-economy-in-us.

51. Sierra Dawn McClain, "Gender Ideology Invades the Foster Care System," *Wall Street Journal*, March 22, 2024, https://www.wsj.com/articles/gender-ideology-invades-the-foster-care-system-washington-oregon-8ee883e0.

52. Jedd Medefind, "New Barna Research Highlights Christian Adoption & Foster Care Among 3 Most Notable Vocational Trends," Christian Alliance for Orphans, February 12, 2014, https://cafo.org/new-barna-research-highlights-christian-adoption-foster-care-among-3-most-notable-vocational-trends.

53. James Madison, "Memorial and Remonstrance Against Religious Assessments, [ca. 20 June] 1785," National Archives, accessed May 14, 2024, https://founders.archives.gov/documents/Madison/01-08-02-0163.

54. Anthony L. Chute, Nathan A. Finn, and Michael A. G. Haykin, *The Baptist Story: From English Sect to Global Movement* (B&H Publishing Group, 2015).

55. Daniel L. Dreisbach, "Origins and Dangers of the 'Wall of Separation' Between Church and State," Imprimis, October 2006, https://imprimis.hillsdale.edu/origins-and-dangers-of-the-wall-of-separation-between-church-and-state.

56. Jordan Lorence, "The End of the Lemon Test," Alliance Defending Freedom, September 12, 2022, https://adflegal.org/article/end-lemon-test.

57. Ashley E. Samelson, "Why 'Freedom of Worship' Is Not Enough," *First Things*, February 22, 2010, https://www.firstthings.com/web-exclusives/2010/02/why-ldquofreedom-of-worshiprdquo-is-not-enough.

58. Jonah Goldberg, *Suicide of the West: How the Rebirth of Tribalism, Populism, Nationalism, and Identity Politics Is Destroying American Democracy* (Crown Forum, 2018).

59. Walter Sánchez Silva, "Famous Atheist Richard Dawkins Says He Considers Himself a 'Cultural Christian,'" Catholic News Agency, April 3, 2024, https://www.catholicnewsagency.com/news/257276/famous-atheist-richard-dawkins-says-he-considers-himself-a-cultural-christian.

60. Derek Thompson, "The True Cost of the Churchgoing Bust," *Atlantic*, April 3, 2024, https://www.theatlantic.com/ideas/archive/2024/04/america-religion-decline-non-affiliated/677951.

61. Louise Perry, "We Are Repaganizing," *First Things*, October 1, 2023, https://www.firstthings.com/article/2023/10/we-are-repaganizing.

62. Scott Waller, Darren Patrick Guerra, and Tim Milosch, "American Democracy Is in Trouble. No, Not like That," *Christianity Today*, March 4, 2024, https://www.christianitytoday.com/ct/2024/march-web-only/american-democracy-is-in-trouble-no-not-like-that.html.

Chapter 2: You Can't Obey God and Hate Your Country

1. Chuck Colson, "Pro Patria," Breakpoint Colson Center, July 3, 1992, https://breakpoint.org/pro-patria-3.

2. Megan Brenan, "Extreme Pride in Being American Remains Near Record Low," Gallup, June 29, 2023, https://news.gallup.com/poll/507980/extreme-pride-american-remains-near-record-low.aspx.

3. Joan C. Williams, "Op-Ed: Even on July 4, the Working Class and the Elites Don't See Eye to Eye," *Los Angeles Times*, July 4, 2017, https://www.latimes.com/opinion/op-ed/la-oe-williams-patriotism-and-the-white-working-class-20170704-story.html.

4. James R. Wood, "Ordering Our Social Loves," Ad Fontes, October 26, 2023, https://adfontesjournal.com/commonwealth/ordering-our-social-loves.

5. "Dissent is the highest form of patriotism (Spurious Quotation)," Jefferson Monticello, https://www.monticello.org/research-education/thomas-jefferson-encyclopedia/dissent-highest-form-patriotism-spurious-quotation.

6. "Charles-Maurice de Talleyrand 1754–1838, French Statesman," Oxford Reference, 2017, https://www.oxfordreference.com/display/10.1093/acref/9780191843730.001.0001/q-oro-ed5-00010627.

7. Trevin Wax, "5 Observations About Younger Southern Baptists," Gospel Coalition, May 5, 2014, https://www.thegospelcoalition.org/blogs/trevin-wax/5-observations-about-younger-southern-baptists.

8. Brian Zahnd, "Weird America," July 4, 2024, https://brianzahnd.com/2024/07/weird-america.

9. Steven B. Smith, *Reclaiming Patriotism in an Age of Extremes* (Yale University Press, 2021), 41.

10. Walter C. Kaiser Jr. and Duane Garrett, eds., *NIV Archaeological Study Bible* (Zondervan, 2006), 669.

11. Timothy Keller, *The Prodigal Prophet: Jonah and the Mystery of God's Mercy* (Penguin, 2018), 10.

12. Keller, *The Prodigal Prophet*, 216.

13. C. S. Lewis, *The Four Loves* (HarperCollins, 2017), 22.

14. Chris Conley, "Confessions of an Unpatriotic Christian," Baptist News Global, June 30, 2021, https://baptistnews.com/article/confessions-of-an-unpatriotic-christian.

15. Mark Tooley, "Pacifism, Stanley Hauerwas and Faithful Witness," Juicy Ecumenism, August 3, 2013, https://juicyecumenism.com/2013/08/03/pacifism-stanley-hauerwas-and-faithful-witness.

16. NPR Staff, "Life After Iconic 1976 Photo: The American Flag's Role in Racial Protest," NCPR, September 18, 2016, https://www.northcountrypublicradio.org/news/npr/494442131/life-after-iconic-1976-photo-the-american-flag-s-role-in-racial-protest.

17. Saint Augustine of Hippo, *On Christian Doctrine* (Aeterna Press, 1958), I, 27.

18. Timothy Keller, *Making Sense of God: An Invitation to the Skeptical* (Penguin, 2016), 92.

19. Michael Reneau and Jen Pollock Michel, "Is Lapsed Patriotism Lapsed Faith?," *The Dispatch*, September 29, 2024, https://thedispatch.com/newsletter/dispatch-faith/is-lapsed-patriotism-lapsed-faith.

20. Gilbert Keith Chesterton, "A Defence of Patriotism," in *The Defendant*, Literature Network, accessed May 2, 2024, https://www.online-literature.com/chesterton/the-defendant/16.

21. Peter Lynas, "What Is It to Be Brave in God's Eyes?," Evangelical Alliance, April 11, 2022, https://www.eauk.org/news-and-views/what-is-it-to-be-brave-in-gods-eyes.

22. Clint Bergen, "Idol of Patriotism," Anabaptist World, February 18, 2019, https://anabaptistworld.org/idol-of-patriotism.

23. Ben Palka, "Millennial Christians Are Often Wrong About Patriotism," *Providence*, January 8, 2019, https://providencemag.com/2019/01/millennial-christians-wrong-patriotism.

24. Richard John Neuhaus, *The Naked Public Square: Religion and Democracy in America* (W. B. Eerdmans, 1984).

25. Lewis, *The Four Loves*, 23.

26. Gilbert Keith Chesterton, *The Collected Works of G. K. Chesterton* (Ignatius Press, 1986), 597.

27. Augustine, *On Christian Doctrine*, 1, 28.

28. Neuhaus, *The Naked Public Square*, 74.

29. John D. Wilsey, "Rightly Ordered Patriotism," Modern Reformation, September 18, 2024, https://www.modernreformation.org/resources/essays/rightly-ordered-patriotism.

30. Jennifer Greenberg, "Honoring Your Father When He's Evil," Gospel Coalition, June 18, 2021, https://www.thegospelcoalition.org/article/honoring-father-evil.

31. Wilfred M. McClay, "How to Think About Patriotism," *National Affairs*, Spring 2018, https://www.nationalaffairs.com/publications/detail/how-to-think-about-patriotism.

32. Eric Patterson and Abigail Lindner, "G. K. Chesterton and the Patriotism of Flag Day," *Providence*, June 14, 2022, https://providencemag.com/2022/06/g-k-chesterton-patriotism-flag-day.

33. Richard J. Mouw, *How to Be a Patriotic Christian: Love of Country as Love of Neighbor* (InterVarsity Press, 2022).

34. Miles Smith, "The History of National Flags in Churches," *First Things*, November 24, 2021, https://firstthings.com/the-history-of-national-flags-in-churches.

35. Theodore Roosevelt, "Lincoln and Free Speech," *Metropolitan* 47, no. 6 (May 1918): 7–8, https://babel.hathitrust.org/cgi/pt?id=uva.x030708290&view=2up&seq=4&size=125.

36. Mouw, *How to Be a Patriotic Christian*, 30.

37. Phillip Yancey, "Where Was God on 9/11?," *Christianity Today*, October 1, 2001, https://www.christianitytoday.com/ct/2001/octoberweb-only/10-22-21.0.html.

38. Yancey, "Where Was God on 9/11?"

Chapter 3: Why Christians Should Be *More* Involved in Politics

1. John Adams, "Letter from John Adams to Abigail Adams, Post 12 May 1780," Adams Family Papers, accessed June 21, 2024, https://www.masshist.org/digitaladams/archive/doc?id=L17800512jasecond.

2. Martin Luther, "The Christian in Society," in *Princeton Readings in Political Thought: Essential Texts from Plato to Populism*, 2nd ed., ed. Mitchell Cohen (Princeton University Press, 2018), 167–171.

3. Michael Dobbs, "Charles Colson, Nixon's 'Dirty Tricks' Man, Dies at 80," *Washington Post*, April 21, 2012, https://www.washingtonpost.com/politics/whitehouse/chuck-colson-nixons-dirty-tricks-man-dies-at-80/2012/04/21/gIQAaoOHYT_story.html.

4. Charles W. Colson, *God and Government: An Insider's View on the Boundaries Between Faith and Politics* (Zondervan, 2010), 381.

5. Ben R. Crenshaw, "Nietzscheans in Negative World," American Reformer, May 18, 2024, https://americanreformer.org/2024/05/nietzscheans-in-negative-world.

6. Carl R. Trueman, "Honorable Conduct in the 'Negative World,'" Ad Fontes, May 21, 2024, https://adfontesjournal.com/web-exclusives/honorable-conduct-in-the-negative-world.

7. "Notional Christians: The Big Election Story in 2016," Barna, December 1, 2016, https://www.barna.com/research/notional-christians-big-election-story-2016.

8. The New Evangelicals, *Christians Living Under an Empire of Terror with Shane Claiborne*, YouTube, May 7, 2024, https://www.youtube.com/watch?v=kNEAhtdMpa4.

9. Andrew T. Walker, *The Nations Belong to God: A Christian Guide for Political Engagement*, Ethics & Religious Liberty Commission, accessed June 23, 2024, https://erlc.com/wp-content/uploads/2024/02/ERL4110_ResearchPDFBook_PoliticEngage_FINAL_020524.pdf, 14.

10. Jonathan Wilson-Hartgrove, "Reviving the Soul of America," Sojourners, December 3, 2019, https://sojo.net/articles/reviving-soul-america.

11. Daniel Darling and Malcom B. Yarnell III, "Public Theology," in *The Authority and Sufficiency of Scripture: Revised and Expanded*, ed. Davis S. Dockery and Malcolm B. Yarnell III (Seminary Hill Press, 2024).

12. Francis A. Schaeffer, *The Complete Works of Francis A. Schaeffer: A Christian Worldview*, vol. 2, *A Christian View of the Bible as Truth* (Crossway Books, 1985), 411.

13. Leslie Allen, "Shalom as Wholeness: Embracing the Broad Biblical Message," Fuller Studio, https://fullerstudio.fuller.edu/shalom-as-wholeness-embracing-the-broad-biblical-message.

14. Matthew Avery Sutton, "Billy Graham Was on the Wrong Side of History," *The Guardian*, February 21, 2018, https://www.theguardian.com/commentisfree/2018/feb/21/billy-graham-wrong-side-history.

15. Martin Luther King Jr., "Letter from a Birmingham Jail," April 16, 1963, African Studies Center, University of Pennsylvania, https://www.africa.upenn.edu/Articles_Gen/Letter_Birmingham.html.

16. Heidi Przybyla, "The Right Way to Cover the Intersection of Religion and Politics," *Politico*, February 29, 2024, https://www.politico.com/news/magazine/2024/02/29/the-right-way-to-cover-the-intersection-of-religion-and-politics-00144261.

17. Kristin Kobes Du Mez, "Some Evangelicals Deny the Coronavirus Threat. It's Because They Love Tough Guys," *Washington Post*, April 2, 2020, https://www.washingtonpost.com/outlook/2020/04/02/conservative-evangelicals-coronavirus-tough-guys.

18. Tim Alberta, *The Kingdom, the Power, and the Glory: American Evangelicals in an Age of Extremism* (HarperCollins, 2023), 279–93.

19. David Fitch, "On Being Pro-Life in the Age of Trump," Fitch's Provocations, September 24, 2024, https://davidfitch.substack.com/p/on-being-pro-life-in-the-age-of-trump.

20. Anthony G. Flood, "In Defense of Lord Acton," January 10, 2020, https://anthonygflood.com/2020/01/in-defense-of-lord-acton.

21. Michael R. Wear, *The Spirit of Our Politics: Spiritual Formation and the Renovation of Public Life* (Zondervan, 2024), 109.

22. Andy Crouch, *Playing God: Redeeming the Gift of Power* (InterVarsity Press, 2013), 25.

23. Warren Throckmorton, "Update on a Spurious Bonhoeffer Quote: Not to Speak Is to Speak, Not to Act Is to Act," *Warren Throckmorton* (blog), November 11, 2016, https://wthrockmorton.com/2016/11/11/update-on-a-spurious-bonhoeffer-quote-not-to-speak-is-to-speak-not-to-act-is-to-act.

24. Walker, *The Nations Belong to God*, 87.

25. Russell Moore, "Political Homelessness Is a Good Start," *Christianity Today*, March 2024, https://www.christianitytoday.com/ct/2024/march/political-homelessness-russell-moore-polarization.html.

26. Mitch Daniels, "Indiana Is Revealing the Real Consequences of One-Party Rule," *Washington Post*, June 18, 2024, https://www.washingtonpost.com/opinions/2024/06/18/republicans-democrats-one-party-state-rule.

27. Wear, *The Spirit of Our Politics*, 114.

28. "Christian Nationalism: A New Approach," Neighborly Faith, accessed May 17, 2024, https://www.neighborlyfaith.org/cn-report-2023.

29. *View of Individuals in Southern Baptist Congregations on Baptist Political Theology*, Land Center for Cultural Engagement, April 2024, https://research.lifeway.com/wp-content/uploads/2024/04/SWBTS-Baptist-Political-Theology-Report.pdf.

30. Winston Churchill, *Churchill by Himself: The Definitive Collection of Quotations*, ed. Richard Langworth (PublicAffairs, 2008).

31. Walker, *The Nations Belong to God*.

32. Stephen Wolfe, *The Case for Christian Nationalism* (Canon Press, 2022), 322.

33. Mark David Hall, *Who's Afraid of Christian Nationalism?: Why Christian Nationalism Is Not an Existential Threat to America or the Church* (Fidelis Books, 2024), 357.

34. Isaac Backus, "An Appeal to the Public for Religious Liberty Against the Oppressions of the Present Day," 1773, Classical Liberals, accessed May 14, 2024, https://classicliberal.tripod.com/misc/appeal.html.

35. Hunter Baker, "How Can We Think Better About Politics as Christians," Ethics & Religious Liberty Commission, June 6, 2024, https://erlc.com/resource/how-can-we-think-better-about-politics-as-christians.

36. Daniel Darling, *A Way with Words: Using Our Online Conversations for Good* (B&H Publishing Group, 2020).

37. Walker, *The Nations Belong to God*, 19.

38. "'Politics is the art of the possible, the attainable—the art of the next best'—Otto von Bismarck," Contemporary Quotations, https://contemporaryquotations.blogs.american.edu/blog/quotes/politics-is-the-art-of-the-possible-the-attainable-the-art-of-the-next-best.

39. Baker, "How Can We Think Better About Politics as Christians."

Chapter 4: Aren't National Myths Just Made Up

1. David McCullough, *The American Spirit: Who We Are and What We Stand For* (Simon & Schuster, 2018), xii.

2. Jeff Diamant, Besheer Mohamed, and Rebecca Leppert, "What the Data Says About Abortion in the U.S.," Pew Research Center, March 25, 2024, https://www.pewresearch.org/short-reads/2024/03/25/what-the-data-says-about-abortion-in-the-us/#how-has-the-number-of-abortions-in-the-us-changed-over-time.

3. John D. Wilsey, "*Jesus and John Wayne*: A Review," *Ad Fontes*, February 9, 2022, https://adfontesjournal.com/book-review/jesus-and-john-wayne-a-review.

4. John D. Wilsey, "Nationalism, Globalism, and American Nationality," Christ Over All, October 2024, https://christoverall.com/article/concise/nationalism-globalism-and-american-nationality.

5. "Westminster Confession of Faith," Administrative Committee PCA, accessed June 4, 2024, https://www.pcaac.org/wp-content/uploads/2022/04/WCFScripureProofs2022.pdf.

6. Daniel Darling, *The Dignity Revolution: Reclaiming God's Rich Vision for Humanity* (Good Book Company, 2018).

7. "Federalist Papers: Primary Documents in American History, Federalist Nos. 51–60," Library of Congress, accessed June 4, 2024, https://guides.loc.gov/federalist-papers/text-51-60.

8. Roosevelt Montás, *Rescuing Socrates: How the Great Books Changed My Life and Why They Matter for a New Generation* (Princeton University Press, 2023), 159.

9. G. K. Chesterton, *Orthodoxy* (Harvard University, 1908), 124.

10. David Dockery, "The Importance of a Christian Worldview," Gospel Project, July 20, 2021, https://gospelproject.lifeway.com/the-importance-of-a-christian-worldview.

11. Sara Tabandeh, *Voices of Wisdom: Karl Marx Quotes* (Sara Tabandeh, n.d.), 15.

12. "How We Got Here," American Revolution Institute of the Society of the Cincinnati, April 5, 2019, https://web.archive.org/web/20210121011701/https://www.americanrevolutioninstitute.org/how-we-got-here-howard-zinn/.

13. William Hogeland, "The Historians Are Fighting," *Slate*, October 30, 2021, https://slate.com/news-and-politics/2021/10/1619-project-historians-controversy-gordon-wood-woody-holton.html.

14. "We Respond to the Historians Who Critiqued the 1619 Project," *New York Times*, December 20, 2019, https://www.nytimes.com/2019/12/20/magazine/we-respond-to-the-historians-who-critiqued-the-1619-project.html.

15. Allen C. Guelzo, "Preaching a Conspiracy Theory," *City Journal*, December 8, 2019, https://www.city-journal.org/article/preaching-a-conspiracy-theory.

16. Orlando Patterson, *Slavery and Social Death: A Comparitive Study* (Harvard University Press, 2018).

17. Jeff Fynn-Paul, *Not Stolen: The Truth About European Colonialism in the New World* (Post Hill Press, 2023), 138.

18. Milton Meltzer, *Slavery: A World History*, updated ed. (Da Capo, 2017).

19. Thomas S. Kidd, *God of Liberty: A Religious History of the American Revolution* (Basic Books, 2017).

20. Mark David Hall, *Proclaim Liberty Throughout All the Land: How Christianity Has Advanced Freedom and Equality for All Americans* (Fidelis Books, 2023), 72.

21. "Benjamin Franklin and Slavery," Benjamin Franklin House, accessed June 4, 2024, https://benjaminfranklinhouse.org/education/benjamin-franklin-and-slavery.

22. Hall, *Proclaim Liberty Throughout All the Land*, 72.

23. Hall, *Proclaim Liberty Throughout All the Land*, 72.

24. Kidd, *God of Liberty*, 147.

25. George Washington, *George Washington: A Collection*, ed. William Barclay Allen (Liberty Classics, 1988), 319.

26. Kay S. Hymowitz, "Uniquely Bad—But Not Uniquely American," *City Journal*, October 16, 2020, https://www.city-journal.org/article/uniquely-bad-but-not-uniquely-american.

27. Wilfred M. McClay, "Of Statues and Symbolic Murder," *First Things*, June 26, 2020, https://www.firstthings.com/web-exclusives/2020/06/of-statues-and-symbolic-murder.

28. Jonah Goldberg, *Suicide of the West: How the Rebirth of Tribalism, Populism, Nationalism, and Identity Politics Is Destroying American Democracy* (Crown Forum, 2018), 34.

29. Hymowitz, "Uniquely Bad—But Not Uniquely American."

30. Frederick Douglass, "What to the Slave Is the Fourth of July?," in *Princeton Readings in Political Thought: Essential Texts from Plato to Populism*, 2nd ed., ed. Mitchell Cohen (Princeton University Press, 2018), 417.

31. "Read Martin Luther King Jr.'s 'I Have a Dream' Speech in Its Entirety," NPR, January 16, 2023, https://www.npr.org/2010/01/18/122701268/i-have-a-dream-speech-in-its-entirety.

32. "Read Martin Luther King Jr.'s 'I Have a Dream' Speech in Its Entirety."

33. C. S. Lewis, *The Weight of Glory* (HarperCollins, 2001), 30–31.

34. Frederick Douglass, "What to the Slave Is the Fourth of July?," 411–26.

35. Richard D. Brown, "On 1619 and Woody Holton's Account of Slavery and the Independence Movement: Six Historians Respond," Medium, September 6, 2021, https://medium.com/@RichardDBrownCT/on-1619-and-woody-holtons-account-of-slavery-and-the-independence-movement-six-historians-respond-b43369ad52d7.

36. Allen C. Guelzo, *Our Ancient Faith: Lincoln, Democracy, and the American Experiment* (Alfred A. Knopf, 2024), 30.

37. Alexis de Tocqueville, *Democracy in America*, vol. 1, part 2, chapter 10 (Floating Press, 2009), 612–13.

38. Charles Marsh, *Strange Glory: A Life of Dietrich Bonhoeffer* (Knopf Doubleday Publishing Group, 2015), 116–27.

39. C. S. Lewis, introduction to *On the Incarnation*, by St. Athanasius, trans. and ed. A Religious of C. S. M. V. (St. Vladimir's Seminary Press, 1993), 4–5.

40. Mark R. Fairchild and Jordan K. Monson, "Was Paul a Slave?," *Christianity Today*, May/June 2024, https://www.christianitytoday.com/ct/2024/may-june/was-paul-saul-tarsus-slave.html.

41. Murray J. Harris, *Slave of Christ: A New Testament Metaphor for Total Devotion to Christ* (InterVarsity Press, 2001), 44.

42. "Resolution on Racial Reconciliation on the 150th Anniversary of the Southern Baptist Convention," SBC, accessed June 5, 2024, https://www.sbc.net/resource-library/resolutions/resolution-on-racial-reconciliation-on-the-150th-anniversary-of-the-southern-baptist-convention.

43. Alan Cross and William Dwight McKissic Sr., *When Heaven and Earth Collide: Racism, Southern Evangelicals, and the Better Way of Jesus* (NewSouth Books, 2014).

44. Ian Olson, "Wesley, Whitefield, and a Gospel That Disrupts," Plough, August 22, 2022, https://www.plough.com/en/topics/faith/witness/wesley-whitefield-and-a-gospel-that-disrupts.

45. Frances FitzGerald, *The Evangelicals: The Struggle to Shape America* (Simon & Schuster, 2017), 40–43.

46. Hall, *Proclaim Liberty Throughout All the Land*, 100.

47. Abraham Lincoln, "Abraham Lincoln's Second Inaugural Address," March 4, 1865, American Battlefield Trust, accessed May 14, 2024, https://www.battlefields.org/learn/primary-sources/abraham-lincolns-second-inaugural-address.

48. Kristin Kobes Du Mez, *Jesus and John Wayne: How White Evangelicals Corrupted a Faith and Fractured a Nation* (Liveright Publishing, 2020).

49. Du Mez, *Jesus and John Wayne*, 297–98.

50. Glenn C. Loury, "The Case for Black Patriotism," *City Journal*, Spring 2021, https://www.city-journal.org/article/the-case-for-black-patriotism.

51. Timothy S. Goeglein, *Toward a More Perfect Union: The Moral and Cultural Case for Teaching the Great American Story* (Fidelis Publishing, 2023), 64.

Chapter 5: The Case for American Exceptionalism

1. F. Scott Fitzgerald, *The Crack-Up* (New Directions Publishing, 2009), 192.

2. "John Winthrop Dreams of a City on a Hill, 1630," American Yawp Reader, accessed June 7, 2024, https://www.americanyawp.com/reader/colliding-cultures/john-winthrop-dreams-of-a-city-on-a-hill-1630.

3. John Newsom, "Joe Biden: 'We Are by Far the Greatest, Powerful, Decent Nation in the World,'" *Winston-Salem Journal*, September 17, 2017, https://journalnow.com/joe-biden-we-are-by-far-the-greatest-powerful-decent-nation-in-the-world/article_40c7d0e8-558e-5c30-af54-0f8ed95d2abb.html.

4. John D. Pierce, "The Abuses and Idolatry of American Exceptionalism," Good Faith Media, August 17, 2021, https://goodfaithmedia.org/the-abuses-and-idolatry-of-american-exceptionalism.

5. John D. Wilsey, *American Exceptionalism and Civil Religion: Reassessing the History of an Idea* (InterVarsity Press, 2015), 88.

6. Wilsey, *American Exceptionalism and Civil Religion*, 65–90.

7. Daniel Darling, *The Dignity Revolution: Reclaiming God's Rich Vision for Humanity* (Good Book Company, 2018).

8. Charles W. Colson, *God and Government: An Insider's View on the Boundaries Between Faith and Politics* (Zondervan, 2010), 345.

9. Wilsey, *American Exceptionalism and Civil Religion*, 217–18.

10. Richard Land, "What Secretary Madeleine Albright Modeled for Us," Ethics & Religious Liberty Commission, April 26, 2022, https://erlc.com/policy-content/what-secretary-albright-modeled-for-us.

11. Brian Zahnd, "American Exceptionalism?," February 20, 2016, https://brianzahnd.com/2016/02/american-exceptionalism-2.

12. Julie Miller, "George Washington, 'The Greatest Man in the World'?," Library of Congress, December 15, 2022, https://blogs.loc.gov/manuscripts/2022/12/george-washington-the-greatest-man-in-the-world.

13. Wendi Maloney, "A President and a King, George Washington and King George III, in a Dangerous Year," Library of Congress, March 2, 2020, https://blogs.loc.gov/loc/2020/03/a-president-and-a-king-george-washington-and-king-george-iii-in-a-dangerous-year.

14. David McCullough, *The American Spirit: Who We Are and What We Stand For* (Simon & Schuster, 2018), 28.

15. Kyle Smith, "George Will's American Exceptionalism," *National Review*, April 6, 2019, https://www.nationalreview.com/corner/american-exceptionalism-george-will-book-the-conservative-sensibility.

16. Thomas Kidd, "Is the Declaration of Independence a Christian Document?," TGC Collective, May 18, 2022, https://www.thegospelcoalition.org/blogs/evangelical-history/is-the-declaration-of-independence-a-christian-document.

17. Jonah Goldberg, *Suicide of the West: How the Rebirth of Tribalism, Populism, Nationalism, and Identity Politics Is Destroying American Democracy* (Crown Forum, 2018), 9, 150.

18. Gilbert K. Chesterton, *What I Saw in America* (Hodder and Stoughton, 1922), 4.

19. Alexis de Tocqueville, *Democracy in America: A New Abridgment for Students* (Lexham Press, 2016), 71.

20. Paul Johnson, *A History of the American People* (Harper Perennial, 1997), 967.

21. Politico Staff, "Marco Rubio's RNC Speech (Text, Video)," *Politico*, August 30, 2012, https://www.politico.com/story/2012/08/marco-rubios-rnc-speech-080493.

22. Christian Union, *"1776 Versus 1789—A Tale of Two Revolutions and America's Present Crisis": A CU Virtual Forum*, YouTube, September 23, 2021, https://www.youtube.com/watch?v=gyWxcJPA8FQ.

23. Konstantin K. Likharev, *Essential Quotes for Scientists and Engineers* (Springer Nature, 2021), 143.

24. "Q & A: Os Guinness on What Freedom in the Balance Looks Like," Interview by Mark Galli, *Christianity Today*, July 3, 2012, https://www.christianitytoday.com/2012/07/os-guinness-freedom-in-balance/.

25. Jim Salter and Dánica Coto, "What We Know About the Young Missionaries and Religious Leader Killed in Haiti," NBC10 Philadelphia, May 25, 2024, https://www.nbcphiladelphia.com/news/national-international/us-missionaries-davy-natalie-lloyd-killed-in-haiti-what-to-know/3868390.

26. Mark Tooley, "American & Christian Duty in Today's World," *Providence*, October 26, 2015, https://providencemag.com/2015/10/american-christian-duty-in-todays-world.

27. Ronald Reagan, "Remarks at a Ceremony Commemorating the 40th Anniversary of the Normandy Invasion, D-Day," June 6, 1984, Pointe du Hoc, France, Voices of Democracy: The U.S. Oratory Project, transcript, https://voicesofdemocracy.umd.edu/ronald-reagan-normandy-speech-point-du-hoc.

28. Charles C. W. Cooke, "My American Dream," *National Review*, July 4, 2019, https://www.nationalreview.com/2019/07/fourth-of-july-my-american-dream.

29. Ronald Reagan, "Address Accepting the Presidential Nomination at the Republican National Convention in Detroit," July 17, 1980, American Presidency Project, accessed June 7, 2024, https://www.presidency.ucsb.edu/documents/address-accepting-the-presidential-nomination-the-republican-national-convention-detroit.

Chapter 6: Christianity Won't Abide Lone Rangers

1. Carl F. H. Henry, *Twilight of a Great Civilization: The Drift Toward Neo-Paganism* (Crossway, 1988), 166.

2. John Adams, "From John Adams to Massachusetts Militia, 11 October 1798," National Archives, accessed May 9, 2024, http://founders.archives.gov/documents/Adams/99-02-02-3102.

3. "Ronald Reagan: Remarks at an Ecumenical Prayer Breakfast in Dallas," American Rhetoric, August 23, 1984, https://www.americanrhetoric.com/speeches/ronaldreaganecumenicalprayer.htm.

4. John Pavlovitz, "Relax Christian, You Don't Have to Go to Church," *John Pavlovitz* (blog), September 4, 2016, https://johnpavlovitz.com/2016/09/04/relax-christian-you-dont-have-to-go-to-church.

5. Elyse Wanshel, "Tucker Carlson Goes into Great Detail About Being 'Physically Mauled' by a 'Demon,'" HuffPost, October 31, 2024, https://www.huffpost.com/entry/tucker-carlson-physically-mauled-by-a-demon_n_6723dca1e4b00acf55d9481a.

6. Skye Jethani, "The Case Against Sermon-Centric Sundays," Premier Christianity, September 20, 2019, https://www.premierchristianity.com/features/the-case-against-sermon-centric-sundays/3530.article.

7. "Imagine Christian mission without the dichotomies of 'us' and 'them,'" reads the marketing copy for one book, https://www.ocms.ac.uk/books/evangelization-or-colonization.

8. Andrea Palpant Dilley, "The Surprising Discovery About Those Colonialist, Proselytizing Missionaries," *Christianity Today*, January/February 2014, http://www.christianitytoday.com/ct/2014/january-february/world-missionaries-made.html.

9. John Stevens, "Tim Keller's Witness at the Parliamentary Prayer Breakfast," Gospel Coalition, July 5, 2018, https://www.thegospelcoalition.org/article/tim-keller-parliamentary-prayer-breakfast.

10. Charles Colson and Nancy Pearcey, *How Now Shall We Live?* (Tyndale House Publishers, 2011), 298.

11. Stephen O. Presley, *Cultural Sanctification: Engaging the World like the Early Church* (Eerdmans, 2024), 17.

12. Daniel Darling, "The Rise of Non-worshipping 'Evangelicals,'" *World*, August 28, 2023, https://wng.org/opinions/the-rise-of-non-worshipping-evangelicals-1693108058.

13. Jim Davis and Michael Graham with Ryan P. Burge, *The Great Dechurching: Who's Leaving, Why Are They Going, and What Will It Take to Bring Them Back?* (Zondervan, 2023).

14. Mark Tooley, "A Christian Nation?," Law & Liberty, February 15, 2024, https://lawliberty.org/a-christian-nation.

15. John Stott, *The Living Church: Convictions of a Lifelong Pastor* (InterVarsity Press, 2011), 19.

16. Gregg R. Allison, *Sojourners and Strangers: The Doctrine of the Church* (Crossway, 2012), 29.

17. Parts of this section were adapted from Daniel Darling, *The Original Jesus: Trading the Myths We Create for the Savior Who Is* (Baker Books, 2015), 126–27.

18. "Erick Erickson: Politics and Faith at a Crossroads," *News Courier*, September 23, 2023, https://www.enewscourier.com/opinion/columns/erick-erickson-politics-and-faith-at-a-crossroads/article_fda16c7e-58a0-11ee-8715-8b6a4df69cb9.html.

19. "What Is the Mission of the Church?," *Credo Magazine*, April 17, 2012, https://credomag.com/2012/04/what-is-the-mission-of-the-church.

20. Ginny Mooney, "Os Guinness Calls for a New Christian Renaissance," Christian Post, June 18, 2011, https://www.christianpost.com/news/os-guinness-calls-for-a-new-christian-renaissance.html.

21. Colson and Pearcey, *How Now Shall We Live?*, 303.

22. Daniel Darling, *The Dignity Revolution: Reclaiming God's Rich Vision for Humanity* (Good Book Company, 2018).

23. Eric Bryant, "'The Next Generation' with Andy Stanley," May 6, 2022, https://ericbryant.org/2022/05/06/the-next-generation-with-andy-stanley.

24. Ayaan Hirsi Ali, "Why I Am Now a Christian," UnHerd, December 25, 2023, https://unherd.com/2023/12/why-i-am-now-a-christian-2.

25. Paul Kingsnorth, "The Cross and the Machine," *The Free Press*, December 25, 2023, https://www.thefp.com/p/paul-kingsnorth-christianity-faith.

26. Joseph Pearce, "Long Defeat and Final Victory," Imaginative Conservative, April 8, 2023, https://theimaginativeconservative.org/2023/04/long-defeat-final-victory-joseph-pearce.html.

27. Louise Perry, "We Are Repaganizing," *First Things*, October 1, 2023, https://firstthings.com/we-are-repaganizing.

28. Mooney, "Os Guinness Calls for a New Christian Renaissance."

29. "Our Ancient Faith: Lincoln, Democracy, and the American Experiment with Allen Guelzo," *Life and Books and Everything* podcast, hosted by Kevin DeYoung, February 14, 2024, https://podcasts.apple.com/us/podcast/life-and-books-and-everything/id1526483896?i=1000645284673&r=3287.

30. "Our Ancient Faith: Lincoln, Democracy, and the American Experiment with Allen Guelzo."

31. Mark Dever, *The Church: The Gospel Made Visible* (B&H Academic, 2012), x–xi.

32. See also Daniel Darling, *Agents of Grace: How to Bridge Divides and Love as Jesus Loved* (Zondervan, 2023).

33. Kristin Kobes Du Mez, *Jesus and John Wayne: How White Evangelicals Corrupted a Faith and Fractured a Nation* (Liveright Publishing, 2020), 7.

34. Charles Colson and Ellen Santilli Vaughn, *The Body: Being Light in the Darkness* (Thomas Nelson, 1994), 73.

35. J. D. Greear, "The Church Isn't a Cruise Ship; It's an Aircraft Carrier," J. D. Greear Ministries, July 8, 2015, https://jdgreear.com/the-church-isnt-a-cruise-ship-its-an-aircraft-carrier.

36. See Daniel Darling, *A Way with Words: Using Our Online Conversations for Good* (B&H Publishing Group, 2020).

37. Matt Smethurst (@MattSmethurst), "The church is the only human institution Jesus started, and the only one inhabited by the Spirit and glory of God. —@TimKellerNYC," Twitter (now X), July 27, 2024, https://twitter.com/MattSmethurst/status/1817285292799443268.

38. Brad Wilcox, *Get Married: Why Americans Must Defy the Elites, Forge Strong Families, and Save Civilization* (HarperCollins, 2024), 32.

39. Wilcox, *Get Married*, 175–78.

40. John Paul II, "Homily of John Paul II," Vatican, November 30, 1986, https://www.vatican.va/content/john-paul-ii/en/homilies/1986/documents/hf_jp-ii_hom_19861130_perth-australia.html.

41. Francis A. Schaeffer, *The Mark of the Christian* (InterVarsity Press, 2013), 22, 52.

42. "5 Facts About Southern Baptist Disaster Relief," Baptist Convention of Iowa, accessed July 28, 2024, https://bciowa.org/5-facts-about-southern-baptist-disaster-relief.

43. George W. Bush, "Rallying the Armies of Compassion," White House Archives, accessed July 28, 2024, https://georgewbush-whitehouse.archives.gov/news/reports/faithbased.html.

44. "Our Mission," Everyone's Wilson, https://everyoneswilson.org/mission.

Chapter 7: The War on the Family

1. Lyndon B. Johnson, "Commencement Address at Howard University: 'To Fulfill These Rights,'" June 4, 1965, American Presidency Project, https://www.presidency.ucsb.edu/documents/commencement-address-howard-university-fulfill-these-rights.

2. "The Negro Family: The Case for National Action," U.S. Department of Labor, March 1965, https://www.dol.gov/general/aboutdol/history/webid-moynihan.

3. Johnson, "Commencement Address at Howard University: 'To Fulfill These Rights.'"

4. Rob Lester, "Daniel Patrick Moynihan's Prophecy," *Compact*, March 4, 2024, https://www.compactmag.com/article/daniel-patrick-moynihans-prophecy.

5. Rich Villodas (@richvillodas), "Here's a few signs that Christians might be caught in the grip of Culture Wars," Twitter (now X), October 18, 2024, https://x.com/richvillodas/status/1847391079210905698.

6. "Just War and Our Cultural Conflict," Clearly Reformed, September 8, 2022, https://clearlyreformed.org/just-war-and-our-cultural-conflict.

7. Ryan N. S. Topping, "The Long War Against the Family (Part I)," *Crisis Magazine*, January 28, 2013, https://crisismagazine.com/opinion/the-long-war-against-the-family-part-i.

8. Topping, "The Long War Against the Family (Part I)."

9. "Decree on the Apostolate of the Laity, Apostolicam Actuositatem, Solemnly Promulgated by His Holiness, Pope Paul VI, on November 18, 1965," Vatican,

accessed July 29, 2024, https://www.vatican.va/archive/hist_councils/ii_vatican_council/documents/vat-ii_decree_19651118_apostolicam-actuositatem_en.html.

10. "Monthly Abortion Provision Study," Guttmacher, March 2025, https://www.guttmacher.org/monthly-abortion-provision-study?gad_source=1&gad_campaignid=1879416845&gbraid=0AAAAAD-Q3tro_FFPOFY_L8K4rBUr-QSLB&gclid=CjwKCAjw3MXBBhAzEiwA0vLXQcrWjROuv7rgk3oDXLFZ6HdLYkpTT7ihTw4XV8AM75gArdPxB8uk-xoCWJ0QAvD_BwE.

11. Aubrie Spady, "Buttigieg's Remark Claiming Men Are 'More Free' with Easy Access to Abortion Sparks Outrage Among Pro-lifers," Fox News, July 30, 2024, https://www.foxnews.com/politics/buttigieg-comment-men-free-access-abortion-deeply-troubling-pro-lifers.

12. Ryan N. S. Topping, "The Long War Against the Family (Part II)," *Crisis Magazine*, January 29, 2013, https://crisismagazine.com/opinion/the-long-war-against-the-family-part-ii.

13. Topping, "The Long War Against the Family (Part II)."

14. "Address of His Holiness Benedict XVI on the Occasion of Christmas Greetings to the Roman Curia," Vatican, December 21, 2012, accessed July 30, 2024, https://www.vatican.va/content/benedict-xvi/en/speeches/2012/december/documents/hf_ben-xvi_spe_20121221_auguri-curia.html.

15. Katie J. McCoy, *To Be a Woman: The Confusion over Female Identity and How Christians Can Respond* (B&H Publishing Group, 2023).

16. USA Today, *Sen. Blackburn Asks Supreme Court Nominee to Define "Woman,"* YouTube, March 23, 2022, https://www.youtube.com/watch?v=BWtGzJxiONU.

17. David Masci, "An Argument Against Same-Sex Marriage: An Interview with Rick Santorum," Pew Research Center, April 24, 2008, https://www.pewresearch.org/religion/2008/04/24/an-argument-against-same-sex-marriage-an-interview-with-rick-santorum.

18. Richard Land and Barrett Duke, "Being Salt and Light in an Unsavory and Dark Age: The Christian and Politics," *Southern Baptist Journal of Theology* 11, no. 4 (Winter 2007): 82–99.

19. Richard Fry, "A Record-High Share of 40-Year-Olds in the U.S. Have Never Been Married," Pew Research Center, June 28, 2023, https://www.pewresearch.org/short-reads/2023/06/28/a-record-high-share-of-40-year-olds-in-the-us-have-never-been-married.

20. Daniel Cox, "The Societal Cost of the Marriage Decline," Institute for Family Studies, March 25, 2024, https://ifstudies.org/blog/the-societal-cost-of-the-marriage-decline.

21. Julissa Cruz, "Marriage: More Than a Century of Change," National Center for Family & Marriage Research, https://www.bgsu.edu/content/dam/BGSU/college-of-arts-and-sciences/NCFMR/documents/FP/FP-13-13.pdf.

22. "U.S. Fertility Rate Drops to Another Historic Low," National Center for Health Statistics, April 24, 2024, https://www.cdc.gov/nchs/pressroom/nchs_press_releases/2024/20240525.htm.

23. Ross Douthat, "The Wild Ideas of Social Conservatives," *New York Times*, April 28, 2015, https://archive.nytimes.com/douthat.blogs.nytimes.com/2015/04/28/the-wild-ideas-of-social-conservatives.

24. John Stonestreet and Shane Morris, "The Predicted Push for Polyamory Is Out in Full Force," Breakpoint Colson Center, February 7, 2024, https://www.breakpoint.org/the-predicted-push-for-polyamory-is-out-in-full-force.

25. Caitlin Emma, "Obama Administration Releases Directive on Transgender Rights to School Bathrooms," *Politico*, May 12, 2016, https://www.politico.com/story/2016/05/obama-administration-title-ix-transgender-student-rights-223149.

26. Dan Quayle, "Address to the Commonwealth Club of California," May 19, 1992, Dan Quayle, accessed August 2, 2024, http://www.vicepresidentdanquayle.com/speeches_StandingFirm_CCC_3.html.

27. Barbara Dafoe Whitehead, "Dan Quayle Was Right," *Atlantic*, April 1993, https://www.theatlantic.com/magazine/archive/1993/04/dan-quayle-was-right/307015.

28. Isabel Sawhill, "20 Years Later, It Turns Out Dan Quayle Was Right About Murphy Brown and Unmarried Moms," *Washington Post*, May 25, 2012, https://www.washingtonpost.com/opinions/20-years-later-it-turns-out-dan-quayle-was-right-about-murphy-brown-and-unmarried-moms/2012/05/25/gJQAsNCJqU_story.html.

29. Melissa S. Kearney, *The Two-Parent Privilege: How Americans Stopped Getting Married and Started Falling Behind* (University of Chicago Press, 2023), 24–25.

30. Kearney, *The Two-Parent Privilege*, 15.

31. Brad Wilcox, *Get Married: Why Americans Must Defy the Elites, Forge Strong Families, and Save Civilization* (HarperCollins, 2024), xiv.

32. Kearney, *The Two-Parent Privilege*, 15.

33. Brad Wilcox et al., "Stronger Families, Safer Streets," American Enterprise Institute, December 13, 2013, https://www.aei.org/research-products/report/stronger-families-safer-streets.

34. W. Bradford Wilcox and Nicholas H. Wolfinger, "Men & Marriage: Debunking the Ball and Chain Myth," Institute for Family Studies, accessed August 2,

2024, https://ifstudies.org/ifs-admin/resources/men-and-marriage-research-brief.pdf.

35. Chris Bullivant and Brad Wilcox, "The Rise of 'Marriage Deserts' and What We Can Do About Them," Institute for Family Studies, July 30, 2024, https://ifstudies.org/blog/the-rise-of-marriage-deserts-and-what-we-can-do-about-them.

36. Pope Francis et al., *Not Just Good, but Beautiful: The Complementary Relationship between Man and Woman* (Plough Publishing House, 2015), 96.

37. Asher Witmer, "Dear Church, Please Stop Idolizing Marriage," September 14, 2018, https://www.asherwitmer.com/stop-idolizing-marriage.

38. Brad Wilcox, "Want to Slash Your Risk for Divorce? Start Going to Church," American Enterprise Institute, February 14, 2024, https://www.aei.org/articles/want-to-slash-your-risk-for-divorce-start-going-to-church.

39. Peter McFadden, "Churches Should Lead a Relationship Revolution," Institute for Family Studies, March 21, 2023, https://ifstudies.org/blog/churches-should-lead-a-relationship-revolution.

40. Russell Moore, "The Sexual Revolution's Coming Refugee Crisis," July 7, 2015, https://www.russellmoore.com/2015/07/07/the-sexual-revolutions-coming-refugee-crisis.

41. Zachary Mettler, "The Good News You Haven't Heard About Marriage: Divorce Rate Hits 50-Year Low," Daily Citizen, September 25, 2023, https://dailycitizen.focusonthefamily.com/the-good-news-you-havent-heard-about-marriage-divorce-rate-hits-50-year-low.

42. Wendy Wang, "The U.S. Divorce Rate Has Hit a 50-Year Low," Institute for Family Studies, November 10, 2020, https://ifstudies.org/blog/the-us-divorce-rate-has-hit-a-50-year-low.

43. Giulia Carbonaro, "Americans Are Becoming Less Accepting of Same-Sex Relationships, Poll Shows," *Newsweek*, June 17, 2023, https://www.newsweek.com/americans-less-accepting-same-sex-relationships-poll-shows-1807422.

44. Christine Emba, "Let's Rethink Sex," *Washington Post*, November 26, 2017, https://www.washingtonpost.com/opinions/lets-rethink-sex/2017/11/26/ d8546a86-d2d5-11e7-b62d-d9345ced896d_story.html.

45. Ericka Anderson, "We Can Turn the Fertility Crisis Around," *World*, August 20, 2024, https://wng.org/opinions/we-can-turn-the-fertility-crisis-around-1724148064.

46. Kevin DeYoung, "It's Time for a New Culture War Strategy," Gospel Coalition, June 17, 2020, https://www.thegospelcoalition.org/blogs/kevin-deyoung/its-time-for-a-new-culture-war-strategy.

Chapter 8: Christians Can't Abandon Schools

1. Noah Webster, "On the Necessity of Fostering American Identity After Independence," *Making the Revolution: America, 1763–1791*, America in Class from the National Humanities Center, accessed August 9, 2024, https://americainclass.org/sources/makingrevolution/independence/text3/websteramericanidentity.pdf.

2. George Washington, "First Annual Address," January 8, 1790, Avalon Project, Lillian Goldman Law Library, accessed August 9, 2024, https://avalon.law.yale.edu/18th_century/washs01.asp.

3. George Washington, "Eighth Annual Address to Congress," December 7, 1796, American Presidency Project, accessed August 9, 2024, https://www.presidency.ucsb.edu/documents/eighth-annual-address-congress.

4. Adam Harris, "George Washington's Broken Dream of a National University," *Atlantic*, September 21, 2018, https://www.theatlantic.com/education/archive/2018/09/founders-national-university/571003.

5. Aditi Sangal et al., "University Presidents Testify Before Congress as US Colleges See More Protests," CNN, May 23, 2024, https://www.cnn.com/business/live-news/college-campus-antisemitism-hearing-05-23-24/index.html.

6. John M. Ellis, "Woke Universities Lead America to a Primitive State," *Wall Street Journal*, November 2, 2020, https://www.wsj.com/articles/woke-universities-lead-america-to-a-primitive-state-11604359918.

7. Alliance Defending Freedom, *William Barr Receives ADF's Edwin Meese III Award*, YouTube, May 21, 2021, https://www.youtube.com/watch?v=3Torq_9HJDg.

8. Judd Legum, "Exclusive: Florida Educators Trained to Teach Students Christian Nationalism," Popular Information, May 28, 2024, https://popular.info/p/exclusive-florida-educators-trained.

9. Ben Shapiro, *The Right Side of History: How Reason and Moral Purpose Made the West Great* (HarperCollins, 2019), 138.

10. Charles W. Colson, *God and Government: An Insider's View on the Boundaries Between Faith and Politics* (Zondervan, 2010), 213.

11. Neil Shenvi and Pat Sawyer, *Critical Dilemma: The Rise of Critical Theories and Social Justice Ideology—Implications for the Church and Society* (Harvest House Publishers, 2023), 89–140. This summary was helpfully adapted from this review: Brittany Shields, review of *Critical Dilemma: The Rise of Critical Theories and Social Justice Ideology—Implications for the Church and Society*, by Neil Shenvi

and Pat Sawyer, Shelf Reflection, May 31, 2023, https://www.shelfreflection.com/blog/critical-dilemma.

12. "Read Martin Luther King Jr.'s 'I Have a Dream' Speech in Its Entirety," NPR, January 16, 2023, https://www.npr.org/2010/01/18/122701268/i-have-a-dream-speech-in-its-entirety.

13. Mike Gonzalez and Katharine Gorka, "How Cultural Marxism Threatens the United States—and How Americans Can Fight It," Heritage Foundation, November 14, 2022, https://www.heritage.org/progressivism/report/how-cultural-marxism-threatens-the-united-states-and-how-americans-can-fight.

14. Daniel Darling, *The Dignity Revolution: Reclaiming God's Rich Vision for Humanity* (Good Book Company, 2018).

15. Erick-Woods Erickson, "The Right Goes Marxist, Trans-Conservative," Erick Erickson's Show Notes, May 16, 2024, https://ewerickson.substack.com/p/the-right-goes-marxist-trans-conservative.

16. "22+ US Literacy Statistics: Literacy Rate, Average Reading Level," May 16, 2024, https://www.brightfuturesny.com/post/us-literacy-statistics.

17. Kara Bettis, "Donna Gaines Showing Neighborly Love Through Literacy," Biblical Recorder, August 14, 2017, https://www.brnow.org/news/Donna-Gaines-showing-neighborly-love-through-liter.

18. "Local Education Inequities Across U.S. Revealed in New Stanford Data Set," Stanford University, April 29, 2016, https://news.stanford.edu/stories/2016/04/local-education-inequities-across-u-s-revealed-new-stanford-data-set.

19. "New Poll: School Choice Support Soars from 2020," American Federation for Children, May 21, 2024, https://www.federationforchildren.org/new-poll-school-choice-support-soars-from-2020.

20. Sarah Rumpf-Whitten, "Condoleezza Rice Defends School Choice, Argues That It Is a Race Issue: 'Are You for School Choice or Not?,'" Fox News, June 21, 2024, https://www.foxnews.com/us/condoleezza-rice-defends-school-choice-argues-race-issue-are-you-school-choice-not.

21. Divya Kumar, "DeSantis Signs 3 Bills Bringing Major Change to Florida Universities," *Tampa Bay Times*, May 15, 2023, https://www.tampabay.com/news/education/2023/05/15/desantis-new-college-higher-education-sb266-christopher-rufo-critical-race-theory-gender-major-changes-legislation-indoctrination.

22. James Taranto, "The Harvard of the Unwoke," *Wall Street Journal*, January 19, 2024, https://www.wsj.com/articles/the-harvard-of-the-unwoke-university-of-florida-is-fixing-higher-education-13f22b77.

23. Becca Wright, "Gov. Lee: University of Tennessee Civics Institute Honors Ideas That 'Make America Great,'" *Knoxville News Sentinel*, May 12, 2022, https://www.knoxnews.com/story/news/education/2022/05/12/gov-bill-lee-university-tennessee-civics-institute-model-country/9730171002; Kate McGee, "Two-Thirds of Board Members Overseeing Texas Public Universities Are Abbott Donors. They're Not Shy About Wielding Influence," *Texas Tribune*, October 18, 2022, https://www.texastribune.org/2022/10/18/greg-abbott-texas-universities-donors.

24. Adam Sabes, "Harvard to Ask Undergraduate Applicants About Time 'They Strongly Disagreed with Someone,'" Campus Reform, August 8, 2024, https://www.campusreform.org/article/harvard-ask-undergraduate-applicants-time-they-strongly-disagreed-someone/26079.

25. "How Does a College Degree Improve Graduates' Employment and Earnings Potential?," Association of Public & Land-Grant Universities, accessed August 11, 2024, https://www.aplu.org/our-work/4-policy-and-advocacy/publicuvalues/employment-earnings.

26. Jim Davis and Michael Graham with Ryan P. Burge, *The Great Dechurching: Who's Leaving, Why Are They Going, and What Will It Take to Bring Them Back?* (Zondervan, 2023), 111.

27. Jessica Lea, "Will Your Teens Lose Their Faith if They Go to College? Ryan Burge on What the Data Shows," ChurchLeaders, November 17, 2023, https://churchleaders.com/news/462908-teens-lose-faith-college-ryan-burge-shows.html.

28. Wendy Wang, "The Link Between a College Education and a Lasting Marriage," Pew Research Center, December 4, 2015, https://www.pewresearch.org/short-reads/2015/12/04/education-and-marriage/.

29. Brad Wilcox, "The Awfulness of Elite Hypocrisy on Marriage," *Atlantic*, February 13, 2024, https://www.theatlantic.com/ideas/archive/2024/02/elitism-marriage-rates-hypocrisy/677401.

30. Francis Schaeffer, "On Education," Francis Schaeffer Study Center, 1982, https://www.schaefferstudycenter.org/francis-schaeffer-on-education.

31. David S. Dockery, "Toward a Theology of Higher Education," *Journal of the Evangelical Theological Society* 62, no. 1 (2019): 5–23, https://etsjets.org/wp-content/uploads/2019/03/files_JETS-PDFs_62_62-1_JETS_62.1_5-23_Dockery.pdf.

32. Noah Webster, "Epilogue: Securing the Republic," in Webster, *On the Education of Youth in America*, 1788, University of Chicago Press, accessed August 11, 2024, https://press-pubs.uchicago.edu/founders/documents/v1ch18s26.html.

Notes

Chapter 9: Restoring "E Pluribus Unum"

1. Jim Mattis, "Jim Mattis: Duty, Democracy and the Threat of Tribalism," *Wall Street Journal*, August 28, 2019, https://www.wsj.com/articles/jim-mattis-duty -democracy-and-the-threat-of-tribalism-11566984601.

2. George Washington, "Farewell Address," September 17, 1796, American Presidency Project, accessed August 26, 2024, https://www.presidency.ucsb.edu /documents/farewell-address.

3. Nathan P. Kalmoe and Lilliana Mason, "Lethal Mass Partisanship: Prevalence, Correlates, and Electoral Contingencies," 2018, https://www.dannyhayes.org /uploads/6/9/8/5/69858539/kalmoe___mason_ncapsa_2019_-_lethal_partisanship _-_final_lmedit.pdf.

4. "Americans View Country as Deeply Divided, but Believe Most Have Much in Common," Ipsos, April 29, 2024, https://www.ipsos.com/en-us/with-honor-ipsos.

5. David Zahl, *Seculosity: How Career, Parenting, Technology, Food, Politics, and Romance Became Our New Religion and What to Do About It* (Fortress Press, 2019), Kindle ed., location 1220.

6. Francis Fukuyama, "Against Identity Politics," *Foreign Affairs*, September /October 2018, https://www.foreignaffairs.com/articles/americas/2018-08-14 /against-identity-politics-tribalism-francis-fukuyama.

7. "The American Dream," Martin Luther King Jr. Research and Education Institute, Stanford University, July 3, 2014, https://kinginstitute.stanford .edu/king-papers/publications/knock-midnight-inspiration-great-sermons -reverend-martin-luther-king-jr-4.

8. Arthur C. Brooks, *Love Your Enemies: How Decent People Can Save America from the Culture of Contempt* (HarperCollins, 2019), Kindle ed., location 2064.

9. Dietrich Bonhoeffer, *Life Together: The Classic Exploration of Christian in Community* (HarperOne, 2009), 35.

10. Margaret E. Banyan, "Civic Virtue," Britannica, accessed August 26, 2024, https://www.britannica.com/topic/civic-virtue.

11. Alexandra Hudson, *The Soul of Civility: Timeless Principles to Heal Society and Ourselves* (St. Martin's Press, 2023), 162.

12. Brian P. Raftery, "Benjamin Franklin and the Civic Virtues of the First American," Grand Canyon University, March 6, 2017, https://www.gcu.edu /blog/criminal-justice-government-and-public-administration/benjamin -franklin-and-civic-virtues.

13. Joe Scarborough, "America Is Doing Just Fine," *Atlantic*, July 10, 2023, https://www.theatlantic.com/ideas/archive/2023/07/uncle-sam-american-military-patriotism/674644.

Chapter 10: Saving America from Your Backyard

1. Edmund Burke, *Edmund Burke: Selected Writings and Speeches* (Regnery Publishing, 1997), 539.

2. Bryan English, text message to author, September 2, 2024.

3. Drew Dyck, *Just Show Up: How Small Acts of Faithfulness Change Everything (A Guide for Exhausted Christians)* (Moody Publishers, 2023), 62.

4. Seth Kaplan, *Fragile Neighborhoods: Repairing American Society, One Zip Code at a Time* (Little, Brown, 2023), 193.

5. Kaplan, *Fragile Neighborhoods*, 193.

6. Gilbert Keith Chesterton, *The Collected Works of G. K. Chesterton*, vol. 20 (Ignatius Press, 2001), 597.

7. Ronald Reagan, "January 5, 1967: Inaugural Address (Public Ceremony)," Ronald Reagan Presidential Library & Museum, https://www.reaganlibrary.gov/archives/speech/january-5-1967-inaugural-address-public-ceremony.

INDEX

Abbott, Greg, 200
Abolitionist movements, 106
abortion, 171
active citizenship, 82, 145–146, 216–217
activism, 92–94, 216–217, 221–224
Acton, Lord, 77
Adams, John, 8, 141–142
Adams, John Quincy, 9
advocacy, performative activism vs, 93–94
Ali, Ayaan Hirsi, 153
alienation, 41–43
Alito, Samuel, 31
Allison, Gregg R., 147–148
America
  creed, 127–128
  culture shift, 77, 153
  culture wars, 168–169
  foreign policy, 135–137
  founding of, 111, 127–128 (*see also* American founders)
  history of (*see* US history)
  isolationism vs interventionism, 133–138
  nihilist view of, 111
  original sin of, 29, 102
  role of Christianity in founding of, 7–13
  source of its greatness, 142
  spiritual awakening in, 155–156
  territorial expansion, 122–123
  uniqueness of (*see* American exceptionalism)
American democracy
  decline in faith of, 23
  dependence on morality and spirituality, 12–13
  doomsday outlook of, 212
  as fragile, 28
  Goldberg's views on, 126–127
  importance of Christianity to, 141
  individualism as threat to, 214–215
  misunderstandings on nature of, 13–14
  as secular enterprise, 24
  Tocqueville's assessment of, 111–112, 128, 214
American exceptionalism
  categories of, 122–123
  Chesterton on, 127–128
  closed, 122–123
  doctrine of, 122
  extending blessings outside its borders, 135–138
  open, 123–124
  stewardship and, 124, 131–134
  triumphalist mindset, 123–124
  understanding of, 130–132
  Washington as example of, 125
American experiment
  connecting to higher purpose, 6
  critical theory and, 192
  education and, 189–190
  importance of Christianity to, 8
  Marxism and, 190
  preservation of, xvii
  as rare, 227
  slavery, as contradiction to, 106–107
  success of, 109, 129
  uniqueness of, 141
  Washington on, 205
American flag, 50–53
American founders
  applying their wisdom to contemporary challenges, 133–134

American founders (*continued*)
Christianity's influence on, 8–9
common grace and, 101
on contradiction of slavery to American experiment, 106–107
First Amendment to the Constitution and, 20–21
on natural rights, 23–24
on producing a well-educated citizenry, 186, 188–189
resisting church-state idea, 19–20
unique vision of, 126–127
vision on political power, 81–82
American identity, reckoning with, 99
American presidents, on Christianity, 10–13
American revolution, 125–126, 129–130
Anabaptists, 42–43
Andersen, Ericka, 183
anti-patriots, 49, 70, 100
ARISE2Read ministry, 196
Athanasius of Alexandria, 141
Atheism, 16
Augustine, 38, 45–46
authority, unlearning poisoned view of, 48

Babylon, 32, 40–41, 43, 46, 72–73, 88
Backus, Isaac, 89
Baker, Hunter, 90, 94
Barr, William, 188
Barrett, Amy Coney, nominating hearing of, 5
"Battle Hymn of the Republic", 70
Bellevue Baptist, 196
Benedict XVI (pope), 172
Berkowitz, Peter, 15
Bismarck, Otto von, 93
Blankenhorn, David, 213
Bonhoeffer, Dietrich, 92, 111, 211
Booker, Cory, 6
Braver Angels, 213–214
Brooks, Arthur, 210
Bryan, William Jennings, 11
Burge, Ryan, 201
Burke, Edmund, 224
Bush, George W., 4, 57, 165
Buttigieg, Pete, 171

Carlson, Tucker, 143
Carney, Timothy P., 181
Carter, Jimmy, xii–xiii
Catholic thinkers, 87
charity, 19
Chesterton, G. K., 13, 40, 45, 59, 127–128, 226
children (*see also* families)
as a burden, 183
family structure's affect on, 176–177
as obstacle to human flourishing, 170–171
of single-parent families, 175–176
Christian Church
active citizenship and, 145–146
as army of compassion, 165
as body of truth, 151–156
Christians retreating from, 142–144
corporate worship experiences, 148–149
as equipping centers, 159–161
in first century, 148–149
government officials connecting with, 219–220
as honorable, 156–159
as local and global, 147–148
mission of, 150
nurturing healthy family life, 179–180
pressure to give up its distinctiveness, 152–153
as priority, 146–147
providing community, 164–166
pursuit of integrity, 157
role of pastors in, 159
as starting point for America's renewal, 145
strengthening families, 162, 179–180
struggling families and, 180–181

Index

teaching effective communications, 160
as work of God, 158–159
working toward unity, 163–164
Christian colleges, 202–203
Christian missions, 144–145
Christian nationalists, 86–90
Christian state, justification in Scripture for, 87–88
Christian unity, 163–164
Christian virtue, 65
Christianity
American founders influenced by, 8–9
enhancing societies, 145
impact on America's founding, 7–13
insistence on truth, 169
Lincoln shaped by, 10–11
Marxism vs, 191
opposition to, 154–155
Second Great Awakening, 156
Christians
duty vs responsibility, 134
imposing political purity tests, 144
political work of, 160–161
in public office, 93
required to speak the truth in love, 151–152, 154
responsibilities to kingdom of God, xvii
responsibilities to nation-states, xvii
retreating from churches, 142–144
seeing US as being like Babylon, 32, 40
Church. *See* Christian Church
Church Ambassador Network, 219–221
church-skeptic narratives, 142–143
church-state idea, 19–20, 87–88
citizenship
active, 82, 146
local stewardship, 224–225
well-educated, 186, 188–189
civic education, 215
civic pilgrimages, 27–28
civic reverence, traditional rituals of, 27
civic virtue, 213–217
civil religion, 22–23
Civil Rights Act of 1964, 167–168
civil rights movement, 116
civility, 210–212
classic liberalism, 15
Clinton, Bill, 4–5
closed American exceptionalism, 122–123
college ministry, 202
colleges and universities. *See* higher education
Colson, Chuck, 62–63, 123, 145–146, 152, 158, 191
common grace, 101
community loyalty, 44–45
compelled love, 47–49
Cooke, Charles C. W., 136–137
corporate worship experiences, 148–149
countercultural truth, 152–153
country love. *See* love of country
covenant marriage, 162
critical theory, 192–194
Crouch, Andy, 80–81
Crouch, Daryl, 166, 222–223
cultural Christians, 23
culture wars, 168–169
cynical persons, xviii

Daniels, Mitch, 84
Davis, Jim, 201
Dawkins, Richard, 23
Dean, Howard, 5
Declaration of Independence, 108–111
DeLullo, Erin, 223
democracy. *See* American democracy
DeSantis, Ron, 200
despotism, 205–206
deterrence, 137
Dever, Mark, 156–157
DeYoung, Kevin, 168–169, 184

disloyalty, 44
disordered love, 47–48
dissent-is-patriotism camp, 30–31
divine power, 77–78
divisiveness
  dehumanizing rhetoric and, 210
  spirit of, 205–207
  as warning of coming civil war, 208–209
divorce, 179, 182
Dockery, David, 103
Doherty, Bill, 213
Douglass, Frederick, 55, 108–109, 110–111
Douthat, Ross, 173–174
Dreisbach, Daniel L., 20
Du Mez, Kristin Kobes, 69–70, 76, 115, 117, 157
Duke, Barrett, 172–173
Dyck, Drew, 221

earthly power vs divine power, 77–78
education. *See* higher education; public education
Eisenhower, Dwight D., 13
Elliot, Jim, 132
emancipation, 118–119
Emba, Christine, 182
Engels, Friedrich, 170
English, Bryan, 220–221
Epistle of Mathetes to Diognotus, xvii
Erickson, Erick-Woods, 150, 194
evangelical movement, as sociological phenomenon, 117
Everyone's Wilson, 223
exilic theology, 41–43

faith, as public exercise, 72–76
familiarity, 46–47, 58
families (*see also* marriage)
  advocating policies for healthy, 181
  as central building block of society, 168
  children and (*see* children)
  Christian Church strengthening, 162, 179–180
  fertility crisis, 183
  gender and, 171–172
  government incentives for, 181
  progressive culture elites' war against, 168–172
  renewal of, 177–178
  single-parent, 175–176, 177
  structure of, 176–177
  struggling, 180–181, 184
  two-parent households, 175–177
Fea, John, 9–10
Finney, Charles Grandison, 115–116
First Amendment to the Constitution, 20–22
Fitch, David, 77
Ford, Gerald, xii
France, 16
Franklin, Benjamin, 9, 106, 215–216, 227
French revolution, 129–130
Fukuyama, Francis, 209

Gaines, Donna, 196
gay marriage, 173–174
gender, as a social construct, 171–172
gender transition surgery, 188
George III, King of England, 125
Gettysburg, Pennsylvania, 207–208
Gettysburg Address, 108
God
  church and (*see* Christian Church)
  command for love, xi–xii, 37
  covenant with Noah, 88
  devotion to, 73
  natural rights as endowed by, 23–24
  ordering love, 39, 141
  place in politics, 74–75
  relationship with, 143, 147, 216
Goeglein, Timothy S., 119–120, 215
Goldberg, Arthur, 17
Goldberg, Jonah, 23, 108, 126, 127
goodness, as source of America's greatness, 142
Gospel, Christian, as political, 71–72
Graham, Billy, 74
Graham, Michael, 201

Index

gratitude
  attentiveness and, 46–49
  capability of losing, 132
  choosing, 109
  expression of, 58
  for home country, 124
  studying history requires, 119–120
Great Commission, 123
Green, Emma, 5
Green Hill Church, 223
Greenberg, Jennifer, 48
Guelzo, Allen C., 104–105, 111, 156
Guinness, Os, 129–130, 131, 151, 155

hagiography, 100–101
Hall, Mark David, 7
Harris, Murray J., 113
Harvard University, 200
Hauerwas, Stanley, 37
healthy patriotism (*see also* patriotism)
  blind loyalty vs, 54
  as necessary posture for Christians, xi
  seeking best for the state, 54–55
  as species of piety, 46
Hemings, Sally, 107
Henry, Patrick, 106–107
heroism, 110
higher education
  Christian colleges, 202–203
  diversifying boards, 200
  economic advantages of, 201
  marriage success and, 201–202
  moral and spiritual formation in, 201–202
  vocational training vs, 200–201
Holland, Tom, 24
Hoover, Herbert, 11
Hosea, 34
Hudson, Alexandra, 214–215
human condition, 27, 101
human dignity, 89–91, 99, 102, 114, 124, 152, 209
human nature, 17, 23, 99, 102, 174 (*see also* natural law)
humility, 93–94, 114, 116, 119–120, 125, 138
Hungary, 137
Huxley, Aldous, 130
Hymowitz, Kay S., 107, 108

imago Dei, 210
incivility, justification for, 210–211
Indian Removal Act, 102–103
individualism, 183, 214–215
ingratitude, xi, 47, 51
injustices in American history, 50–52, 77, 97–98, 103–106, 131, 193–194 (*see also* slavery)
interventionism, 133–138
isolationism, 133–138

Jackson, Andrew, 102–103
Jackson, Ketanji Brown, 172
January 6, 2021 events, xiv–xv
Jay, John, 106
Jefferson, Thomas, 17–18, 107
Jeremiah (prophet), 40–41, 43, 72–73, 166, 217
Jeroboam II, King, 33–34
Jethani, Skye, 143–144
Jim Crow racism, 29, 98, 102, 115, 168, 193–194
John Paul II (pope), 162
Johnson, Lyndon B., 167–168
Johnson, Mike, 3–4
Johnson, Paul, 128
Jonah, 33–36
Jones, Robert P., 4
just law, 74–75

Kaplan, Seth, 224, 225
Kearney, Melissa S., 176
Keller, Timothy, 34, 35, 38–39, 145, 161
Kidd, Thomas S., 107, 126
kindness
  exercising, 65–66, 211
  niceness vs, 66
King, Martin Luther, Jr., 55, 74–75, 109, 209–210

kingdom of Heaven, 71, 73
Kingsnorth, Paul, 153

Land, Richard, 124, 136, 172–173
Landsmark, Ted, 37–38
Lapp, David, 213
Lee, Bill, 200
Lemon test, 20–21
Lew, John, 107–108
Lewis, C. S., 23, 36, 38, 110, 112
Lincoln, Abraham, 10–11, 55, 108, 116
Lindner, Abigail, 51
lived experience, 193
localism, 221–226
Locke, John, 15
Loury, Glenn C., 118
love of country
  Biblical example of, 33–36
  compelled to, 47–49
  defining, 30–32
  even when imperfect, 98–99
  extreme examples of, 32–33
  false binary between love of God and, 38–40
  love of God over, 36
  as natural, 46–47
  objection to, 32–33
love of God, 37–40
love of humanity, 58–59
love(s)
  disordered, 47–48
  for the familiar, 46–47
  God's command for, xi–xii, 37
  learning Christian definition of, 48
  ordering of, 39, 141
  spiritual, 211–212
loving our neighbors, 73–74, 94
loyalty
  alternative to, 44
  blind, 102
  as citizens, 52–53
  to community, 44–45
  to Jesus, 53
  patriotism and, 31, 54

Macdonald, Norm, 121
Madison, James, 19–20, 101
Manifest Destiny, 122–123
marriage
  biblical view of, 178
  college graduates and, 201–202
  community health and, 180
  divorce and, 179, 182
  plummeting rates of, 173
  redefining, 172–174
  same-sex, 173–174, 182
Marx, Karl, 103, 170
Marxism, 190–191 (*see also* critical theory)
Mattis, Jim, 209
McClay, Wilfred M., 49–50
McCullough, David, 126
McKinley, William, 11
Mercy Clinic, 223
Montás, Roosevelt, 101
Moore, Russell, 180–181
moral law, 22–24, 74–75
moral movement, 70–71
morality, higher education and, 201–202
More, Thomas, 39
Mount Vernon, 125
Mouw, Richard J., 55–56
Moynihan, Daniel Patrick, 167–168

National Museum of African American History, 29, 102
nationalism vs patriotism, 33
Native Americans, 102–103, 106
natural law, 11, 75, 88, 182
natural rights, as endowed by the Creator, 23–24
Naylor, Rebekah, 223
negative freedom, 131
neo-isolationism, 134
Neuhaus, Richard John, 14–15, 18, 44–45
neutrality, 13–18
New York Times, The 1619 Project, 104–105, 110

Index

news media, imbalanced reaction to religion and politics, 3–7
Noll, Mark A., 116

Obergefell v. Hodges, 173–174
Onishi, Bradley, 7
open American exceptionalism, 123–124
oppressed class, 192
ordered loves. *See* love(s)

patriotic symbols
  American flag, 50–53
  attacks on, 50–51
patriotism (*see also* anti-patriots; healthy patriotism; US history)
  alienation and, 42–43
  definition of, 31–32, 50
  dissent as form of, 30–31
  hard work as form of, 226
  injustices and, 97–98
  level of, 29–30
  localist view of, 222–224
  loyalty and, 31, 54
  nationalism vs, 33
  overview, 226–227
  Pledge of Allegiance and, 53
  rightly ordered, 217–218
  as sense of "we-ness," 55–56
  spiritual advantage of, 45, 226
Patterson, Eric, 51
Paul the Apostle, Saint, 65, 78–79, 113–114, 148–149, 157
Pavlovitz, John, 143
"peace through strength" doctrine, 137
performative activism, 93
Perry, Louise, 24, 153
Perry, Samuel L., 4
Peter, Saint, 65–66, 73
Platt, David, 5
Pledge of Allegiance, 53
polarization of America, 208–209 (*see also* divisiveness)
political campaigns, existential nature of, 165
political Christians, apocalyptic warnings about, xii–xiii
political homelessness, 83–84
political leaders, statements on God's providence, 3–6
political parties, Christians identifying with, 82–86
political power
  avoidance of, 67
  citizens' share in American, 79–82
  danger of authority and, 62–63
  desire for, 69–70
  Graham's indifference to, 74
  granted by God, 78–79
  practice of giving up, 125
  reverence around the presidency, 62–63
  stewarded for good ends, 80–81
  as temporal, 64
  temptations to, 63–64, 76–77
political system, Christian's place in, 66–67
political theology, 77–79
politics
  as all-consuming idol, 67
  approach to, 90
  as art of the possible, 93
  in Christian Gospel, 71–72
  definition of, 69
  engaging in, 69–70
  as exercise in seeking power, 80–81
  God's place in, 74–75
  involvement in local, 225–226
  in its rightful place, 63–64
  motivations for entering, 90
positive freedom, 131–132
power. *See* divine power; political power
presidency, reverence for, 62–63
Presley, Stephen O., 146
pro-life movement, 55
Protestant thinkers, 87
public education (*see also* higher education)

public education (*continued*)
American founders' concern for quality, 186, 188–189
battle of ideas on, 189–190
caste system in, 197
Christians active participation in, 196–197
church opportunities in shaping, 196
Ivy League schools, 187
K-12, 187–188, 195–199
LGBT curriculum, 188
Marxist assumptions in school curricula, 190–191
political divide on plight of, 186–189
school choice, 197–199
student socioeconomic status and, 197
voucher programs, 198
Washington's passion for, 185–186
public engagement, localism and, 221–224
public schools. *See* education
public square, 14–15, 18, 20, 68–69, 160–161
public theology, 72–76

Quayle, Dan, 175–176

racism. *See* Jim Crow racism
Reagan, Ronald, 135, 137, 142, 227
Religious Freedom Restoration Act of 1993, 89–90
religious institutions. *See* Christian Church
revolutions, as common in history, 126 (*see also* American revolution)
Rice, Condoleezza, 198
Roosevelt, Franklin D., 11–12, 135
Roosevelt, Theodore, 54
Rubio, Marco, 129
Rush, Benjamin, 106

Salt Network, 202
Samelson, Ashley E., 22
same-sex marriage, 173–174, 182
Sanger, Margaret, 171
Santorum, Rick, 172
Sasse, Ben, 200
Schaeffer, Francis A., 72, 163, 202–203
school choice, 197–199
schools of citizenship, 214–215
Schumer, Chuck, 6
Schweiger, Beth Barton, 98–99
Scripture
influence on Declaration of Independence, 108–109
Pete Laverick, 113–118
praise of "heroes", 110
slavery and, 113–114
twisting in name of injustice, 117–118
secular society, as historical aberration, 13
segregation, 74
sentimental persons, xviii
September 11 terrorist attacks, 56–58
Shapiro, Ben, 190–191
single-parent families, 175–176, 177
1619 Project, 104–105, 110
slavery
American founders on, 10, 106–108
Bible verses pro and con, 113–114
contradiction between democracy and, 111–112
demise of, 108–109
denunciation of, 115–116
emancipation, 118–119
extensiveness of, 105–106
Greco-Roman vs chattel, 113–114
Jefferson's views on, 17–18
justification for, 113–114
proper response to history of, 102
as worldwide, 105–106
Smith, Al, 11–12
Smith, Miles, 52–53
Smith, Steven B., 33
socialism, 170
Southern Baptist Convention, 114, 165

Index

Soviet Union, 137
spiritual formation, 91–94, 201–202
spiritual love, 211–212
State of the Union address, 185–186
stewardship, 124, 131–132, 133–134, 138, 224–225
"strict separation" theory, 16–17
Supreme Court
  Lemon test and, 20–21
  "strict separation" theory, 16–17

Ten Commandments, 18
theocracy, 86–90
Thompson, Derek, 23
Timothy, Saint, 141
Tocqueville, Alexis de, 111, 128, 142, 214
Tooley, Mark, 133, 147
Topping, Ryan N. S., 169–172
Travis Avenue Baptist Church, 223
triumphalist exceptionalism, 123–124
Trueman, Carl R., 65
Truman, Harry, 12–13
Trumbull, John, 125
Trump, Donald, 5
truth, countercultural, 152–153
two-parent households, 175–177

unity, Christian, 163–164
unjust law, 75
US history (*see also* America)
  chattel slavery (*see* slavery)
  consideration of the good in, 119–120
  exploring within your community, 224–225
  injustices in, 30–32, 77, 97–98, 103–104, 131, 193–194, 218
  interpreting, 99–101
  secular view of, 14
  study of, 119–120
  temptation to glamorize, 103
  Zinn's recasting of, 104

Vander Plaats, Bob, 219–220
VanDrunen, David, 88
victimhood mindset, 193–195
vocational training, 200–201
Vonnegut, Kurt, 18
voter turnout, 84
voucher programs, 198

Walker, Andrew T., 69, 83, 88, 92
Wang, Wendy, 182
Warren, Elizabeth, 6
Washington, George, 8–9, 107, 125, 185–186, 205–206
Wax, Trevin, 32, 150
Wear, Michael R., 80, 85
Webster, Noah, 204
welfare, definition of, 73
"we-ness", 55–58
Wesley, John, 115
Westminster Confession of Faith, 100–101
Whitefield, George, 115–116
Whitehead, Andrew, 4
Whitehead, Barbara Dafoe, 175
Wilberforce, William, 92
Wilcox, Brad, 162, 177, 202
Will, George, 126
Wilsey, John, 8, 46, 98–99, 122
Wilson, Woodrow, 11
Winthrop, John, 122
Wolfe, Stephen, 89
Wood, James R., 30
Woodberry, Robert, 144–145
Woodward, Kenneth L., 6
World War I, 135
Wright, N. T., 178

Yagoda, Herman, 50–51
Yancey, Phillip, 57–58

Zahl, David, 207
Zahnd, Brian, 32, 77
Zinn, Howard, 30, 104

ABOUT THE AUTHOR

DANIEL DARLING is a pastor and the author of several books, including *Agents of Grace*, *The Dignity Revolution*, and *The Characters of Christmas*. He currently serves as the director of the Land Center for Cultural Engagement at Southwestern Baptist Theological Seminary and is a fellow at the Ethics & Religious Liberty Commission of the Southern Baptist Convention. He is also a columnist for *World* and a contributor to *USA Today*.